Gothic Immortals

Fuseli, *The Rosicrucian Cavern* (1803)

Gothic Immortals

The Fiction of the Brotherhood of the Rosy Cross

Marie Roberts

ROUTLEDGE
LONDON AND NEW YORK

First published 1990
by Routledge
11 New Fetter Lane, London EC4P 4EE

Simultaneously published in the USA and Canada
by Routledge
a division of Routledge, Chapman and Hall, Inc.
29 West 35th Street, New York, NY 10001

Printed in Great Britain by
T.J. Press (Padstow) Ltd, Padstow, Cornwall

British Library Cataloguing in Publication Data

Roberts, Marie
Gothic immortals: the fiction of the brotherhood of the Rosy Cross
1. Gothic novels in English. Influence of
Rosicrucianism. 1745–1837
I. Title
823′.0872

Library of Congress Cataloging in Publication Data

Roberts, Marie.
Gothic immortals: the fiction of the brotherhood of the
Rosy Cross/Marie Roberts.
p. cm.
Includes index.
ISBN 0-415-02368-8
1. English fiction – 19th century – History and criticism.
2. Rosicrucians in literature. 3. Gothic revival (Literature).
4. Occultism in literature. 5. Godwin, William, 1756–1836. St.
Leon. 6. Lytton, Edward Bulwer Lytton, Baron, 1803–1873
– Knowledge – Occultism. I. Title
PR868.R75R67 1990 89-5983
823′.009′37 – dc19 CIP

ISBN 0–415–02368–8

For Catherine, Emrys,
Marie, Janet, Wimbo
and in Memory of Laly and Nogga

Contents

Contents

List of Plates

The plate section appears between chapters 4 and 5.

Acknowledgements

I would like to thank Sascha and Ezra Talmor the editors of *History of European Ideas* for permission to include a revised version of my article 'Rosicrucian or Cross-Rosism in Hegel's *Phenomenology*' and Stan Linden the editor of *Cauda Pavonis* for his courteous consent in allowing me to make use of my article 'The English Rosicrucian Novel.' The publishers of *British Poets and Secret Societies* (Croom Helm, 1986) have kindly permitted me to reuse some of the material in the present work. Thanks are due to the Goethe Museum in Frankfurt for permission to reproduce the Fuseli and to the Museo del Prado in Madrid for authorising the reproduction of the paintings by Goya. My gratitude is extended to those who commented on all or part of the manuscript at various stages especially Christine Battersby, Bill Hutchins, Bill Ruddick, and Angus Ross, the editors at Routledge, Denise O'Hagan, Kay Edge, Sue Bilton and Margaret Lipscomb, and my colleagues in the Literary Studies department at Bristol Polytechnic, especially Marian Glastonbury, Helen Taylor, Kate Fulbrook, Renée Slater, Rosie Bailey, Sue Habershaw, Robin Jarvis and Jennifer Green. Deserving of special mention are Chris Baldick for much valued help and advice, Alan Wills for his wizardry with computer systems which has been of invaluable assistance and David Lamb for his constant encouragement. I would also like to express my appreciation to family, friends and colleagues for their support and enthusiasm for this project which started out as a Ph.D. thesis. Delays in getting to press could be blamed upon mythological beasts such as Bulwer-Lytton's 'Dweller of the Threshold', but for all the errors in the text, I must take sole responsibility.

1

The Brotherhood of the Rosy Cross

I suspect that the Brethren of the Rosy Cross are a fiction.
Leibniz [1]

The image of the Gothic immortal has been overshadowed by one of its more unsavoury varieties: that of the deathless vampire in the form of Nosferatu or some other Eastern European aristocrat. The notoriety of Dracula helped discredit the idea of bodily immortality through his insatiable thirst for blood which marked him out as the most loathsome of human parasites. Scarcely more inviting than the vampire is the Wandering Jew, another member of the cabal of Gothic immortals. There are occasional sightings of this morose and melancholy figure as he meanders through Gothic literature emerging on close encounter as a melodramatic character, with his mesmeric stare and fiery cross branded on his forehead. The most infamous blasphemer is Faust, who through the diabolic ministrations of Mephistopheles relinquishes his eternal soul for the immortality of the flesh. Similarly the alchemical secret of the *elixir vitæ* (elixir of life) could be passed on like a deadly virus infecting future generations with the pestilence of never-ending life. This is the stigma borne by the unhallowed tribe of Gothic immortals whether they be Medieval satanists, dark magi of the Renaissance or hosts of the undead stirring from some Transylvanian burial ground.

Apart from this roll-call of miscreants, there was a species of immortal who evoked the redemptive powers of myth by using the gift of eternal life for the purposes of benevolence. This was the Brotherhood of the Rosy Cross, for whom immortality was a blessing and not a curse. But unlike the vampire, Wandering Jew, or werewolf, the Rosicrucian has proved to be an elusive prey for the historian, since his distinguishing feature is his power of invisibility. The advantages of the vampirologist are not afforded to those in pursuit of members of the brotherhood. For example, mirrors reflect back their image and they are able to tolerate sunlight. Unimpeded by the necessity of having to lug a coffin round with them on their travels, neither are they obliged to take up nocturnal residence in a graveyard or crypt. They are immune to the protective properties of garlic, and the crucifix holds no terror for this Christian brotherhood.

Yet the adepti of the Rosy Cross, along with all the other Gothic immortals, are culpable in having cheated the great leveller, death. Our sense of the moral necessity of death is embodied in myths like the staking of the revenant and the shunning of the Wandering Jew. The Rosicrucians, however benign their aims, risk transgressing this powerful taboo by turning the sacred immortality of the soul into a travesty and snubbing the angel of death. Their only legitimate immortality may be found in literature, where their eternal wanderings are mapped out in the Gothic novel.

The secret organisation of Rosicrucians announced its supposed existence to the world in the form of two manifestos which were published between 1614 and 1615. Scholars still debate whether or not this clandestine brotherhood ever actually existed or if it was merely an elaborate hoax. It may seem curious to embark upon a study of a society reputed to be so secret that it was even believed to be invisible. No one had ever met a Rosicrucian or even been able to contact one. Nonetheless, the idea of such a fraternity inspired the formation of a number of later Rosicrucian societies, while the manifestos themselves expressed an identifiable way of thinking. These currents of thought contributed to a tradition of the Rosy Cross out of which emerged a fictional genre, the 'Rosicrucian' novel.

This designation was first employed by Edith Birkhead when she identified William Godwin as the first novelist to 'embody in a romance the ideas of the Rosicrucians which [so] inspired Bulwer-Lytton's *Zicci, Zanoni* and *A Strange Story*.'[2] Commencing with Godwin's *St Leon* (1799), various novels will be analysed here as examples of Rosicrucian fiction, including P. B. Shelley's *St Irvyne or The Rosicrucian* (1810), Mary Shelley's *Frankenstein* (1818) and Charles Maturin's *Melmoth the Wanderer* (1820). These Gothic novels, it will be argued, manifest the influence of the Rosicrucian tradition on English literature, since the ideas planted by the manifestos and the mystical traditions associated with the Rosy Cross germinated in the form of a Rosicrucian novel populated with Gothic immortals.

The term 'Rosicrucian' is generally believed to have been derived from the Latin *rosa* (rose) and *crux* (cross). Certainly Rosicrucian societies are symbolised by the rose and cross, from which the name of the legendary founder of the original brotherhood, Christian Rosencreutz, had been devised. It is likely, however, that the Rosicrucian idea was started by Johann Valentin Andreæ (1586-1654), the Lutheran theologian, whose family arms bore the symbols of the rose and cross.[3] These emblems also appear on the seal used by Martin Luther, which signifies the association between the Rosicrucian Enlightenment and the Lutheran Reformation. Their Christian connotation may be found in the Crucifixion imagery of the rose, which is indicative of the dying Christ on the blood-stained cross. The Rose-Cross symbolism was evocative of the Protestant backlash to Hapsburg hegemony preceding the outbreak of the Thirty Years' War in 1620, which has been documented by Frances Yates in *The Rosicrucian Enlightenment.*

The Rosicrucian manifestos heralded the arrival of the Brotherhood of the Rosy Cross. The *Fama Fraternitatis or a Discovery of the Fraternity of the Most Noble Order of the Rosy Cross* (1614) followed by the *Confessio Fraternitatis or The Confession of the Laudable of the Most Honourable Order of the Rosy Cross, written to All the learned of Europe* (1615)[4] both advocated social and political reform, set out the rules of the order and narrated the life-story of Rosencreutz. According to the *Fama,* he was born in 1378 to a noble family which had become impoverished. At the age of five he was placed in a monastery and educated in the classics until called upon to accompany one of the monks on a pilgrimage to Jerusalem. Unfortunately the brother died in Cyprus, so Rosencreutz had to travel to Jerusalem alone. *En route* he stayed at Damascus, where he heard the teachings of wise men who received him 'not as a stranger, but as one whom they had long expected.'[5] From this prophetic beginning, Rosencreutz's wanderings turned into a search for knowledge. He learned about physics and mathematics, during which time his increased proficiency in Arabic enabled him to translate into Latin the mysterious *Book M* which contained the secrets of the universe. At Fez, Rosencreutz was introduced to the 'Elementary Inhabitants, who revealed unto him many of their secrets.'[6]

After spending two years there studying the Cabala and other occult sciences, Rosencreutz sailed to Spain in order to impart his wisdom to the learned of Europe, so that they might 'rule and order all studies according to those sound and sure foundations.'[7] But Rosencreutz's proposals for reform were so ridiculed that he decided to form his own society, which would be devoted to bringing about universal change through a radical epistemology. Starting with eight members, Rosencreutz formed a fraternity of the Rose and Cross whose first task was to invent a magical language and script for the purpose of writing the *Book of Nature,* a compilation of all knowledge. The rules of the Rose-Cross brethren were laid out as follows:

1. That none of them should profess any other thing than to cure the sick, and that *gratis*. None of the posterity should be constrained to wear one certain kind of habit, but therein to follow the custom of the country.
2. That every year upon the day C. they should meet together in the house S. Spiritus, or write the cause of his absence.
3. Every brother should look about for a worthy person, who, after his decease, might succeed him.
4. The word C. R. should be their seal, mark, and character.
5. The Fraternity should remain secret one hundred years.[8]

After the death and burial of Rosencreutz, his disciples reopened his tomb ten years prior to the publication of the *Fama*. 1604 marked the year when the door of his vault was opened to send his message reverberating throughout Europe with the eventual appearance of the manifestos.

Rosencreutz's life furnishes a prototype for the career of the Rosicrucian hero in the novel, who also bears a family resemblance to the philosophical magi associated with the occult traditions of the Rosy Cross. Yates identifies as key Rosicrucian figures Cornelius Agrippa (1486-1535), Paracelsus (1493-1541), and John Dee (1527-1608). Agrippa's sorcery and alleged necromantic activities influenced Mary and P. B. Shelley's treatment of the Rosicrucian themes while Paracelsus's writing on prolongevity provided Godwin with source-material for *St Leon*. The Paracelsian blend of magic, medicine and science was characteristic of the Rosicrucian elements which Bulwer-Lytton explored in *A Strange Story*. John Dee, another model for the Rosicrucian hero, even plays a minor role in Maturin's *Melmoth the Wanderer*. Yates's classification of Agrippa, Paracelsus and Dee as Rosicrucians is based on the following criteria:

> I should like to try to persuade sensible people and sensible historians to use the word "Rosicrucian." This word has bad associations owing to the uncritical assertions of occultists concerning the existence of a sect or secret society calling themselves Rosicrucians the history and membership of which they claim to establish .... The word could, I suggest, be used of a certain style of thinking which is historically recognizable without raising the question of whether a Rosicrucian style of thinker belonged to a secret society.[9]

A number of Rosicrucian societies did emerge from the body of myth and symbolism contained within the Rosicrucian manifestos, such as Andreæ's Christian Union,[10] and the Invisible College which, according to Yates, was the ancestor of the Royal Society. One of its members, Robert Boyle, makes reference in his correspondence to 'our invisible college' while in a letter to Francis Tallente in 1646, he describes the college as follows:

> The best on't is, that the corner-stone of the *invisible,* or (as they call themselves), the *philosophical* college, do now and then honor me with their company … men of so capacious and searching spirits, that school-philosophy is but the lowest region of their knowledge … persons that endeavor to put narrow-mindedness out of their countenance, by the practice of so extensive a charity, that it reaches into everything called man, and nothing less than universal good-will can content it. And indeed they are so apprehensive of the want of good employment, that they take the whole body of mankind for their care … their chiefest fault … is that there are not enough of them.[11]

Membership of the Invisible College contained such luminaries as Elias Ashmole, Kenelm Digby, Robert Child, and later Christopher Wren, John Wilkins, and Robert Hooke. Many of these joined the Royal Society when it was seeking the patronage of the newly crowned Charles II in 1660.[12] The founding of the Royal Society has always been seen as the advent of a new period of rationality which witnessed the rise of mechanistic science and the correspondent decline of operative magic.

This apparent demarcation is evident from the contrast between the occult pursuits cultivated by the Invisible College such as the search for the *lapis philosophicus* (philosopher's stone) and the *elixir vitæ*, and the predisposition of the Royal Society to meet the demands of orthodox science. Yet in fact, the preoccupations of the Invisible College overlapped with those of the Royal Society. As Charles Webster has pointed out, the role of magic in synthesising the Newtonian revolution has been devalued by the tendency to overstate the relationship between science and rationality.[13] He claims that there was a less radical epistemological shift between the ages of Paracelsus and Newton than has been previously imagined. The rise of mechanistic science during the seventeenth century was grounded in a tradition of scientific magic. Instrumental in this cross-fertilisation were the Rosicrucians as a species of magician-scientists.

The Rosicrucian tradition was based upon a corpus of occult knowledge derived from the Hermetic-Cabalistic traditions of the Renaissance which led on to a distinctive mode of thinking. The mythologies of the brotherhood concerning Rosencreutz, the philosopher's stone and the elixir of life, contain a revolutionary message urging social, political and spiritual change. This radical vision is preserved within literature through the utopianism of Andreæ, Francis Bacon and Tommaso Campanella. The residual influence of these thinkers may be detected on later writers such as Swift, who satirised the Brethren of the Rosy Cross in *Gulliver's Travels* (1726) and *A Tale of a Tub* (1704). Another area of literary influence points to the poetic mythologies contained in Villars's *Comte de Gabalis* (1670), Pope's *Rape of the Lock* (1714), and the anonymous *Bridegroom of the Fay* (1727). Rosicrucian allegory threads its way through Andreæ's *The Chemical Wedding* (1616), which was a forerunner of the Rosicrucian novel.

Literature did much to create and then perpetuate the myths surrounding the Brotherhood of the Rosy Cross. Novelists in particular exploited such Rosicrucian legends as the existence of a spirit-world, the elixir of life and the perpetual burning lamp. To a great extent, the Rosicrucians became the property of the creative writer. Some critics protested that literature perpetuated 'false and unreasonable statements'[14] in regard to the Rose-Cross fraternity. F. Leigh Gardner in *Bibliotheca Rosicruciana* chastises those poets and writers of romance who have 'shed a halo of unreality about the Rosicrucians'[15] since 'no true Rosicrucian Adept has asserted his power to make Gold at will, or to possess such an elixir of life as could enable men to avoid death altogether, or indefinitely.'[16] Gardner recognises that the manifestos do not advocate the pursuit of the philosopher's stone and the elixir of life in order to gain freedom from poverty, old age and death. Instead they indicate that these objectives can only be realised through an evolutionary progression encompassing the spiritual development of the human race.

The second Rosicrucian manifesto, the *Confessio*, is emphatic that only through God may the secrets of nature be unlocked. The author asks, 'Were it not a precious thing, that you could always live so, as if you had lived from the beginning of the world, and, moreover, as you should still live to the end thereof?'[17] and even tries to dissociate the Brotherhood of the Rosy Cross from seekers of the philosopher's stone who hoped to discover the secrets of the transmutation of base metal into gold alchemy and the elixir for their own selfish gain. 'False Alchemists'[18] and those blinded by the glittering of gold should be denied the elixir of life:

> let them think, that although there be a medicine to be had which might fully cure all diseases, nevertheless those whom God hath destined to plague with diseases, and to keep under the rod of correction, sure shall never obtain any such medicine.[19]

It is revealed further in the *Confessio* that the brotherhood will only become visible to those who are chosen by God. But for those pursuing riches and knowledge of the Rosy Cross in defiance of His will, the brotherhood will remain forever out of reach:

> it shall be so far from him whosoever thinks to get the benefit and be partakers of our riches and knowledge, without and against the will of God, that he shall sooner lose his life in seeking and searching for us, than to find us, and attain to come to the wished happiness of the Fraternity of the Rosy Cross.[20]

In a number of Rosicrucian novels, the consequences of this blasphemy are dramatised, sometimes to the heights of Gothic melodrama. Melmoth in Maturin's *Melmoth the Wanderer* and Margrave in *A Strange Story* are two demonic villains who forfeit their souls by renouncing their creator for perpetual life. Through the novel, the ideals of the Rosy Cross have been in danger of being tarnished and the Rosicrucian character of being misrepresented, for according to Gardner:

> The name "Rosicrucian" has suffered greatly from the pretensions of men who falsely claiming membership have made exaggerated, false and unreasonable statements regarding the powers and possessions of the Fraters of the Rose and Cross.[21]

Nevertheless, later apologists such as Michael Maier explained how strains of occult and mystical thought became accredited to Rosicrucianism. Sigmund Richter in 1710 claimed that the philosopher's stone could enable a Rosicrucian to prolong his life indefinitely. In his *True and Complete Preparation of the Philosophers' Stone of the Brotherhood from the Order of the Golden and Rosy Cross* (1710) Richter, writing under the pseudonym 'Sincerus Renatus,' revealed that each brother was given a portion of the stone which would enable him to extend his life-span for another sixty years. Since the allotted span had been prescribed by the Bible as three score years and ten, an extra sixty years was effectively worth two life-spans. Each Rosicrucian was entitled to these additional years on condition that he obeyed a number of rules. Some of these related directly to the philosopher's stone, which was never to be carried in the form of oil but only as a 'powder of first projection,'[22] contained in a metal box. The short-cut magical methods advocated by various apologists inspired creative writers to reinforce and perpetuate such distortions of the Rosy Cross tradition.

Rosicrucian fiction emerged during the Enlightenment with Godwin's *St Leon* in 1799. It is rather uncanny to consider that it was Godwin, a political philosopher and social reformer who launched this mystical genre. He may have been drawn to adopt the Rosicrucians' reputed immortality as a literary theme by current scientific theories on life-extension which will be discussed in more detail in chapter two. The eighteenth-century interest in prolongevity is one example of how the Enlightenment tried to actualise some of the aspirations laid out by the Rosicrucians of the Renaissance. Bulwer-Lytton's treatment of the French Revolution in *Zanoni* is the best illustration of how the Enlightenment may be regarded as the legitimate heir of the Renaissance.

The five novelists to be discussed explore the artistic possibilities presented by the legendary philosopher's stone and elixir of life which had become part of the Rosicrucian tradition. The term 'immortal,' which characterises the hero or villain of this type of novel, will be applied to those who regard their life-extension as a perpetual earthly existence. These characters soon discover the anguish and tedium of coping with immortality, since loneliness and guilt force them to wander in search of spiritual fulfilment. Chameleon-like, a resurrected Faust or Wandering Jew, the Rosicrucian hero is a composite of the heretical and fallen, seeking out from among the arcane repositories of magic and myth forbidden springs of ancient knowledge, arcadian fountains of perpetual youth and archetypal elixirs of eternal life. Godwin confronts the neurosis brought about by perpetual life in his psychological study of the eternal wanderer, *St Leon*. Contrasting with this is Shelley's melodramatic portrayal of the Rosicrucian in *St Irvyne*. In Mary Shelley's 'Mortal Immortal' and *Frankenstein*, the pursuit of the elixir of life is turned into a parable for the transition from the socially integrated man of the eighteenth century to the alienated individual of the Romantic era. In 'Mortal Immortal' she plots the perversity of scientific reason in trying to fix a formula for immortality. Her treatment of the sacrilege of science pales before the blasted and withering damnation wreaked upon Maturin's Melmoth, whose Rosicrucian heresy may be viewed as a second Fall of mankind. Finally, the triumph of the Rosicrucian sage is celebrated in Bulwer-Lytton's *Zanoni* (1842), where the true conquest of death is seen as a fusion between the actual and the ideal, symbolised by the rose and cross, emblems of the Brotherhood of the Rosy Cross.

Rosicrucianism, by functioning as a synthesis for opposing principles, reflects important intellectual movements which have been described by Hegel and others. For example, the Rosicrucian novel preserves the complex interplay between reason, magic and science. In Mary Shelley's 'Mortal Immortal' and *Frankenstein*, a balance between experimental magic and scientific discovery is maintained; also for the additional reason that P. B. Shelley, with his interests in magic and science, inspired the characterisation of Victor Frankenstein. For Godwin, the pursuit of immortality had a socio-economic context, which, as a continuation of eighteenth-century rationality, fulfilled Enlightenment expectations concerning the potential perfectibility of mankind. *St Leon* is a case-history documenting the errors which arise when the elixir of life is deployed to further the ambition and greed of the individual rather than to benefit society at large. Ironically, the sceptical atmosphere of the French Revolution provides the setting for Bulwer-Lytton's most Rosicrucian novel, *Zanoni*, where he demonstrates the interdependence of rational Enlightenment and mystical illumination. In Bulwer's *A Strange Story*, Alan Fenwick discovers that the tensions between magic and science may be resolved through the acceptance of a Rosicrucian world-view. Through the acquisition of the *elixir vitæ,* the Gothic immortal finds himself at the nexus of a series of traditional opposites including magic and science, mortality and eternal life, the secular and the divine.

The aspirations of Rosicrucian idealism re-emerge in the Romantic individualism exhibited in the novel. The way in which Rosicrucianism was adapted for fiction meant that the main interest centred upon the immortality of the Rosicrucian character. The flexibility of the elixir of life theme was such that it could be utilised by an Enlightenment thinker, Godwin, explored within Shelley's and Maturin's Gothic novels, adapted for Mary Shelley's Romanticism, and then reworked within the Victorian fiction of Bulwer-Lytton. The acquisition of bodily immortality formed part of the arcanum of secret teaching which traditionally has been regarded as prohibited. Indeed, the most important characteristic of the Rosicrucian novel is the pursuit and acquisition of such forbidden knowledge.

Forbidden Knowledge

It has always been within the province of the Christian Church to legitimise or outlaw branches of knowledge. Not surprisingly, religious orthodoxy condemned the occult practices associated with the Rosicrucians, particularly the cultivation of supernatural powers such as control over mortality. In almost all the Rosicrucian novels discussed, the consequences of the sacrilegious meddling with the sacred mysteries of life and death may be traced back to the indefatigable curiosities of the hero, whose penitential wanderings are the outcome of his enslavement by his own selfish desires.

The Rosicrucians had been associated with diabolical transactions in order to gain prohibited knowledge since 1623, as indicated by the anonymous pamphlet, *Effroyables Pactions faites entre de Diable et les prétendues Invisibles.*[23] The author claimed that members of the College of Rosicrucians had signed a pact in their blood with a necromancer called Raspuch. The transaction was allegedly witnessed by the demon Astaroth, who had taken the form of a beautiful youth. The Rosicrucians agreed to perform various blasphemous acts for Satan in return for a number of powers such as invisibility, dematerialisation and the ability to speak all languages fluently. The hero of Bulwer-Lytton's *Zanoni* is renowned for this last attribute. The reason why knowledge of all languages was considered such an asset for the Rosicrucian seer was so that the necessity of conquering death could be communicated to all races. In 1623, which was the same year as the *Effroyables Pactions* appeared, placards were displayed in the streets of Paris announcing:

> We, the deputies of our Head College of the Rosy Cross, now sojourning, visible and invisible, in this town, by grace of the Most High, towards Whom the hearts of sages turn, do teach, without the help of books of signs, how to speak the language of every country wherein we elect to stay, in order that we may rescue our fellow men from the error of death.[24]

The redemption of humanity from death was a blasphemy which Francis Bacon viewed as a second Fall because it represented the reversal of the consequences of mankind's first disobedience. When Adam ate the forbidden fruit from the Tree of Knowledge of Good and Evil, he gained instead knowledge of suffering and of the inevitability of disease, old age and death. The belief in a universal medicine or *elixir vitæ* which could 'cure' the 'diseases' of illness, old age and even death has always been compelling. Byron's Manfred uses this imagery of disease in his vision of a Golden Age which has produced an 'undiseased mankind.'[25] As an allegory of epistemology, the Fall marks the transition of the individual from a state of primordial consciousness to that of self-consciousness, and so the Rosicrucian sage aspires towards the higher state of universal consciousness in order to regain power over nature. But the moral basis for control over the powers of nature would be more justifiable in terms of a collective action which would benefit the human race and not merely service the selfish inclinations of the solitary individual. For the fictional wanderer, the individualism engendered by his solitary quest is reinforced by his attainment of the elixir of life, which repudiates Godwin's notions of equality and justice. The Rosicrucian hero mirrors the human race yet his individuality denies it. The outcome of this is that the sage is pitted against nature as well as against mankind. Thus the condemned magus is a portrait of a wanderer whose ultimate progression to universal consciousness has been arrested by his ego or an over-developed sense of self. Such a pronounced sense of individuality acts as a negation of the universal. Therefore, the self-consciousness of the sage results in a denial of the divine not because of a god in the magician but because the magician himself strives to become the conqueror of nature. At this point, the magus becomes both the master and slave of his will. The enslavement of the Rosicrucian hero by his own passions may be seen in the lust and debauchery which beset St Leon and Melmoth at the onset of their disillusionment with protracted existence. Manfred expresses such turbulence:

> My solitude is solitary no more,
> But peopled with the Furies.[26]

Manfred fails to recognise that he is the slave of his own passions since he fails to subjugate them through the power of his will:

> Slaves, scoff not at my will!
> The mind, the spirit, the Promethean spark,
> The lightning of my being, is as bright,
> Pervading, and far-darting as your own,
> And shall not yield to yours, though coop'd in clay![27]

Seekers after forbidden knowledge, such as Faust, had always assumed that control over the spirit-world was crucial, yet as Hegel's master-slave dialectic exemplifies, the spirits ultimately gain control and, in this case, bring his immortal existence to a demonic close. Even though Byron introduces a variation to this eschatological probability in Manfred, most heroes of the novels succumb to the power of the Furies. The sage's desire for mastery over nature through its subjugation to his will is the very impulse which prevents him from integrating with nature. This is not merely the problem of the Rosicrucian hero but also that of the *Übermensch,* since harmony with nature, cannot be achieved through the dominance of the will.

Such an impossibility was recognised in the manifestos, where it is stated that the power of the philosopher's stone and *elixir vitæ* may only be exercised once mankind had been reconciled with nature. Thus, in order to reverse the effects of the Fall and to achieve this reconciliation, the adept again tries to acquire forbidden knowledge. But after obtaining the elixir of life, the Rosicrucian experiences even greater alienation than before, now ostracised not only from nature but also from himself and from human society. Hence the anguish of Byron's immortal, Manfred, who by severing his last link with nature and mankind finds himself in 'A wandering hell in the eternal space.'[28] St Leon, Frankenstein's monster, Melmoth and Zanoni echo his lament:

> My spirit walk'd not with the souls of men,
> Nor look'd upon the earth with human eyes;
> The thirst of their ambition was not mine,
> The aim of their existence was not mine;
> My joys, my griefs, my passions, and my powers,
> Made me a stranger.[29]

Manfred's conquest of death has alienated him from life and particularly from his own species. Though outwardly a mortal, he now has 'no sympathy with breathing flesh.'[30] This is the dilemma for the Rosicrucian protagonist, whose career throughout the novel magnifies and re-enacts the Fall and consequent alienation of Adamite man from nature.

The Rosicrucian's estrangement from nature may be viewed as Promethean since the adept has offended the gods by stealing immortality. Eventually eternal life, by becoming unendurable, turns into its own punishment. The immortal's wanderings are penitential for his bid to usurp the powers of a god. The wanderer's predicament, whether to identify himself as human or divine, is shared by every individual who may be 'In doubt to deem himself a God or Beast.'[31] As in Mary Shelley's *Frankenstein* and Maturin's *Melmoth,* the outsider is forced to parody and even challenge his creator. The process by which this apotheosis of ourselves as both human and godlike is central to the Rosicrucian predicament since the immortal wanderer embraces immortal consciousness from within the mortal state. Nevertheless, the ultimate goal for the seeker lies in acquiring self-knowledge. The metaphysics of tragedy is that the Gothic immortal cannot confront himself within his eternal existence. Only through death can he achieve such self-realization. But this wisdom is denied to the possessor of eternal life. According to Lukács, the tragic hero must experience the point of intersection between life and death:

> the ethic of tragedy must have as its categorical imperative the continuance unto death of everything that has begun; nor is it only that the psychology of tragedy is a science of death-moments, of conscious last moments when the soul has already given up the broad richness of existence and clings only to what is most deeply and intimately its own. Quite apart from these and many other negative reasons, death is also – in a purely positive and life-affirming sense – the immanent reality of tragedy. The experiencing of the frontier between life and death is the awakening of the soul to consciousness or self-consciousness.[32]

Yet the possession of the *elixir vitæ,* by dispensing with death, prevents the seeker from acquiring this knowledge. The elixir also creates an obsession with self so that the Rosicrucian comes to regard the pursuit of immortality as the only reality, and so becomes maniacally imprisoned within himself. It is this incarceration which is experienced by Tennyson's Tithonus, who reflects 'Me only cruel immortality / Consumes.'[33] Tithonus is less fortunate than most immortals since he has forfeited his eternal youth and so languishes in a sibylline state contemplating the ravages of time which he claims

> left me maim'd
> To dwell in presence of immortal youth,
> Immortal age beside immortal youth,
> And all I was in ashes.[34]

Tithonus goes on to ask:

> Why should a man desire in any way
> To vary from the kindly race of men,
> Or pass beyond the goal of ordinance
> Where all should pause, as is most meet for all?[35]

The lure of forbidden knowledge is the chronic ailment of human nature, which relentlessly hankers after ever-receding goals such as self-knowledge. The idea of a Golden Age or utopia, the pursuits of the philosopher's stone and the elixir of life are powerful metaphors beckoning for the integration of mankind with the divine principle in a reharmonisation with nature. These aspirations are not necessarily irrational but suggest that category-formations in human beings could follow similar universal paths articulated by myth, which can function as a means of enabling the mind to evade unwelcome or irreconcilable contradictions. The spiritual and poetic dimensions of myth are contained within aspects of Rosicrucianism such as the conquest of death and the godlike state of absolute knowledge.

Belief in a pansophy or universal wisdom as expressed in the manifestos is exploded by Roland Barthes in his denunciation of the fallacy that knowledge has finite parameters:

> There is a single secret to the world, and this secret is held in one word; the universe is a safe for which humanity seeks the combination: Einstein almost found it, this is the myth of Einstein. In it, we find all the Gnostic themes: the unity of nature, the ideal possibility of a fundamental reduction of the word, the unfastening power of the word, the age-old struggle between a secret and an utterance, the idea that total knowledge can only be discovered all at once, like a lock which suddenly opens after a thousand unsuccessful attempts... discovery, on the contrary, has a magical essence, it is simple like a basic element, a principal substance, like the philosopher's stone of the hermeticists.[36]

The desire for forbidden knowledge through the attainment of the philosopher's stone and the elixir of life has been mirrored in an intensified form through art and particularly through the Rosicrucian novel.

The Philosopher's Stone and Elixir of Life

> Who craves excess of day
> Scorning the common span
> Of life, I judge that man
> A giddy wight who walks in folly's ways.
>
> Sophocles[37]

Mainstream Rosicrucian fiction is concerned with the fate of the transgressor who defies the Creator by recommitting the sin of Adam for the expectation of unlimited life. The *elixir vitæ* becomes a secular version of the Holy Grail, allegoric of the protagonist's struggle to reconcile himself to the prospect of an immortal existence.

Long Livers, which purports to be *A Curious History of Such Persons of both Sexes who have liv'd several Ages, and grown Young again*[38] is a fantasy of rejuvenation written during the eighteenth century. Robert

Samber in claiming to be the author of this curiosity conveniently ignores de Longeville Harcouet, who had translated it previously from the French. In his preface, Samber employs a masonic metaphor drawn from the legendary building of King Solomon's Temple when he addresses the Rosicrucian Illuminati as 'living stones' who must build up 'a spiritual House.'[39] He warns them not to let the uninitiated 'look behind the veil'[40] and to protect the secrets of the *Book of Nature* and the *Book M* mentioned in the manifestos. Samber's use of the name 'Eugenius Philalethes,' which was the pseudonym of Thomas Vaughan, the author of the Rosicrucian allegory *The Spiritual Mountain*[41] helps to place *Long Livers* within a tradition of Rosicrucian writing.

Another eighteenth-century novel written by a self-proclaimed Rosicrucian adept is *Chrysal* (1761). The novelist, Charles Johnstone, apologises for producing a 'mystic tale' within a 'sceptical age'[42] since his hero is a spirit who has been conjured up by an alchemist engaged upon a 'mysterious process.'[43] Chrysal invites the reader to share the secret of the *opus magnum:*

> I shall trace the operations of nature through her most secret recesses, and illustrate the truth of what I say, by a detail of the various incidents of my being, in my present state, to prepare thee for the reception and proper use of that *grand secret* which I shall afterwards communicate.[44]

The *elixir vitæ* was believed to be a by-product of the process of transmutation which led to the attainment of the *opus magnum.* It was also regarded as the property of the devil, partly because it was believed to unleash demonic forces and give the possessor power over life and death. Often this entailed surrender of the receiver's soul to Satan, as in Hoffmann's account of *The Devil's Elixir* (1815-16) which promised the hero power over others:

> I unlocked the cabinet – I seized the box – opened it – beheld the bottle, drew the cork, – and in an instant had swallowed a deep and powerful draught! It seemed immediately as if fire streamed through my veins, and filled me with a sensation of indescribable delight! I drank more (but sparingly) and the raptures of a new and glorious life began at once to dawn on my perception .... It was ambition that possessed me, I should have once more the power of obtaining that noblest of earthly supremacies, an empire over the mind of others![45]

In William Harrison Ainsworth's *Elixir of Life* (1881), the villainous Cyprian de Rougemont is prepared to disturb the dead in order to realise his dream of eternal life. Breaking into his ancestor's tomb, he reminds himself: 'My ancestor's wondrous power was of infernal origin – the result, in fact, of a compact with the Prince of Darkness.'[46] At the entrance of the crypt Rougemont reflects that 'The old Rosicrucian has kept his secret well; but the devil has helped me wrest it from him.'[47] Ainsworth's description of the sepulchre is derived from the Rosicrucian manifestos. In the *Fama,* for instance, the tomb of Christian Rosencreutz is described as having seven sides with corners eight feet high and lit by an inner sun or perpetual-burning lamp. The brass inscription over the tomb of Rosencreutz reads *'Hoc universi compendium unius mihi sepulchrum feci'* ('This compendium of the universe I made [in my lifetime] to be a tomb').[48] The corpse itself lies 'whole and unconsumed'[49] and clasps in its hand a parchment book which, next to the *Bible,* the fraternity claim as their greatest treasure. In *The Elixir of Life,* Rougemont enters a septilateral chamber about eight feet high which is illuminated by the 'ever-burning lamp of the Rosicrucians.'[50] Upon a gold plate are engraved the same words as on the brass plate described in the *Fama.* Like the body of Christian Rosencreutz, the corpse of Rougemont's ancestor has been preserved. A large book bound in black vellum and fastened with bronze clasps has been placed upon the body. In this book Rougemont discovers the recipe for a potion which he administers to his arch-enemy, the immortal Auriol. The effect of the drink is to weaken Auriol's resistance to signing a pact with Rougemont, who identifies himself as the devil. Here Ainsworth has conflated a number of traditions such as the Faustian predicament over a diabolic transaction, the opening of the tomb of Christian Rosencreutz and the immortality of the Rosicrucian hero.

The Elixir of Life opens at the turn of the century in the prophetic year 1600. The alchemist, Dr Lamb, is exultant at having discovered the secret of perpetual life, proclaiming that he is 'the possessor of the wondrous secret, which the greatest philosophers of all ages have sought to discover – the miraculous preservative of the body against decay.'[51] But just as he tries to drink the magical potion, it is stolen from him by his great-grandson Auriol, who consumes it himself. Following this, Auriol is beset by a series of misfortunes leading to his impoverishment. Crippled by gambling debts, he is forced to seek out the help of the Satanic figure, Rougemont, who promises him wealth in exchange for signing a bond which will bring about his eternal damnation. During these infernal negotiations, Auriol is coaxed into drinking another elixir. He discovers that this is an 'infernal potion' which 'without destroying life, shatters the brain, and creates maddening fancies.'[52] Auriol's nightmare dilemma from which he is eventually cured by his great-grandfather, Dr Lamb, is in being doomed to an immortal existence at the same time as he loses his reason. Here there is a poetic irony since the seeker of unlimited knowledge is punished with madness. This is an example of how those whom the gods destroy they first make mad. The predicament of the 'mortal immortal' is that his rationality has been circumscribed within the finite. Thus he may find himself unable to cope with the prospects of an eternal existence which may lie beyond the limits of reason.

A less dramatic treatment of the bid for perpetual life may be found in Thomas Moore's romance, *The Epicurean* (1827). The narrative is set in the second century and concerns Alciphron, a young Epicurean philosopher, who is advised to journey to Egypt in search of the secret of immortality. On his arrival, he is instructed by a stranger to 'go unto the shore of the dark Nile, and thou wilt find the eternal life thou seekest.'[53] Determined to discover some spell or talisman 'to make the spirit within us deathless as the stars' and to 'open to its desires a career like theirs, burning and boundless throughout all time,'[54] Alciphron visits the Temple of the Moon, where he witnesses the spectacle of nymphs dancing for the goddess Isis. From there he sails to Necropolis, the City of the Dead, where he gazes upon the visage of the god Osiris. Finally, he ventures into a pyramid to undergo the initiation of fire, water and air.[55] Many details of this coincide with the description in the Abbé Jean Terrasson's *Sethos* (1732) of the hero and heroine's inauguration into the rites of an Egyptian brotherhood. *Sethos* also supplied one of the sources for the libretto of Mozart's masonic opera *The Magic Flute* (1791).[56]

The Epicurean also reflects the influence of the charismatic Count Cagliostro (Giuseppe Balsamo, 1743-95), who had introduced new rituals into Freemasonry from Rosicrucian Hermeticism, allegedly derived from the secret hieroglyphics inscribed on Egyptian tombs. This colourful character captured the imagination of Schiller, who modelled his ghost-seer on Cagliostro in *Der Geisterseher* (1789) and Veit Weber, who based his sorcerer in *Die Teufelsbeschworung* (1791) on the famous charlatan. Cagliostro, who was believed to possess many of the occult powers attributed to the members of the Brotherhood of the Rosy Cross, provided Rosicrucian novelists with a prototype for the Gothic immortal.

As mentioned earlier, historical figures such as Dee, Agrippa and Paracelsus provided novelists like Godwin and Mary Shelley with models for their Rosicrucian heroes. But the real importance of this kind of novel lies in its capacity to explore the invariably tragic consequences for the immortal wanderer embarking on the pursuit of immortality. The extent to which novelists enter into this kind of inner exploration varies from one novel to another. For example, *St Irvyne,* the most Gothic novel to be discussed, scarcely engages in any psychological exploration, unlike *Zanoni*, which Edwin M. Eigner describes as a metaphysical novel. *Zanoni, St Leon, Melmoth the Wanderer* and *A Strange Story,* may be regarded as fictional representations of explorations in consciousness. The sense of the eternal experienced by their Rosicrucian heroes is also captured by Byron in his wandering immortal Manfred, who laments:

> I tell thee man! I have lived many years
> Many long years, but they are nothing now
> To those which I must number: ages – ages
> Space and eternity – and consciousness.[57]

In order to understand the tragedy of the Rosicrucian hero as the prisoner of his own purgatorial existence, it is necessary to analyse the consciousness of the paradoxical state of mortal immortality in terms of a self-imposed alienation.

The Eternal Wanderer

The alienated consciousness of the post-Enlightenment figure is represented in the novel through the wanderings of the isolated Rosicrucian. The Gothic immortal experiences estrangement from both external reality and inner consciousness. David Punter, in *The Literature of Terror,* draws attention to the Gothic heroes whose social isolation draws them into the realms of the diabolical and the divine. Punter applies Marx's theory of alienation to his argument, saying:

> Under capitalism, Marx argues, man is further alienated from the natural world: under this heading we can place the emphasis on landscape in Gothic, the dialectic between the fading world of reality and the creation of expressionistic substitutes for a realm which is vanishing from sight.[58]

Later examples of the Rosicrucian novel such as *Zanoni* and *A Strange Story* coincided with the theories of alienation which had been formulated by Marx during the 1840s. The Rosicrucian hero passes through all the stages of alienation which Marx had shown to have emerged from the political economy of capitalism: (1) the alienation of man from his labour and its product; (2) the alienation of man from nature; (3) the alienation of man from his own species; (4) the alienation of man from himself. As the following Marxist analogy will demonstrate, the Rosicrucian novel is not ahistorical but is a product of its own socio-economic context.

1. The first type of alienation concerns man's alienation from the product of his labour. According to Marx, the worker becomes externalised through his product so that 'it exists outside him, independent and alien, and becomes a self-sufficient power opposite him, that the life he has lent to the object affronts him, hostile and alien.'[59] Mary Shelley's *Frankenstein* illustrates how the worker becomes severed from his product, which in Marx's terms now stands in opposition to him as an autonomous power. Frankenstein's monster resists the control of its maker. Instead it harnesses impersonal forces resulting in the destruction of the creator by his creation.

2. The alienation of man from nature may be exemplified by Frankenstein's unnatural creation. Moreover, the Rosicrucian sage divorces himself from nature by artificially extending his life. In the novel, the Rosicrucian hero re-enacts Original Sin by robbing for a second time the Tree of Knowledge of Good and Evil. The mythology of the Fall may be viewed as a symbolic enactment of the transition from consciousness to self-consciousness brought about by mankind's separation from a state of nature or primæval innocence. Yet in its purest sense, Rosicrucianism is a tradition which, consciously or unconsciously, strives to reverse the effects of the Fall in order to reunite mankind with nature. Nevertheless, the Rosicrucian hero invariably achieves the opposite of this goal by reinforcing the alienation between himself and nature through his selfish pursuit of immortality.

3. Marx views the consequences of alienated labour as the estrangement of man from his 'species-being.' The alienation of man from man is illustrated by the Rosicrucian tradition through the wanderer who despite plundering the resources of vitality and life-extension can have no real share in human activity. As Bulwer's immortal, Mejnour, so aptly comments in *Zanoni,* 'I have no life in mankind.'[60] The immortal wanderer is a non-productive being who consumes his way through eternity by having no life in his species. For Marx, productive life is species life, because man is a productive being who actualises himself through labour. Since the Rosicrucian protagonist produces nothing, he becomes the equivalent of an aristocrat wandering the earth in search of some meaningful action. St Leon's failure to find any meaning to his existence leads him to descend into a hedonistic orgy of self-destruction through the excesses of sensory and material pleasure. The wanderer who fails to find conscious vital activity, like Maturin's Melmoth and Bulwer-Lytton's Margrave, may become instead an incarnation of evil, which is antagonistic towards the interests of the human race. This loss of humanity dehumanises the wanderer, who reverts almost atavistically to the level of a creature gov-

erned by mere animal appetites. Margrave, the immortal villain in *A Strange Story,* exemplifies such an individual who has stripped himself of all humanity. Sir Philip Derval despairs that he cannot 'bring human laws to bear upon a creature armed with terrible powers of evil,' since Margrave has become a monster 'for without metaphor, monster it is, not man like ourselves' who has acquired 'arts superior to those of ordinary fugitives.'[61]

4. The final type of alienation lies in man's estrangement from himself when his existence ceases to conform with his essence. The psychosis of the Rosicrucian hero, whose immortality is at odds with his mortal state, is an underlying theme of the Rosicrucian novel. In one sense, the wanderer has overcome an important source of alienation, the fear of death. But unfortunately, this inevitably results in a dislocation from life, which thrives upon a counterpoint with impending death. Since this particular *Angst* is rooted in the values endorsed by society, it is clear that the role of the immortal within literature cannot be examined ahistorically.

David Punter draws attention to the historic significance of Gothic novels as a literature of alienation and locates its inception in the period of early industrial change, which heralded the disruption of well-established social structures and traditions. He explains how even the traditional sense of time which was usually regulated by the seasons was displaced by a new pattern of time, 'the time of the machine and the time of the employer.'[62] The timelessness experienced by the wandering immortal, who has lost all sense of time, represents the temporal and spatial disorientation brought about by increased industrialisation. For example, Godwin's Rosicrucian hero St Leon finds himself unable to distinguish between divisions of time, saying 'Months, years, cycles, centuries! To me all these are but as indivisible moments. I shall never become old.'[63] The ensuing boredom brought about by his protracted existence is indicative of an age entering upon the perils of a mechanised world where the division of labour diminishes the vitality of human activity. The spirit of rebellion which lurks in the depths of the Rosicrucian novel may be identified in the figure of the Gothic immortal who, as a survivor of death, has transgressed the border between the human and the divine. Punter views the immortal wanderers as 'individualist disruptives' who 'burst out of the eighteenth century suddenly and furiously'[64] in a revolt against the constraints of an ordered society.

The historical context for the emergence of the Rosicrucian novel was the period of the Enlightenment when Godwin wrote *St Leon.* The prospect of life-extension appealed to the materialism of eighteenth-century thinkers as reason outwitting nature. Paul Louis Landsberg's observation that consciousness of death is most acute in periods of social disorganisation[65] may be extended to include the corresponding surges of interest in life-extension. The French Revolution, which is the setting for *Zanoni*, marked a major turning point in the history of ideas as a charter for absolute freedom shattering existing hierarchies and tearing down the moral order in a culmination of wholesale destruction. The most radical expression of such anarchy lies in the refusal to submit to eventual death. This represents a rejection of the ultimate threshold or the final restraint placed upon society and the individual. If morality is viewed as a system of hypothetical imperatives, then death must be the stamp of that moral code. Since death ratifies these social values, the Rosicrucian, by defying his allotted life-span, is inevitably a force for anarchic disarray.

The five novelists who will be discussed in the following chapters treated their protagonists in a number of different ways. Godwin's hero, St Leon, who possesses the potential to instigate an anarchistic breakdown of society, eventually submits to death. Though immortality for Shelley symbolised revolutionary change, in *St Irvyne* this ideal is subordinated to the whims of Gothic terror. Mary Shelley portrays her immortals as seekers who fall into the Rose-Cross tradition of magician-scientists, while Maturin condemns the wandering immortal as heretical. Finally, through the hero of *Zanoni*, Bulwer legitimises the mortal immortal as an individual searching for mystic truth. Such diversity may be found among these five authors, whose work spans several periods of literary history ranging from the emergence of the Gothic through to the Romantic novel, and from the period of the Enlightenment up to the Victorian age.

Notes

1. *Secret Societies*, ed. Norman Mackenzie (London, 1967). See Francis Yates, *The Art of Memory* (Harmondsworth, 1978) p. 421 for details relating to Leibniz's Rosicrucian interests.
2. See Edith Birkhead, *The Tale of Terror: A Study of the Gothic Romance* (London, 1921), p. 116 and Marie Roberts, 'The English Rosicrucian Novel,' *Cauda Pavonis*, 8, no. 1 (Spring, 1989), pp. 7-11.
3. See Yates, *The Rosicrucian Enlightenment* (St Albans, 1972) p. 98 and Montgomery, *Cross and Crucible*, 1, p. 195 who quotes from Luther's *Table Talk 'Mysterium Sigilli D[octors] M[artini] L[utheri]'* is revealed:

circulus		*consummatum*
rosa		*gaudium*
cor	significat	*cordis*
crux		*in cruce*

4. *The Chemical Wedding of Christian Rosencreutz* written by Andreæ is believed to be a third Rosicrucian manifesto.
5. *Fama*, quoted by Yates, *The Rosicrucian Enlightenment*, p. 285.
6. Ibid., p. 284.
7. Ibid., p. 285
8. Ibid., p. 288
9. Yates, 'The Hermetic Tradition in Renaissance Science,' p. 263.
10. The actual plans for the '*Societas Christiana*' were laid out in two works he published in 1619–20 called *Modell of a Christian Society* and *The Right Hand of Christian Love Offered.*
11. R. S. Wilkinson, 'The Hartlib Papers and Seventeenth-Century Chemistry,' *Ambix*, 15 (February, 1968), p. 59. See Marie Roberts, 'The Flying Island and the Invisible College in Book Three of *Gulliver's Travels*,' *Notes and Queries* (September, 1984), pp. 391-3.
12. This was the year Dryden celebrated in '*Annus Mirabilis*: The Year of Wonders, 1666: An Historical Poem,' in *The Poems and Fables of John Dryden*, ed. James Kinsley (London, 1970), pp. 42-105.
13. See Charles Webster, *From Paracelsus to Newton: Magic and the Making of Modern Science* (Cambridge, 1982).
14. *Bibliotheca Rosicruciana*, ed. F. Leigh Gardner (London, 1923), p. xxi.
15. Loc. cit.
16. Loc. cit.
17. Yates, *The Rosicrucian Enlightenment*, p. 299.
18. Ibid., p. 305.
19. Ibid., p. 306.
20. Loc. cit.
21. *Bibliotheca Rosicruciana*, ed. Gardner, p. xxi.
22. Christopher McIntosh, *The Rosy Cross Unveiled: The History, Mythology and Rituals of an Occult Order* (Wellingborough, 1980), p. 73.
23. See ibid., pp. 70-1.
24. Ibid., p. 70.
25. Byron, *Poetical Works*, ed. Frederick Page and John Jump (London, 1970), p. 403.
26. Ibid., p. 397.

27. Ibid., p. 392.
28. Ibid., p. 390.
29. Ibid., p. 396.
30. Loc. cit.
31. Pope, *An Essay on Man*, ed. Maynard Mack (London, 1950), III, p. 55.
32. Georg Lukács, *Soul and Form* (Cambridge, Massachusetts, 1974), p. 161.
33. *The Poems of Tennyson*, ed. Christopher Ricks (London, 1969), p. 1114.
34. Ibid., p. 1115.
35. Loc. cit.
36. Quoted by John Brockman and Edward Rosenfeld, *Real Time* (London, 1973), pp. 155-6.
37. Sophocles, *Oedipus at Colonus* from *Sophocles*, trans. F. Storr (London, 1924), I, p. 261.
38. Samber does not acknowledge that this book is actually a translation published in 1715.
39. *Early Masonic Pamphlets*, ed. D. Knoop, G. P. Jones, D. Hamer (Manchester, 1945), p. 44.
40. Ibid., p. 43.
41. See *A Christian Rosenkreutz Anthology*, ed. Paul M. Allen (New York, 1968) pp. 393–6.
42. Charles Johnstone, *Chrysal: Or The Adventures of a Guinea* (London, 1761), I, p. 3.
43. Ibid., p. 2.
44. Ibid., p. 3.
45. Ernest Theodor Amadeus Hoffmann, *The Devil's Elixir* (London, 1829), I, pp. 74-5.
46. William Harrison Ainsworth, *Auriol: The Elixir of Life* (London, 1881), p. 131.
47. Ibid., p. 128.
48. Yates, *The Rosicrucian Enlightenment*, p. 291.
49. Ibid., p. 292.
50. Ainsworth, *Elixir of Life*, p. 129.
51. Ibid., p. 14.
52. Ibid., p. 131.
53. Thomas Moore, *The Epicurean* (Paris, 1827), p. 13.
54. Ibid., p. 12.
55. Alciphron fails in his quest for life-extension. Instead he converts to Christianity through which he hopes to achieve spiritual immortality. As a result of helping an Egyptian priestess, Alethe, who is martyred for her Christian faith, Alciphron is sentenced to hard labour and dies as a prisoner.
56. See Jean Terrasson, *The Life of Sethos: Taken from Private Memoirs of the Ancient Egyptians*, trans. Lediard (London, 1732) and Jacques Chailley, *The Magic Flute, Masonic Opera: An Interpretation of the Libretto and the Music*, trans. Herbert W. Weinstock (London, 1972), pp. 35-7.
57. Byron, *Poetical Works*, ed. Page and Jump, p. 395.
58. David Punter, *The Literature of Terror, A History of Gothic Fctions from 1765 to the Present Day* (London, 1980), p. 417.
59. Karl Marx, *Economic and Philosophical Manuscripts* (1844), ed. David McLellan (Oxford, 1972), p. 135.
60. Bulwer-Lytton, *Zanoni* (London, 1853), p. 154.

61. Bulwer-Lytton, *A Strange Story: An Alchemical Novel* (London, 1973), p. 160.
62. Punter, *The Literature of Terror*, p. 413. See also E. P. Thompson, 'Time, Work-Discipline, and Industrial Capitalism,' *Past and Present: Journal of Historical Studies*, 38 (1967), pp. 56-97.
63. Godwin, *St Leon: A Tale of the Sixteenth Century* (New York, 1972), p. 163.
64. Punter, *The Literature of Terror*, p. 120.
65. See Paul Louis Landsberg, *The Experience of Death: The Moral Problem of Suicide* (London, 1953), pp. 7-8.

2

William Godwin's Darkness of Enlightenment

> If we would know man in all his subtleties, we must deviate into the world of miracles and sorcery.
>
> Godwin [1]

It is surprising to discover that William Godwin, the author of *An Enquiry Concerning Political Justice* (1793) played an important role in the development of the Rosicrucian novel. The anomaly this presents is why Godwin, a political reformer and anarchist philosopher, should have become the founder of a branch of Gothic fiction inspired by the mystical Brothers of the Rosy Cross? As we shall see, his seminal Rosicrucian novel, *St Leon*, gave expression to some of the anarchistic ideas of the *Enquiry*, while its main plot reflected his interest in life-extension which was currently being considered by medical scientists and Enlightened philosophers.

In his essay, 'Of the Duration of Human Life' (1831) and in the *Enquiry*, Godwin advances the idea that a prolonged life-span could be a material possibility if brought about through the advocacy of reason. Instead of relegating the subject of immortal existence to the theoretical spaces of metaphysical speculation, Godwin was prepared to treat it as an empirical contingency and radical alternative, thus antagonising theologians and conservatives like Malthus. Though fascinated by the legend of an elixir of life, as evident from *St Leon* and his esoteric biographical work *Lives of the Necromancers* (1834), Godwin regarded such magical panaceas as dangerous illusions running counter to his own line of thought. *St Leon*, which was inspired by the forerunner to Rosicrucian fiction, John Campbell's *Hermippus Redivivus: The Sage's Triumph over Old Age and the Grave* (1744), captures this dual response.

The Sleep of Reason Produces Monsters

According to William Hazlitt, paradox was the keynote to Godwin's character, which consisted of 'a strange composition of contrary qualities:'[2]

> He has written against matrimony, and has been twice married. He has scouted all the commonplace duties, yet he is a good husband and a kind father .... He is a cold formalist, and full of ardour and enthusiasm of mind; dealing in magnificent projects and petty cavils; naturally dull, and brilliant by dint of study; pedantic and playful; a dry logician, and a writer of romances.[3]

Choosing not to allow his antithetical roles of philosopher and poet to polarise reason and imagination, Godwin insisted instead upon the interdependency of rationality and the creative imagination, reason and passion, arguing in the *Enquiry*:

> passion is so far from being incompatible with reason that it is inseparable from it .... We are no longer at liberty to consider man as divided between two independent principles, or to imagine that his inclinations are in any case inaccessible through the medium of his reason.[4]

By rejecting a static model of reason for a more dynamic one, Godwin was able to account for the excesses of the imagination within his own theory of human nature. Ford K. Brown locates the point where reason and enthusiasm intersect by making a comparison between the philosopher and the poet William Blake: 'The two were the opposite extremes of eighteenth-century thought, but had much in common, Blake advocating Enthusiasm very rationally, Godwin advocating Reason with great enthusiasm.'[5] In pursuing an analytical distinction to an extreme position, Godwin brought about a dialectical reversal so that reason became its own antithesis, irrationality. Don Locke compiles some responses to this tendency in his critique of Godwin's philosophy, *A Fantasy of Reason*:

> Godwin is regarded still as the supreme fantast of reason. 'Reason seems to have had the same effect on him as mere enthusiasm has on other men,' wrote the essayist John Churton Collins. 'What sobers most men intoxicated him. What quenches them gave him fire. And perhaps no other work carries reason to such patently unreasonable lengths.' 'It is a curious instance of extreme principles,' complains the *Dictionary of National Biography*, 'advocated with the calmness of one-sided logic.'[6]

The importance of ascertaining Godwin's attitude towards reason is that he regarded the legendary goal of the Rose-Cross Brethren, immortality, as both rational and legitimate. In *Lives of the Necromancers*, the shadowy Rosicrucians are dimly silhouetted:

> Nothing very distinct has been ascertained regarding the sect, calling itself Rosicrucians. It is said to have originated in the East from one of the crusaders in the fourteenth century; but it attracted no public notice till the beginning of the seventeenth century. Its adherents appear to have imbibed their notions from the Arabians, and claimed the possession of the philosopher's stone, the art of transmuting metals, and the elixir vitæ.[7]

Attracted to the notion of the Rosicrucians as alchemists laying claim to the secret of eternal youth, Godwin typifies those thinkers of the Enlightenment, such as Condorcet, who had inherited the fascination of the Florentine Neoplatonists with longevity and immortality. Some of these Renaissance scholars had been captivated by the idea that an individual could transcend the limits of mortality imposed by nature through the use of magical incantation. Progressive and radical Enlightenment thinking desirous of secularising Christian eschatology put its faith in reason as the agent which could conquer death. Godwin's attraction to the fabled elixir of life was attributable in part to this climate of revisionist teleology. The expectation that immortality would materialize into a scientific reality was in circulation when Godwin started writing *St Leon*.

An Enlightenment Panacea: The Cure for Death

The Scientific Revolution had established a rational foundation for prolongevity which developed during the Enlightenment. Godwin's interest in life-extension had been shared by Descartes, Bacon, Franklin and Condorcet, who were all committed to the view that material immortality was a distinct possibility. Godwin, however, disagreed with Bacon, Franklin and Condorcet that the answer was contingent upon 'the growing perfection of art'[8] or science. He believed that immortality would come about through nature during the course of evolution. The perfectibility of the human race if perceived as a gradual process emerging from the supremacy of reason and pre-eminence of truth would then precipitate perpetual improvements in knowledge thus enabling the prolongation of life to emerge from 'the immediate and unavoidable operation of an improved intellect.'[9] Godwin believed that the amelioration of mankind would inevitably lead to the conquest of death so that immortality would eventually be achieved. In accordance with his doctrine of self-determination, he was convinced that the individual would be the matrix for this moral progress which could be measured in terms of the prolongation of life through the exercise of 'mind over matter,' and insisted that faith in prolongevity would increase life-expectancy and so lengthen lives accordingly.

Marshalling examples of psychomatic phenomena, Godwin inferred from these that the power of the mind is capable of arresting even bodily decay. Observing in medicine that good news frequently improves the condition of patients while bad tidings may accelerate or even cause illness, he noted: 'There is nothing of which the physician is more frequently aware than of the power of the mind in assisting or retarding convalescence.'[10] Satisfied that voluntary control over bodily functions was the key to perfect health and infinite life-extension, Godwin observed that the circulation of the blood was subject to effects caused by 'certain thoughts, and states of the thinking faculty.'[11] From this it follows that the mind may exert control over the operations of the body. Arguing for the mastery of the will over the cycles of nature, he reasoned that the mind which is essentially progressive will break out of its prescribed boundaries.

This formulation of the power of the will had been influenced by Thomas Holcroft, an advocate of the mind-over-matter doctrine, who probably provided Godwin with a model for the hero of *St Leon*. Treating pain as an illusion and death and disease as symptoms of man's mental ineptitude,[12] Holcroft was optimistic that the individual would soon be able to overcome the mortal condition through the power of the will. In the following dialogue, Holcroft explains to Thomas Ogle how fatal accidents arise from error:

> It is nonsense to say that we must die; in the present erroneous system I suppose that I shall die, but why? because I am a fool:– "Hurra" said I, "but if a man chops your head off it will be impossible to chop your head off: chopping off heads is error, but if a tree falls on you and crushes you?– men will know how to avoid falling trees:– but trees will not fall: falling of trees arises from error.'"[13]

As he rightly predicted, Holcroft did indeed die, but the circumstances surrounding his death were curious. Charles Lamb wrote to his friend

Thomas Manning that Holcroft's heart had completely ossified following a severe illness during which he had kept himself alive through his mental powers 'long after another person would have given up.'[14] Lamb goes on to report that 'the physicians all concurred in positively saying he would not live a week, many weeks before he died.'[15] In his essay, *Dreams at the Dawn of Philosophy,* Isaac Disraeli dismisses Holcroft's theory that longevity may be achieved through the power of the mind as just as incredible as the occult explanations of his Hermetic predecessors:

> The late Holcroft, Loutherbourg and Cosway, imagined that they should escape the vulgar era of scriptural life by reorganizing their old bones and moistening their dry marrow; and their new principles of vitality were supposed by them to be found in the powers of the mind; this seemed more reasonable, but proved to be as little efficacious as those other philosophers, who imagine they have detected the hidden principle of life in the eels frisking in vinegar, and allude to "the bookbinder" who creates the book-worm.[16]

Holcroft's belief in mind-over-matter helped to shape Godwin's vision of a perfected humanity which would evolve eventually into a race of immortal beings. In the *Enquiry*, Godwin predicted that first mankind would overcome the need for sleep, since before death can be banished we must first obliterate its image, sleep. In 1772, Antoine-Angélique Chomel voiced the conflicting view that those with a sound physique and the ability to sleep long and deeply would live longer than others. If this were so then the next major problem to surmount would not be death but insomnia, for which he had no cure![17] Like Chomel, many prolongevity theorists believed that sleep could stave off ageing and death. Godwin's daughter, Mary Shelley mentions the Seven Sleepers of Ephesus in one of her short stories about suspended animation.

During the Enlightenment, gerontology was bound up with notions of degeneration. Scientists like Buffon considered theories of botanical exhaustion alongside the hypothesis that gravity, by becoming more powerful, was exerting more pressure on the human body.[18] Hypotheses such as these had the advantage of being able to account for the prolonged lifespans of the Biblical patriarchs who had survived, allegedly, for several centuries. During the eighteenth century, the preoccupation with mortality turned on the finite capacities of the human body. Medical experts argued that human physiology wore out, artificial light deteriorated the eyes while noise eroded the ear-drums. The digestive system was also exhausted by the food and drink consumed during a lifetime.

Scientists explored ways in which the human life-span could be extended. Three years before the publication of *St Leon*, the physician Christopher Hufeland, a disciple of the major exponent of longevity, Conaro, published *The Art of Prolonging Life* (1796). Hufeland, who was a member of the Weimar group and friend of Goethe, Schiller and Herder, claimed that the human life-span could be extended to two hundred years. His approach to prolongevity advocated a macrobiotic life-style embracing more than the idea of temporal extension since it was targeted at improving the quality of life.

Another way of eliminating the factors responsible for death, such as disease and senescence, was through social engineering, which had been proposed by the physician-philosopher Cabanis, who in turn had been inspired by Condorcet. Though sympathetic towards Condorcet's belief that mankind is endowed with a perfectibility to which it is impossible to assign a limit,[19] Godwin would have rejected the further suggestion that indefinite prolongation of human existence should be brought about by selective breeding. Such a criterion for universal longevity clashed with his guiding principle of equality. Likewise the prospect of a solitary Rosicrucian greedily coveting the elixir of life would also have been anathema. Instead, Godwin promoted the kind of socio-philosophical reforms which would free all individuals from the statutory limits of life prescribed by Christianity. Anti-clerical eighteenth-century thinkers who regarded the prolongation of life as an extension of Enlightenment idealism would have welcomed this radical thinking.

According to Kant, the concept central to the process of enlightening or *Aufklärung* is liberty: 'To this enlightening however nothing is required but LIBERTY.'[20] The most radical expression of this freedom was the liberation from mortality, which threw into reverse the metaphysical and biological certainty of death. Resistance to the eventuality of death as the supreme assertion of the individual will was in tune with Godwin's philosophical anarchism. In the wake of the Scientific Revolution, the Enlightenment had redrawn the boundaries of knowledge and redefined the material and moral universe. The pursuit of immortality formed part of this revised epistemology, making thinkers now more inclined to question the limits of mortality.

Godwin's complaint in his *Essay on Sepulchres,* that death reduces human beings to 'mere creatures of abstractions and mathematical or syllogistic deduction,'[21] is repudiated by St Leon, whose post-revolutionary sensibilities and Romantic awakening goad him to challenge the instinctive acceptance of death.

Godwin and Malthus

Before writing his Rosicrucian novel Godwin had already defended the right to material immortality in his *Enquiry*. His section on 'Health and the Prolongevity of Human Life' had offended Thomas Malthus, who in retaliation subtitled his *Essay on the Principles of Population, On the Speculations of Mr Godwin, M. Condorcet, and Other Writers* (1798). As an advocate of population control, Malthus believed that Godwin's recommendations for life-extension could only exacerbate the problems of over-population by leading to food shortages, outbreaks of epidemics and widespread poverty. Godwin had already anticipated these objections through the arguments put forward by Robert Wallace in *Various Prospects of Mankind, Nature and Providence* (1761), predicting that population rises would level out and then drop in accordance with the ascendancy of reason, on the grounds that sexual desire would be recognised as an animal function which the intellect would surely learn to despise:

> One tendency of a cultivated and virtuous mind is to diminish our eagerness for gratification of the senses. They please at present by their novelty, that is, because we know not how to estimate them. They decay in the decline of life, indirectly because the system refuses them, but directly and principally because they no longer excite the ardour of the mind. The gratifications of sense please at present by their imposture. We soon learn to despise the mere animal function, which, apart from the delusions of intellect, would be nearly the same in all cases; and to value it only as it happens to be relieved by personal charms or mental excellence.[22]

According to Godwin the widespread use of birth-control was inevitable given that future generations would be governed by utilitarian considerations, intent on curbing population increases in proportion to factors relating to life-extension and improved health. As a clergyman, Malthus was opposed to contraception on the grounds that it impeded nature. Neither was he prepared to consider life-extension as a viable option for society, because it conspired against nature. Malthus had noted that philosophers such as Godwin and Condorcet had, by denying divine immortality in fact secularised Christian eschatology by trying to create a Heavenly City on Earth:

> I cannot quit this subject without taking notice of these conjectures of Mr Godwin and Mr Condorcet, concerning the indefinite prolongation of human life, as a very curious instance of the longing of the soul after immortality. Both these gentlemen have rejected the light of revelation which absolutely promises eternal life in another state. They have also rejected the light of natural religion, which to the ablest intellects in all ages, has indicated the future existence of the soul. Yet so congenial is the idea of immortality to the mind of man, that they cannot consent entirely to throw it out of their systems .... What a strange and curious proof do these conjunctions exhibit of the inconsistency of scepticism![23]

Malthus goes on to argue that Godwin and Condorcet in their search for immortality succumb to the superstitious forces which they profess to have overcome:

> After all their fastidious scepticisms ... they introduce a species of immortality of their own ... in the highest degree, narrow, partial and unjust. They suppose all the great, virtuous, and exalted minds, that have ever existed, or that may exist for some thousands, perhaps millions of years, will be sunk in annihilation; and that only a few beings, not greater in number than can exist at once upon the earth, will be ultimately crowned with immortality. Had such a tenet been advanced as a tenet of revelation, I am very sure that all the enemies of religion, and probably Mr Godwin and Mr Condorcet among the rest, would have exhausted the whole force of their ridicule upon it, as the most puerile, the most absurd, the poorest, the most pitiful, the most iniquitously unjust, and, consequently, the most unworthy of the Deity, that the superstitious folly of man could invent.[24]

Godwin's proposals for life-extension were part of a utopian vision which is described in the *Enquiry Concerning Political Justice*:

> Other improvements may be expected to keep pace with those of health and longevity. There will be no war, no crimes, no administration of justice, as it is called, and no government. Beside this, there will be neither disease, anguish, melancholy, nor resentment. Every man will seek, with ineffable ardour, the good of all.[25]

In this system, utilitarianism was accompanied by the cultivation of benevolence, the Humean foundation for his system of ethics which he believed would 'tend to the prolongation of human life.' Towards the end of *St Leon*, his immortal hero eventually realises this and so devotes himself to benevolent action.

Godwin believed that prolongevity was a natural and inevitable consequence of human progress. In a proleptic passage, he proselytises:

> Nothing can be more irreconcilable to analogy than to conclude, because a certain species of power is beyond the train of our present observations, that it is beyond the limits of the human mind .... If it could have been told to the savage inhabitants of Europe in the times of Theseus and Achilles that man was capable of predicting eclipses and weighing the air, of reducing to settled rules the phenomena of nature so that no prodigies should remain, and of measuring the distance and size of the heavenly bodies, this would not have appeared to them less incredible than if we had told them of the possibility of maintaining the human body in perpetual youth and vigour .... The sum of the arguments which have been here offered amounts to a species of presumption that the terms of human life may be prolonged, and that by the immediate operation of intellect, beyond any limits which we are able to assign.[26]

While anticipating no limits to the mental capacity of the individual to increase his or her life-span, Godwin cautions against the futility of getting embroiled in the discourse of immortality:

> It would be idle to talk of the absolute immortality of man. Eternity and immortality are phrases to which it is impossible for us to annex any distinct ideas, and the more we attempt to explain them the more we shall find ourselves involved in contradiction.[27]

The way in which he depicts St Leon immersing himself in the problems of eternity for his own personal advancement is a paradigm of how the rational pursuit of immortality can degenerate into irrationality.

Godwin's interest in moral and spiritual deterioration led him to explore his hero's folly in trying to short-cut the evolutionary path towards immortality by using the elixir of life. As a consequence, St Leon's life-extension becomes a living abuse of the Rosicrucian tradition which, as a system of magic and science, had the capacity to unite the secular aspirations for human perfectibility of both the Renaissance and the Enlightenment.

Lives of the Necromancers

Godwin devoted himself to the study of Rosicrucians, occultists and operative magicians in his biographical *Lives of the Necromancers: An account of the most eminent persons in successive ages, who have claimed for themselves, or to whom has been imputed by others, the exercise of magical power* (1834) where he announces that his avowed intention in writing the book was 'to exhibit a fair delineation of the credulity of the human mind. Such an exhibition cannot fail to be productive of the most salutary lessons.'[28] Areas of credulity are classified under the headings of 'Rosicrucians,' 'Necromancy,' 'Alchemy,' 'Fairies,' 'Talismans and Amulets,' 'Chiromancy,' 'Physiognomy' and 'Astrology.' Also mentioned are 'Sylphs and Gnomes,' 'Salamanders and Undines,' who are inhabitants of the Rosicrucian spirit-world. Anxious that his work should not be mistaken for a treatise on occultism, Godwin dismisses these entries as products of auto-suggestion and superstitious fears, reminding the reader that:

> the work I have written is not a treatise of natural magic. It rather proposes to display the immense wealth of the faculty of imagination, and to show the extravagances of which man may be guilty who surrenders himself to its guidance.[29]

He narrates the lives of a number of famous occultists such as Pythagoras, Albertus Magnus, Cornelius Agrippa and John Dee for the purpose of casting doubt upon the authenticity of the magical powers attributed to them:

> No sooner do we imagine human beings invested with these wonderful powers, and conceive them as called

> into action for the most malignant purposes, than we become the passive and terrified slaves of the creatures of our own imaginations, and fear to be assailed at every moment by beings to whose power we can set no limit, and whose modes of hostility no human sagacity can anticipate and provide against. But, what is still more extraordinary, the human creatures that pretend to these powers have often been found as completely the dupes of this supernatural machinery, as the most timid wretch.[30]

Godwin's scepticism extended to miracles. His taxonomy of the irrational included several Biblical characters intermingled with his catalogue of necromancers. His admiration for magicians as explorers of the incredulous may have been tempered by the need to legitimise his own interest in documenting the misguided wanderings of the mind:

> The errors of man are worthy to be recorded, not only as beacons to warn us from the shelves where our ancestors have made shipwreck, but even as something honourable to our nature, to show how high a generous ambition could soar, though in forbidden paths, and in things too wonderful for us.[31]

For Godwin, human beings, though 'partners of gods,'[32] were also capable of rejecting 'the sceptre of reason:'[33]

> We long to be something, or to do something, sudden and unexpected, to throw the furniture of our apartment out at the window, or, when we are leaving a place of worship, in which perhaps the most solemn feelings of our nature have been excited, to push the grave person that is just before us, from the top of the stairs to the bottom. A thousand absurdities, wild and extravagant vagaries, come into our heads.[34]

In his essay on 'The Rebelliousness of Man,' Godwin puts forward three explanations for such irrational behaviour: a love of novelty, the pursuit of adventure and a craving for power. The fictional Rosicrucian character, having inherited all the weaknesses of a fallen mankind, pines for power over life and death, being at the same time fallible, human and eternal. If the Rosicrucian dream were realised within such circumstances then the consequences could be alarming, as Godwin suggests:

> If man were an omnipotent being, and at the same time retained all his present mental infirmities, it would be difficult to say of what extravagances he would be guilty. It is proverbially affirmed that power has a tendency to corrupt the best dispositions. Then what would not omnipotence effect?[35]

Godwin argues that omnipotence feeds the power-seeker's irrational tendencies. He extends his hypothesis by speculating on the outcome of bestowing supernatural powers upon an imaginary individual: 'But, to bring the irrationality of man more completely to the test .... Let us imagine him to be gifted with the powers of the fabled basilisk, "to monarchise, be feared, and kill with looks."'[36] Godwin believed it inevitable that such an individual would abuse these powers of nature particularly since magic itself trafficked in the unnatural. Throughout his writings, magic is regarded as an agent of radical change which is indicative of spiritual and moral decay. For Godwin, the occult was the apotheosis of human irrationality, an idea which he sought to express in his novels.

An early example is *Imogen*, described as *A Pastoral Romance from the Ancient British, a fantasy of magic and intrigue.* Claiming that the story was a translation from an ancient Welsh Druidic legend, Godwin parodies the Ossianic tradition. Martha Winburn England notes that in this caricature of Celtic folk-lore Godwin does not believe in the magical powers which supply the dynamics of his plot in the way that Milton believes in the magic wand in *Comus* (1634) and Johnson in the 'Happy Valley' in *Rasselas* (1759).[37] Godwin was, however, curious about those who believed implicitly in the power of magic and who were ready to defend its rationality.

In *St Leon*, Godwin spotlights the errors of reason brought about by his Rosicrucian hero's pursuit of the supernatural. Documenting how science may be subverted into superstition and rational pursuits turned into irrationality, *St Leon* is a case-history illustrating how easily the quest for the philosopher's stone and the elixir of life can degenerate into an abuse of immortality.

St Leon – a Rosicrucian Novel

> It is well known that the philosopher's stone, the art of transmuting metals into gold, and the *elixir vitæ*, which was to restore youth, and make him that possessed it immortal; formed a principal object of the studies of the curious for centuries.
>
> Godwin[38]

Godwin's exposure of the hollow tyranny of the philosopher's stone in *St Leon* is calculated to show that the secret of alchemical transmutation and eternal life are futile goals for which domestic affection and inner peace have been needlessly sacrificed, and that limitless wealth, freedom from disease, weakness and death are unimportant compared to the domestic affection of family life. This emphasis upon the importance of family life is significant since *St Leon* was written shortly after his wife, Mary Wollstonecraft, died giving birth to Mary Shelley. The novel was written as a tribute to her memory and lovingly portrays her as Marguerite, St Leon's wife.

The story concerns Count Reginald de St Leon, a descendant of one of the oldest families in France, who after pursuing a military career embarks upon a period of gambling. Two years later he meets Marguerite Louise de Damville, whom he eventually marries. They have several children and share a few years of domestic happiness. But eventually St Leon returns to his former life at the gambling tables of Paris. As he approaches financial ruin he becomes disillusioned with Parisian life and returns to his wife and family, retreating with them to a place of obscurity in Switzerland. It is here that St Leon enjoys an idyll of pastoral simplicity, but after a while he longs to return to the world of power and influence. After a number of setbacks, he encounters a mysterious old man called Zampieri on the verge of death, who turns out to be the possessor of the philosopher's stone and the elixir of life. Before the stranger dies in a state of disillusionment with his own life, he imparts his occult knowledge to St Leon. Initially overjoyed by his acquisition of the secrets of alchemical transmutation and eternal life, St Leon soon discovers that his newly-found wealth only arouses the envy and suspicion of his neighbours. Persecuted by the authorities and besieged by a mob, he begins to experience the miseries of the stranger's legacy. His son Charles leaves home in protest against his father's disgrace, while Marguerite dies believing that her husband has betrayed her. Consequently, St Leon wanders from country to country, exiled to an immortal existence. While searching for the peace he has forfeited, he is hounded by the Inquisition and eventually imprisoned by them for heresy. On escaping to Hungary, St Leon decides to mobilise his knowledge of the occult arts by putting into practice the principles of universal benevolence, and to this end enlists the support and friendship of Bethlem Gabor. Unfortunately, this turns out to be an unwise move since Gabor turns out to be an arch-villain who imprisons St Leon for his alchemical secrets. After his release, St Leon meets up with his son who fails to recognise him. He conceals his identity from Charles, who is on the verge of marrying the beautiful Pandora. After Charles at first accuses his father of trying to steal the affections of Pandora, the story ends on a bitter-sweet note with St Leon, the self-imposed exile, witnessing the reconciliation of Pandora and his estranged son.

Godwin wrote *St Leon* to alleviate his financial difficulties, since his mounting debts had begun to alienate such friends as Francis Place, making it imperative for him to produce a best-seller which would rival the success of his psychological thriller, *Caleb Williams* (1794). It is only fitting that Godwin, in striving for literary immortality, should choose as the hero for his next novel one who discovers the secret of eternal life. He noted that: 'In those days it was deemed a most daring thought to attempt to write a novel, with the hope that it might hereafter rank among the classics of a language.'[39] Following the completion of *Caleb Williams*, Godwin confessed 'I despaired of finding again a topic so rich of interest and passion.'[40] The attraction to the supernatural for his next novel was a reaction against *Caleb Williams*, for as Godwin readily acknowledged:

> One caution I have particularly sought to exercise: "not to repeat myself." *Caleb Williams* was a story of very surprising and uncommon events, but which was supposed to be entirely within the Laws and established course of nature, as she operates in the planet we inhabit.[41]

The 'mighty trifle'[42] which established Godwin as a novelist tells the story of Caleb Williams, who is appointed secretary to the eccentric Squire Falkland. Gradually, Williams's suspicions grow that Falkland is the murderer of the tyrannical land-owner Tyrrel, who has died earlier in mysterious circumstances. Although remaining loyal to Falkland by protecting his secret, he is cruelly persecuted by his employer, who eventually imprisons him. Williams manages to escape and proceeds to lay a charge of murder against Falkland. Lacking any incriminating evidence, he manages to extract a confession from the murderer through the sincerity of his own testimony. According to Godwin, *Caleb Williams* had been designed 'to comprehend, as far as the progressive nature of a single story would allow, a general review of the modes of domestic and unrecorded despotism by which man becomes the destroyer of man.'[43] *St Leon* is a continuation of this pattern of destruction, this time by drawing attention to the tragic squandering of immortal life.

Godwin decided to combine elements of the Gothic novel and the psychological thriller with Rosicrucianism. The result was *St Leon*, which he described as follows: 'The story of *St Leon* is of the miraculous class; and its design [is] to mix human feelings and passions with incredible situations, and thus render them impressive and interesting.'[44] Godwin had noted the demand in England for translations of German Gothic novels. One English writer, Matthew Gregory Lewis, had steeped himself in the methods and techniques of *Schauerromantik* in *The Monk* (1796) in order to capitalise on the current vogue for *Sturm und Drang* literature. Godwin introduced the Rosicrucian novel by adapting the legends of the philosopher's stone and the elixir of life to the Gothic formula. In 1795 the *Monthly Review* drew attention to the attraction of the Rosicrucian arcana for the novelist:

> The Platonic idea of influencing demons or disembodied spirits by human rites and adjurations, of learning secret phenomena from their revelations, and of accomplishing by their intervention, important purposes of this world, had scarcely been mentioned, much less credited, since the time of the old Alchemists and Rosicrucians, until some modern novelists chose once more to familiarise the superstition; partly in order to expose it, and partly in order to extract from it new sources of the terrible.[45]

The original title of *St Leon* had been the *Opus Magnum*, which had acknowledged the central importance of the philosopher's stone and elixir to the plot. But subsequently dissatisfied with this, Godwin changed it to the less esoteric title of *Natural Magic* and then to *The Adept* before finally deciding on *St Leon*. Godwin may have taken this surname from the Cabala with which the Rosicrucians had been associated, since the name of the author of one of the most influential Cabalistic texts was Moses de Leon. In view of the reputation of the Rosicrucians as alchemists, Godwin may have appropriated the surname from Cohausen's *Hermippus Redivivus*, in which the town of Leon is identified as the place where the adept Nicholas Flamel discovered the secrets of alchemy. In the same work there is a reference to Leonicus, who having mastered the art of longevity read a lecture at the age of 96. St Leon may be a contraction of the name of Leonicus, who was also determined to extend his natural lifespan.

In the novel, St Leon is the hero's family name, which Godwin links with the tradition of the Rosy Cross through the Red Cross knights of the Crusades. St Leon describes how his mother had hoped 'to render me the worthy successor of the counts de St Leon, who had figured with distinguished reputation in the wars of the Holy Land.'[46] Some sources claim that the Rosicrucians were descended from the Knights Templar, a military order associated with the Crusaders. Godwin makes this connection in his own definition of the Rosicrucian sect in *Lives of the Necromancers,* where he points out that 'it is said to have originated in the East from one of the crusaders in the fourteenth century,'[47] before going on to characterise the Rosicrucians by their knowledge of alchemical transmutation and the *elixir vitae.*

Alchemist and Adept

Alchemy and adeptship are two key aspects of Godwin's portrayal of St Leon as a Rosicrucian adept. His treatment of the Rosicrucian theme contributed to the nineteenth-century perception of the tradition of the Rose and Cross which was influenced by Renaissance occultism.[48] Two such works listed in Godwin's library catalogue,[49] Francis Bacon's *Historia Vitæ et Mortis* (1620) and Paracelsus's *De Vita Longa* (1566) would have provided him with source material for the story of St Leon's immortal existence. In *De Vita Longa,* Paracelsus argues persuasively for the prolongation of life by pointing out that since no specific time has been determined for a person's death then it could be postponed indefinitely. To counter theological objections, particularly charges of blasphemy, Paracelsus reasons that prolongevity is not contrary to nature, since the creator has provided the necessary ingredients for the manufacture of the elixir. It is significant that these arguments are rehearsed in *St Leon* in defence of the hero's decision to take the life-prolonging potion.

Another work by Paracelsus listed in Godwin's library catalogue is *De Transfiguratione Metallorum Libellus* (1593). Even though this treatise furnished Godwin with details of alchemical transmutation, he does not divulge the mechanics of alchemy in *St Leon.* The reason for this may be because Godwin believed that such an account might actually perpetuate the very superstition he was trying to dispel. In *Lives of the Necromancers,* Godwin roundly dismissed alchemy as a product of the 'lawless imagination of man'[50] which contributed to the 'catalogue of supernatural doings,'[51] and this is surely how he would have regarded Paracelsus's *De Transfiguratione Metallorum Libellus*.

Transmutation is approached by way of the moral problems faced by the alchemist. In the novel, Zampieri and St Leon practise this unhallowed art. Godwin employs hermetic imagery to symbolise not only material prosperity but also greed. Like Zampieri, St Leon discovers that alchemy 'had planted the sordid love of gold in my heart, there, by its baneful vegetation, to poison every nobler and more salubrious feeling.'[52] For the true adept, material alchemy was merely symbolic of the spiritual transmutation which purified the individual on the road to mystical enlightenment. With St Leon, the converse of this occurs, so that his alchemical pursuits accelerate his spiritual deterioration. Even when St Leon loses interest in gold-making and goes on to describe gold as 'mere dross and dirt,'[53] he remains obsessed by alchemy itself, and confesses:

> The secrets of the stranger had given me a particular relish for this kind of pursuit. There are habits of the mind and modes of occupying the attention, in which, when once we have engaged, there seems a sort of physical impossibility of ever withdrawing ourselves.[54]

The enslavement to alchemy is illustrated by an episode in the novel when St Leon is imprisoned by Bethlem Gabor, who tries to exploit his ability to manufacture gold. Yet the alchemical skills which attract Gabor repel Marguerite, for as St Leon is forced to admit, 'she believed me an alchymist [*sic*], a character which she viewed as base, degrading, and insensible.'[55] In an embittered outburst, Marguerite accuses him of betraying her saying: 'For a soldier you present me with a projector and a chemist, a cold-blooded mortal, raking in the ashes of a crucible for a selfish and solitary advantage.'[56]

St Leon's isolation, brought about by his possession of the elixir of life, enables him to embark upon the solipsistic existence of the wandering immortal. Initially he is seduced by the prospect of perpetual youth and freedom from sickness and death:

> I am invulnerable to disease. Every sun that rises, finds the circulations of my frame in the most perfect order. Decrepitude can never approach me. A thousand winters want the power to furrow my countenance with wrinkles, or turn my hairs to silver.[57]

Because he is spiritually unprepared for his mortal immortality, St Leon has short-cut the evolutionary path to life-extension which had been forecast by some Enlightenment thinkers. In addition to this, he has defiled the progress towards unity with the creator advocated by the Rosicrucian manifestos. Like Caleb Williams, St Leon has been selected by fate for an exceptional purpose. In both novels, the hero's downfall is brought about by his longing for prohibited knowledge. For example, Falkland tantalises Williams to unearth a dangerous secret, while Zampieri awakens in St Leon undreamed-of ambition:

> The alchemist had amused me with descriptions of various processes for the transmutation of metals, had exhibited his crucibles and retorts, and employed a sort of dramatic *coup d'oeil* for the purpose of awakening my curiosity and stimulating my passions.[58]

The fall of St Leon is a fable concerning mankind's perennial desire to obtain sacred or prohibited knowledge. Often this hidden wisdom is related to the secrets of life and death, as in Godwin's tragedy, *Faulkener* (1807), where the hero feels himself to be:

> Drawn as by some magician's powerful spell,
> To seek the sacred spring that gave me life?[59]

St Leon tries to justify meddling with occult mysteries by asking 'Shall I shut myself the gate of knowledge and information?' For the Enlightenment thinker such wilful ignorance would have been akin to epistemological sacrilege. Yet St Leon's intention to procure prohibited knowledge is, according to Godwin, the denial of wisdom:

> The midnight oil was held to be the signal of infernal machinations. The paleness of study and the furrows of thought were adjusted to be the tokens of diabolical alliance. He [the adept] saw, in the transactions of that night, a pledge of the eternal triumph of ignorance over wisdom.[60]

St Leon's possession of the *elixir vitae* has enabled him to escape the mortality which had resulted from Original Sin. His realisation that he has contrived a second Fall is evident from the imagery which he uses to convey his impressions of his companions: 'The first sensation I derived from their prosperity, as I have already said, was pleasure: my second was that which the devil might have felt, when he entered paradise for the seduction of our first parents.'[61] Power of omniscience has given him a Luciferian state of being. He even declares 'I was like a god,'[62] but goes on to admit, 'The reader may, if he pleases, despise me for the confession; but I felt I was not formed for the happiness of a god.'[63] St Leon may have felt that god-like happiness could only be obtained from the act of creation, but this is denied him and so he resolves to find satisfaction in improving the material world by 'spreading improvements, dispensing blessings, and causing all distress and calamity to vanish from before me.'[64] Benevolence is the prerequisite to St Leon's happiness as an immortal, but this he cannot sustain. Instead, arrogance and pride triumph, for, having forfeited his mortality, he longs to take his place among the gods, saying 'Methought the race of mankind looked too insignificant in my eyes .... I could have been well content to be partaker with a race of immortals, but I was not satisfied to be single in this respect.'[65]

Even though St Leon complains about his solitude, he is not prepared to share his secret of immortality with anyone else. Instead he locks away the secret inside himself saying:

> I may whisper it to the woods and the waters, but not in the face of man. Not only am I bound to suppress the knowledge of the important secret I possess, but even the feelings, the ruminations, the visions, that are for ever floating in my soul.[66]

Initially, St Leon's possessive individualism means that he has coveted the formula for the *elixir vitae* out of a sense of self-interest. Later, however, he preserves this secrecy for altruistic reasons once he has realised that the diffusion of this knowledge would be detrimental to society.

The conflict between self-interest and altruism is contained within the wider ethical construct of the Enlightenment, which encompassed both elitism and egalitarianism. Ironically, St Leon has achieved the moral and social stasis which had bewitched those eighteenth-century thinkers who wanted to preserve their civilisation from change and decay. As St Leon complains, 'for me the laws of nature are suspended; the eternal wheels of the universe roll backward.'[67] By achieving the absolute, St Leon has lost the dynamic quest for knowledge which drives on the seeker. Even his metaphysical speculations have degenerated into a solipsistic contemplation of self upon which he reflects, 'What adept or probationer of the present day would be content to resign the study of God and the profounder secrets of nature, and to bound his ardour to the investigation of his own miserable existence?'[68]

St Leon is following out the same tragic destiny as Zampieri, whose life-story is a litany of despair. Zampieri's eye-witness description of historical events identifies him as a Rosicrucian sage. He tells St Leon of his travels:

> I have wandered through every region of the earth, and have found only disappointment. I have entered the courts of princes; I have accompanied the march of armies; I have pined in the putridity of dungeons. I have tasted every vicissitude of splendour and meanness; five times have I been led to the scaffold, and with difficulty escaped a public execution. Hated by mankind, hunted from the face of the earth, pursued by every atrocious calumny, without a country, without a roof, without a friend.[69]

Marguerite begins to realise that her husband can no longer sustain any meaningful human relations since he has become a 'solitary, cold, self-centred individual'[70] alienated from his fellow-species. The real price he has paid for the possession of the philosopher's stone is alienation. Unprepared for this contingency, St Leon has turned himself into a lonely immortal, wandering the earth in search of the unattainable goals of lasting friendship and unbroken peace, regarding himself as one who must endure perpetual isolation in the belief that an 'immortal can form no true and real attachment to the insect of an hour.'[71] To such a being the cycles of mankind appear to be that of a mayfly, for as St Leon points out, 'months, years, cycles, centuries! To me all these are but as indivisible moments.'[72] When he realises that solitude must accompany this timeless existence, the prospect seems to be almost unendurable. Cast out from nature, he laments, 'Man was not born to live alone. He is linked to his brethren by a thousand ties; and, when those ties are broken, he ceases from all genuine existence.'[73] St Leon's mastery of death has turned him into the slave of eternity, for he now begins to view his immortality as a form of non-existence, saying; 'it was all a lie; I was no youth; I was no man; I was no member of the great community of my species.'[74] Now a living negation of himself and consumed by nihilism, he declares 'I am nothing to any human being: I am alone in the boundless universe.'[75] His life has become a living death, since he believes that he who dedicates his days to an endless sorrow is the worst and most degraded of suicides.

St Leon atones for his guilt by resolving to undergo the sufferings inflicted upon him by persecutors such as Bethlem Gabor, who derives sadistic satisfaction from witnessing the 'sublime desolation of a mighty soul.'[76] St Leon's greatest expiation is in continuing to live, for as he points out, 'I could not resolve to die: death had too many charms to suit the self-condemnation that pursued me. I found a horrible satisfaction in determining to live, and to avenge upon myself the guilt I had incurred.'[77] He urges, 'Let no man, after me, pant for the acquisition of the philosopher's stone.'[78] The lesson to be learnt from the pursuit and acquisition of the elixir of life is that freedom from mortality enslaves the individual in an endless syndrome of life-in-death and death-in-life from which there is no escape. The chronic discontent engendered by such a predicament was also capable of breaking out into social disruption.

The Anarchy of Immortality

The potential danger of the mortal immortal as an instrument of anarchy is immediately recognised by the authorities; hence St Leon's persecution by Church and state. The philosopher's stone is a metaphor for the chaos threatening the moral, social and political order, for as Zampieri warns: 'It might overturn kingdoms, and change the whole order of human society into anarchy and barbarism.'[79] The *elixir vitæ*, by challenging Christian eschatology and its promises of a future life, throws the teachings of the Church into jeopardy. If the secrets of alchemical transmutation were freely available then these would also weigh down the Invisible Hand regulating market forces. St Leon's unlimited wealth has the capability of disrupting the economic balance of the country, while his life-extension poses a threat to the social and spiritual fabric of the state. The government views the prospect of a race of immortals as a subversive menace. St Leon himself, reflecting upon the frailty of the mechanisms of social control which impose a tenuous order upon human society, contrasts the permanence of his immortality with the mutability of society, the rise and fall of empires which he expects to outlive. Yet St Leon, who is an immutable being, is also a catalyst for radical change. His career traces out a Rousseau-type drama in its revolutionary promise to overthrow institutions.

The novel was published in the same year that William Pitt introduced legislation against secret societies and trade unions through the Combination Acts (1799).[80] A vehicle for the ideas contained in Godwin's anarchistic *Enquiry Concerning Political Justice*, *St Leon* provided Godwin with an outlet for his frustration at the government's attempt to suppress suspected revolutionary activists in 1794. St Leon's internment by the inquisitorial forces of law and order parallels the government's harassment of its author. Godwin regarded effective anarchic activity as a collective enterprise not to be undertaken by an individual acting alone. In the preface to *Caleb Williams* he argues:

> Can anything be more distinct than such a proposition on the one hand and a recommendation on the other that each man for himself should supersede and trample upon the institutions of the country in which he lives? A thousand things might be found excellent and salutary, if brought into general practice, which would in some cases appear ridiculous, and in others be attended with tragical consequences, if prematurely acted upon by a solitary individual.[81]

By using magic as the agent of his anarchism, St Leon threatens not only to destroy tyrannical institutions but also to undermine human values, as his son Charles points out: 'Magic dissolves the whole principle and arrangement of human action, subverts all generous enthusiasm and dignity, and renders life itself loathsome and intolerable.'[82] Godwin in his essay 'On the Exoteric and Esoteric in Philosophy and Theology' attacks those secret societies which employ magic as the instrument of political change, accusing them of resorting to the expedient of cloaking their occult lore behind a set of doctrines contrived to gain greater public acceptability. The menace of a hidden organisation armed with anarchic ideals and occult powers, like the Illuminati, was exploited in such German Gothic novels as Grosse's *Horrid Mysteries,* which Godwin had read before writing *St Leon.*

In his other novels anarchy makes itself felt on a number of different levels. For instance, in *Mandeville,* the hero experiences a similar sense of moral chaos as St Leon, saying:

> For me the order of the universe was suspended; all that was most ancient and established in the system of created things was annulled; virtue was no longer virtue, and vice no longer vice. This utter subversion related to me, and me alone.[83]

Similarly, the moral topography of the drama *Antonio* (1800) is one in which the hero is born 'Rude from the hand of chaos, cradled with Wild Winds.'[84] As a radical thinker, Godwin was fascinated by moral catastrophe which threatened to tear down the edifice of social order. But as a philosopher, he recognised how difficult it is to systematise the anarchic tendencies within human nature. In his *Italian Letters* he writes:

> It is vain that the philosopher sits in his airy eminence, and seeks to reduce the shapeless mass [of man] into form, and endeavours to lay down rules for so variable and inconstant a system: Nature mocks his efforts, and the pertinacity of events belies his imaginary hypothesis.[85]

St Leon personifies the rebellion and disobedience which is pervasive and universal throughout the human race. Godwin's essay on 'The Rebelliousness of Mankind' recognises the importance of ensuring that individuals are never overwhelmed by social systems. St Leon is confronted by the paradox facing Rousseau, namely that to gain survival entails a loss of humanity. Ironically, by conquering death and losing all moral restraint, St Leon has denied for himself the ultimate in radical change. He has lost his revolutionary capabilities and forfeited his humanity. No longer mortal, St Leon now regrets that he has tried to realise the Rosicrucian dream of eternal life through his pursuit of the philosopher's stone. The novel is a warning to those Enlightened thinkers who sought to short-cut the path of human progress which Godwin believed may only be achieved by evolutionary means.

St Godwin

Godwin attracted critical attention as the first English writer to incorporate in a romance the idea of a Rosicrucian hero. The appearance of such a fantastic fiction at the time of the Enlightenment made some critics feel rather uneasy: 'During the mania of the philosopher's stone, such a tale might have had its use: but it is now as obsolete as would be a farce or novel designed to ridicule astrology and the casting of nativities.'[86] The incredible plot of the tale prevented the empirically-minded from perceiving St Leon's quest for self-knowledge as a parable of the *Zeitgeist*. In the preface to *Fleetwood* Godwin pointed out that his friends had denounced *St Leon* as: 'a vicious style of writing; that Horace has long ago decided, that the story we cannot believe, we are by all the laws of criticism, called upon to hate.'[87] Praised by Byron and Shelley, *St Leon* met with both critical and commercial success running into six editions during Godwin's life-time. It was hailed by Hazlitt as one of the most splendid and impressive works of his time; and Horne Tooke assured Godwin that 'you write better each time than the time before.'[88] But these laudations were by no means universal. In 1800 a scathing parody of the novel appeared called *St Godwin: A Tale of the 16th, 17th and 18th Century* (1800) by Count Reginald de St Leon, whose real name was Robert

Dubois. Ridiculing as crass sentimentality Godwin's description of idyllic domesticity, Dubois parodies Godwin's eulogies of Marguerite and the children: 'I can merely say, that I believe they were like most other people's children, sometimes good and sometimes naughty, but more frequently the latter. Such then was 'my family as they surrounded me in the year 1544.'[89] Dubois, having conveyed the improbability of Godwin's idyll of family-life, has little difficulty in casting doubt on the plausibility of the plot. He also attacks Godwin's verbosity with such interjections as 'every little in this way helps to fill the pages, *and* that is all I have got to do,'[90] and at the same time chastises Godwin for neglecting to develop the descriptive passages which would build up an atmosphere of Gothic terror: 'I wish I had Mrs Radcliffe by me, for I am at a stand; I know this is the place for description, but I cannot get on.'[91] Mimicking Godwin's desire for approval from his reader with such asides as 'Hey, do not you think that is a good round period? Not quite so simple as the case required perhaps, but the two last words are thumpers, that is enough for me,'[92] he peppers his parody with unkind jibes such as 'I could be infinite. But, I beg pardon, I fear I am writing too well, I will endeavour to descend.'[93] He goes on to a vicious attack upon Marguerite, the idealisation of Mary Wollstonecraft, the author of *A Vindication of the Rights of Woman* (1792): 'I cannot see how the chattering of a foolish woman concerns any one but her husband, I shall keep it to myself.'[94] In *St Godwin,* St Leon's aspirations towards benevolence are besmirched through puns on the name 'Hungary,' the country in which the hero attempts to put his principles into practice. St Leon's misguided hero-worship of the villainous Bethlem Gabor also provides Dubois with ammunition:

> the sight of his right eye was extinguished, and the cheek half shot away .... Such was the amiable creature I elected for my bosom friend .... He cursed mankind, he rose up in *fierce defiance of eternal providence;* and your blood curdled within you as he spoke: Such was Bethlem Gabor: I COULD NOT HELP ADMIRING HIM![95]

Dubois's attempt to debase St Leon's noble intentions thinly disguises his main intention of deflating Godwin's pomposity at the cost of Godwin's desire for public approval. There is no evidence that *St Godwin* was taken seriously, but it must have been savoured by Godwin's enemies, especially the concluding passage:

> thinking from my political writings, that I was a good hand at *fiction,* I turned my thoughts to novel writing.– These I wrote in the same pompous inflated style as I had used in my other publication; hoping that my fine, high-sounding periods would assist to make the unsuspecting reader swallow all the insidious reasoning, absurdity, and nonsense, I could invent. The plan succeeded for some time, but at last they burlesqued my works, and made me look like a fool.[96]

Hermippus Redivivus

The inspiration behind *St Leon* was *Hermippus Redivivus,* which Godwin acknowledged had 'suggested the first hint of the present performance'[97] to him. The alleged author, John Campbell, claimed that the treatise was a translation from the German of Johann Heinrich Cohausen. Yet Godwin was convinced that *Hermippus Redivivus,* the biography of an adept who had conquered death, was Campbell's own invention. The writer of the essay 'On the Prolongation of Life' assumed in 1832 that the author was Cohausen, of whom he wryly notes: 'The author of *Hermippus Redivivus* was John Henry Cohausen, a German physician, who did not quite make good his own theory, but died in a sort of nonage, when he was only eighty-five years of age.'[98] Dr Johnson had already assigned the authorship of *Hermippus Redivivus* to Campbell saying:

> Campbell is a man of much knowledge, and has a good share of imagination. His *Hermippus Redivivus* is very entertaining, as an account of the Hermetick philosophy, and as furnishing a curious history of the extravagances of the human mind. If it were merely imaginary, it would be worth nothing at all.[99]

There is even a doubt expressed in the text itself that Hermippus Redivivus had ever existed as a historical person but was instead an 'Invention of some malicious Wit amongst the Ancients.'[100] Certainly, the treatise bears all the hallmarks of a Rosicrucian-type hoax, which suggests that *Hermippus Redivivus* was a product of the 1740s and not of the ancient world. There is a further clue in the verbal echo of the *Corpus Hermeticum* written during the second century A. D., which the Renaissance Neoplatonists wrongly believed to have been the much earlier source of Plato's work.

Rejuvenation and longevity are the main themes in this supposed history of Hermippus Redivivus who allegedly lived for 150 years plus 5 days with the aid of the breath of young women. The author makes a mock appeal to the authority of the ancients to authenticate the viability of such methods by noting such variants as the claim attributed to Pliny that Hermippus Redivivus lived even longer by inhaling the breath of young men! The presumed author, Campbell, regarding death as unnatural, argues that disease is 'Superinduced by the Follies and Vices of Men, which carry in them naturally the Seeds of Death.'[101] He cites examples of individuals who prolong their lives by purifying themselves from the moral contamination of folly and vice. Campbell also speculates that prolongevity may be aided by a mysterious preparation containing human blood. In his brief history of hermetic philosophy, he refers to the longevity of the Biblical Patriarchs and to Roger Bacon's *De Prolongatione Vitæ* in support of his central argument that life-extension is really accessible to all of us:

> We have no more a right to complain that the Secret of preserving long life is not discovered to us, than that the Art of baking Bread, of melting Ores, and refining Metals, or indeed any other Art was not revealed to our ancestors in the earliest Ages of the World, but left to be the Reward of their Industry and Sagacity.[102]

He goes on to argue that rejuvenation and prolongevity deserve serious attention:

> Now, if there be a Possibility of renovating human Nature, why on the one side should we not Study it? Or why on the other, should this kind of Study be treated as a vain and fanciful Thing? If the Office of a Physician be Honourable; if there be something Noble and God-like in curing Diseases, in stopping the progress of Pain and Misery, and warding off the dart of Death for a few Years....[103]

Campbell tries to broaden the appeal for quests associated with the philosopher's stone and the *elixir vitæ*, which Godwin observed had 'formed a principal object of the studies of the curious for centuries.'[104] Turning his attention to the Rosicrucians, for whom he declares prolongevity was a privilege of membership, he claims to have derived his information from *Arcana Totius Naturæ Secretissima* (1630) by Peter Mormius, a self-appointed ambassador for the Rosicrucians who even tried to represent the *Collegium Rosanium* at the States-General. Unfortunately, Mormius's ambassadorial mission failed, partly due to the adverse reception of his book, which had prompted the theological professors of Leyden to condemn the tenets of the Brotherhood of the Rosy Cross by recommending that members of the order should be regarded as being on the verge of insanity since they threatened the inviolability of the Church and the peace of the State.

Mormius's description of a meeting in 1620 with an old man called Rose who was a member of the brethren has similarities with St Leon's encounter with Zampieri. Though Mormius refuses to be admitted into the order, he manages to unearth some of its mysteries while employed as the old man's servant. Mormius identifies the Rosicrucian secrets to be Perpetual Motion, the art of transmuting metals, and the Universal Medicine, the cure for death. Campbell argues that the Universal Medicine, which was derived from the philosopher's stone, accounted for the fabled longevity of the Rosicrucian adepts. Campbell goes on to document the life of Nicholas Flamel, whom he introduces as a 'well-known Rosicrucian sage.'[105] Flamel's adventures may well have provided Godwin with a model for St Leon's career, since both are mortal immortals. Like St Leon, Flamel and his wife Perrenelle are harassed because of the adept's reputation as a sorcerer. Eventually they are forced to pretend that they died in a fire in Switzerland. Both St Leon and Flamel are French and are persecuted for their magical arts, thus being forced to find refuge in Switzerland. As mentioned earlier, the name of Godwin's hero may have been derived from Leon, the town where Flamel discovers the secrets of the philosopher's stone from the *Book of Abraham the Jew*. This book is described in the nineteenth-century story, *The Lying Raven*, by Ninian Bres, where the narrator records his encounter with Flamel and Perrenelle:

> As the couple came abreast of the spot where I stood, Flamel turned toward me and seemed about to speak, but Perrenelle drew him quickly on, and they were almost at once lost in the crowd. You ask how I am so confident that this was Nicholas Flamel? I tell you that I have spent many hours in the *Bibliothèque Nationale*, poring over *Figures d'Abraham Juif:* look carefully at the first side of the fifth leaf and there, in the lower right-hand corner of the representation of those who seek for gold in the garden, you will see the face that searched mine that evening of the boulevard du Temple, and that has haunted my dreams ever since.[106]

Flamel's possession of the elixir was recorded by the seventeenth-century traveller Paul Lucas, who had been informed by a Turkish sage that 'true philosophers had the secret of prolonging life for anything up to a thousand years.'[107] Lucas was further assured by the Turk that 'Flamel is still living; neither he nor his wife has yet tasted death.'[108]

Yet Campbell points out that even the most celebrated adepti such as Roger Bacon, Raymond Lully and Basil Valentine did not want to sustain the burden of eternal life indefinitely and so resigned themselves to death. An example of a mortal immortal not yet disillusioned with his life-extension is Signor Gualdi, whose career is described in *Hermippus Redivivus*. In the preface to *St Leon,* Godwin includes a long quotation about Signor Gualdi. The narrative tells of how Gualdi in 1687 meets a nobleman in Venice and invites him to view his collection of pictures. The Venetian accepts and during the viewing he recognises a portrait of his host in a painting by Titian, who had died 130 years earlier. The implication of this is that Signor Gualdi had discovered the secret of the philosopher's stone. As Godwin points out in his conclusion to the tale, 'Many stories, besides this of Signor Gual have been told, of persons who were supposed to be in possession of those wonderful secrets, in search of which hundreds of unfortunate adventurers wasted their fortune and their lives.'[109] *St Leon* is yet another episode in the saga of the *elixir vitæ,* but its primary importance lies in its seminal role of establishing the genre of the Rosicrucian novel which led on to Shelley's *St Irvyne.*[110]

Notes

1. Godwin, *Lives of the Necromancers: or, An account of the most eminent persons in successive ages, who have claimed for themselves, or to whom has been imputed by others, the exercise of magical power* (London, 1834), preface, p. vii. For a graphic representation of reason and its antithesis see Plate 1: *El sueno de la rason produce monstruos* which is no. 43 of the *Caprichos*. Goya's full commentary is: 'Imagination deserted by reason, begets impossible monsters. United with reason she is the mother of all the arts, and the source of all their wonders.'
2. Hazlitt, *Conversations with Northcote* in *Complete Works of William Hazlitt*, ed. P. P. Howe (London, 1930-31), XI, p. 235.
3. Loc. cit.
4. Godwin, *Enquiry Concerning Political Justice and its Influence on Modern Morals and Happiness*, ed. Isaac Kramnick (Harmondsworth, 1976), pp. 135-6.
5. Ford K. Brown, *The Life of William Godwin* (London, 1926), p. 40.
6. Don Locke, *A Fantasy of Reason: The Life and Thought of William Godwin* (London, 1980), p. 9.
7. Godwin, *Lives of the Necromancers*, pp. 35-6.
8. Godwin, *Enquiry Concerning Political Justice*, p. 771.
9. Loc. cit.
10. Ibid., p. 772.
11. Ibid., p. 774.
12. Holcroft directed much of Godwin's thinking on death and immortality. In 1788 he persuaded Godwin to become an atheist. It is possible that Holcroft's atheism, by excluding the prospect of a spiritual after-life, motivated his desire for material immortality. A year later, Godwin helped Holcroft come to terms with the suicide of his son. See *Tragical Consequences or A Disaster at Deal being an unpublished letter of William Godwin, Wed. Nov. 18, 1789* (London, 1921).
13. Quoted by E. Colby, *A Bibliography of Thomas Holcroft* (New York, 1922), p. 15.
14. *The Letters of Charles and Mary Lamb*, ed. E. V. Lucas, 3 vols (London, 1935), II, p. 68.
15. Loc. cit.
16. Isaac Disraeli, *Dreams at the Dawn of Philosophy* in *Curiosities of Literature*, ed. B. Disraeli (London, 1863), III, p. 286.
17. See John McManners, *Death and the Enlightenment: Changing Attitudes to Death among Christians and Unbelievers in Eighteenth-century France* (Oxford, 1981), p. 113.
18. Ibid., p. 114.
19. See Antoine-Nicolas de Condorcet, *Sketch for a Historical Picture of the Progress of the Human Mind* (1793-4). For a discussion of the theories on life-extension see Gerald J. Gruman, *A History of Ideas about the Prolongation of Life: The Evolution of Prolongevity Hypotheses to 1800* (1966).

20. *The Age of Enlightenment: An Anthology of Eighteenth-Century Texts*, ed. Simon Eliot and Beverley Stern, 2 vols (London, 1979), 2, p. 251.
21. Godwin, *Essay on Sepulchres, or A proposal for erecting some memorial of the illustrious dead in all ages on the spot where their remains have been interred* (London, 1809), p. 4.
22. Godwin, *Enquiry Concerning Political Justice*, p. 776. See W. P. Albrecht and C. E. Pulas, 'Godwin and Malthus,' *Publications of the Modern Language Association*, 70 (June, 1955), pp. 552-5.
23. Thomas Robert Malthus, *An Essay on the Principle of Population, as it Affects the Future Improvement of Society, with Remarks on the Speculations of Mr Godwin, M. Condorcet, and Other Writers* (London, 1798), pp. 240-2. See also Godwin, *Of Population – An Enquiry concerning the Power of Increase in the Number of Mankind, Being an answer to Mr Malthus's essay on that subject* (London, 1820).
24. Loc. cit.
25. Godwin, *Enquiry Concerning Political Justice*, pp. 776-7.
26. Ibid., pp. 775-6.
27. Ibid., p. 776.
28. Godwin, *Lives of the Necromancers*, preface, p. v.
29. Ibid., preface, p. xii.
30. Ibid., preface, p. x.
31. Ibid., p. 7.
32. Godwin, *Thoughts on Man, His Nature, Productions and Discoveries: Interspersed with some particulars respecting the author* (London, 1831), p. 93.
33. Ibid., p. 94.
34. Loc. cit.
35. Ibid., p. 98.
36. Ibid., p. 99.
37. Martha Winburn England, *Felix Culpa* appended to Godwin, *Imogen: A Pastoral Romance from the Ancient British* (New York, 1963), p. 109.
38. Godwin, *St Leon* (New York, 1972), advertisement, pp. vii-ix.
39. Ibid., p. v.
40. Loc. cit.
41. Godwin, *Caleb William*, preface (1805), p. 13.
42. Ibid., preface (1832), p. 12.
43. Ibid., preface (1794), p. 5.
44. Ibid., preface (1805), p. 13. *St Leon* was later turned into a drama which was published in London by Edward Churton in 1835.
45. Lawrence Flammenberg, *The Necromancer*, trans. Peter Teuthold (London, 1968), pp. xv-xvi.
46. Godwin, *St Leon*, p. 3.
47. Godwin, *Lives of the Necromancers*, p. 35.
48. For some insights into his methods of research see Godwin, *Caleb Williams*, preface (1832), p. 11.

49. See Godwin, *Catalogue of the Curious Library of that very eminent and distinguished author, William Godwin* (London, 1836) and Edmund Blunden, 'Godwin's Library Catalogue,' *Keats-Shelley Memorial Bulletin*, 9 (1958), pp. 27-9.
50. Godwin, *Lives of the Necromancers*, p. 29.
51. Loc. cit.
52. Godwin, *St Leon*, p. 130.
53. Ibid., p. 93.
54. Ibid., p. 258.
55. Ibid., p. 247.
56. Ibid., p. 210.
57. Ibid., p. 2.
58. Ibid., p. 144.
59. Godwin, *Faulkener* (London, 1807), p. 5.
60. Godwin, *St Leon*, p. 290.
61. Ibid., p. 302.
62. Ibid., p. 377.
63. Loc. cit.
64. Ibid., p. 167.
65. Ibid., p. 164.
66. Ibid., p. 161.
67. Ibid., p. 2.
68. Ibid., p. 2.
69. Ibid., p. 127.
70. Ibid., p. 363.
71. Ibid., p. 296.
72. Ibid., p. 163.
73. Ibid., p. 282.
74. Ibid., p. 448.
75. Ibid., p. 413.
76. Ibid., p. 401. Godwin's information on Bethlem Gabor was probably derived from *Cabala: Sive Scrina Sacra: Mysteries of State and Government in Letters of Illustrious Persons and great agents; in the Reigns of Henry the Eighth, Queen Elizabeth, King James and the late King Charles* (London, 1654) which is listed in his library catalogue. See also Alexander Fest, 'Bethlem Gabor in English Literature,' *The Hungarian Spectator* (November, 1913), p. 89.
77. Godwin, *St Leon*, p. 83.
78. Ibid., p. 466.
79. Ibid., p. 135.
80. E. P. Thompson, *The Making of the English Working Class* (Harmondsworth, 1968), pp. 546-65.
81. Godwin, *Caleb Williams*, preface (1805), p. 14.
82. Godwin, *St Leon*, p. 474.

83. Godwin, *Mandeville, A Tale of the Seventeenth Century in England*, 3 vols (London, 1817), III, p. 135.
84. Godwin, *Antonio: A Tragedy in 5 Acts* (London, 1800), p. 50.
85. Godwin, *Italian Letters of the History of the Count de St Julian*, ed. Burton R. Pollin (Lincoln, 1965), p. 32.
86. Christopher Moody, 'Godwin's *St Leon, A Tale*,' *The Monthly Review*, 33 (1800), p. 25.
87. Godwin, *Fleetwood or, The Man of Feeling*, 3 vols (London, 1805), preface.
88. Quoted by Locke, *A Fantasy of Reason*, p. 147.
89. Count Reginald de St Leon, *St Godwin: A Tale of the 16th, 17th and 18th Century* (London, 1800), p. 7.
90. Ibid., p. 27.
91. Ibid., pp. 28-9.
92. Ibid., p. 32.
93. Ibid., p. 39.
94. Ibid., p. 42.
95. Ibid., pp. 175-6.
96. Ibid., p. 234.
97. Godwin, *St Leon*, preface.
98. 'On the Prolongation of Life,' *The Retrospective Review*, 7 (1832), p. 76.
99. James Boswell, *Life of Johnson* (London, 1791) reprint (London, 1958), I, p. 258.
100. John Campbell, *Hermippus Redivivus: or, The Sage's Triumph over Old Age and the Grave* (London, 1744), p. 5.
101. Ibid., p. 12.
102. Ibid., p. 101.
103. Ibid., pp. 86-7.
104. Godwin, *St Leon*, preface, pp. vii-ix.
105. Ibid., p. 121.
106. Quoted by Neil Powell in *Alchemy, the Ancient Science* (London, 1976), pp. 40–50.
107. Ibid., p. 46.
108. Loc. cit.
109. Godwin, *St Leon*, p. ix.
110. Regarding inter-connections between the Rosicrucian novelists, Shelley, Godwin's son-in-law, admired *St Leon* while in 1828 Godwin and Bulwer-Lytton became close friends. According to C. Regan Paul, *William Godwin: His Friends and Contemporaries* (London, 1876), II, pp. 305–4, Godwin handed over the notes for his projected novel, *Eugene Aram*, to Bulwer-Lytton. It is possible that Bulwer may have stimulated Godwin's interest in Rosicrucianism. Godwin's receptivity to Bulwer-Lytton's ideas is evident from his declaration to him: 'I now avow myself your convert.' See Paul, *William Godwin: His Friends and Contemporaries*, II, p. 307.

3

Percy Bysshe Shelley: A Gothic Immortal

> You talk like a Rosicrucian, who will love nothing but a sylph, who does not believe in the existence of a sylph, and who yet quarrels with the whole universe for not containing a sylph.
>
> Peacock[1]

Science and Magic

Percy Bysshe Shelley, who became Godwin's son-in-law, continued the line of the Rosicrucian literary tradition with his novel, *St Irvyne* (1801). His own leanings towards magic and science granted him an immediate affinity with the Rosicrucian outlook. This synthesis was characteristic of Rosicrucianism, and may have been responsible for Shelley's attraction towards the Brotherhood of the Rosy Cross. Although Shelley's scientific pursuits have been fairly well documented, Carl Grabo points out in *The Magic Plant: The Growth of Shelley's Thought* that the poet's induction into the marvellous and supernatural remains a blank in his biography.[2] Grabo suggests that Shelley probably had access at his home in Field Place to a number of occult writers such as Paracelsus, along with the blend of science and myth to be found amongst the writings of Erasmus Darwin. Confessing to Godwin that 'he pored over the reveries of Albertus Magnus and Paracelsus'[3] with an enthusiasm which almost amounted to belief, Shelley's reading of Paracelsus's alchemical treatises may have accounted for his boyhood belief in an imaginary alchemist who lived in the attic of Field Place. Likewise Darwin's scientific writings may have inspired not only his poetry but also the series of boyish experiments he conducted at Field Place while on holiday from Eton.[4] Shelley continued to pursue his magico-scientific interests during term-time, brewing strange and fiery liquids to the chorus of:

> Double, double, toil and trouble;
> Fire burn, and cauldron bubble.[5]

On one such occasion, Mr Bethel, who was Shelley's tutor and reputed to be the dullest man in Eton, suddenly came across his pupil engaged on a dangerous-looking experiment. After enquiring into the purpose of this, Mr Bethel was given the following reply, 'Please sir, I am raising the devil.'[6] The consequences of this were that the tutor received an electric shock from touching Shelley's mysterious apparatus. This was not to be the only occasion when the poet's dabblings in scientific experiments threatened to be potentially dangerous. Hogg, for example, recalls that while at Oxford

> It seemed but too probable that in the rash ardour of experiment he [Shelley] would some day set the college on fire, or that he would blind, maim, or kill himself by the explosion of combustibles ... he used to speak with horror of the consequences of having inadvertently swallowed ... some mineral poison, I think arsenic, at Eton.[7]

Many of Shelley's early attempts to amalgamate science and magic found their way into Mary Shelley's fiction, most notably in *Frankenstein* (1818) and 'The Mortal Immortal' (1834). In each story, the hero is inspired to extend the frontiers of science into the realm of magic by the writings of the renowned occultist Cornelius Agrippa. It is tempting to interpret this as a direct reference to Shelley, particularly since he had read Agrippa. He conveys his early enthusiasm for such reading material in a letter to Godwin, saying 'I was haunted with a passion for the wildest and most extravagant romances. Ancient books on chemistry and magic were pursued with an enthusiasm of wonder, almost amounting to belief.'[8]

Since the 'ancient books of chemistry' would have dealt with alchemy it is probable that these, along with Shelley's ventures into science, had heightened his fascination with the occult. The legacy of the poet's scientific interests is apparent in his pragmatic attitude towards the supernatural. One boyhood prank involved a midnight expedition to the tomb of Warnham Church where he intended to use a spell in order to summon a ghost. Although the outcome of this necromantic experiment is not known, it illustrates an attraction towards the occult which is expressed in the early poem, 'Hymn to Intellectual Beauty' where Shelley writes:

> While yet a boy I sought for ghosts, and sped
> Through many a listening chamber, cave and ruin,

And starlight wood, with fearful steps pursuing
Hopes of high talk with the departed dead.
I call on poisonous names with which our youth is fed;
I was not heard – I saw them not.[9]

Eventually, Shelley channelled his energies towards the life of the imagination rather than towards the development of a scientific mind. Nevertheless, it is likely that he had been attracted to the Rosicrucian tradition because it encompassed both magic and science.

The Bavarian Illuminati

The Brotherhood of the Rosy Cross had not been the only secret society to capture Shelley's imagination; there was also the Bavarian Illuminati. His association with secret societies such as the Illuminati, the Assassins, and the Rosicrucians was really an imaginative identification, since he never actually belonged to any of them. The nearest Shelley had come to joining a clandestine brotherhood was when he tried to create his own. Mainly through literature, he explored esoteric societies for their Gothic appeal, while some like the Rosicrucians also laid claim to many of the ideals of Romanticism.

In the wake of the French Revolution, the secret societies were the dark spectres haunting the mass-movements of Europe. Gothic novelists had seized upon them as metaphors of terror. As Walter Scott observed, no novelist was 'so obtuse as not to image forth a profligate abbot, an oppressive duke, a secret and mysterious association of Rosycrucians [sic] and Illuminati, with all their properties of black cowls, caverns, daggers, electric machines, trap-doors, and dark lanterns.'[10] Shelley was attracted to the popular image of the secret societies subversively gnawing at the fabric of Western civilisation. He regarded them as agencies for those dark mysterious forces which dethroned kings, dismounted generals and toppled governments. In 1799, the British government passed an act banning secret and seditious societies. In 1811, Shelley published a novel about a Rosicrucian. He may have been drawn to the revolutionary beginnings of the Rose-Cross brethren who had attracted a following as a Protestant resistance movement during the previous century. In his novel *St Irvyne or The Rosicrucian*, Shelley explores the impact of the most radical implication of any revolution, the conquest of death.

After the continental witch-hunts of the 1790s, he found himself drawn to the Bavarian Illuminati, which was dedicated supposedly to anarchy and revolution. An early version of this society was the Assassins, a Near Eastern sect, which inspired Shelley's prose work of that title.[11] His romantic view of this brutal secret society indicates that he had interpreted the activities of the Assassins in the same favourable light as had the Illuminés. The Bavarian Illuminati had been institutionalised by Adam Weishaupt (1748-1830) at the University of Ingoldstadt in 1776. Regarding themselves as guardians of the Rational Enlightenment, the Illuminati contrived and conspired to illuminate the world with the light of reason until, as Weishaupt forecasts:

> Princes and nations will disappear without violence from the earth, the human race will become one family and the world the abode of reasonable men. Morality alone will bring about this change imperceptibly .... Why should it be impossible that the human race should attain to its highest perfection, the capacity to guide itself?[12]

Drawn to the atheism and liberalism of this cause, Shelley contacted the radical Leigh Hunt about organising a band of 'enlightened unprejudiced members' in order 'to resist the coalition of the enemies of liberty.'[13] Shelley insisted that his proposed society would be instrumental in activating political and social reform, since 'it has been for want of societies of this nature that corruption has attained the height at which we now behold it.'[14]

It is likely that his proposals had been influenced by Robert Clifford's translation of the Abbé Barruel's *Memoirs Illustrating the History of Jacobinism* (1797–8) an exposé of alleged Masonic, Rosicrucian and Illuminist activities. Portraying the secret societies as precipitators of the French Revolution based on an anti-monarchical and anti-ecclesiastical conspiracy, the *Memoirs* trace the origins of the French Revolution from the Illuminati in Ingoldstadt to the Freemasons, philosophers and Jacobins, and then to the mobs on the street. Thomas Jefferson Hogg claimed that one of Shelley's favourite books at Oxford was Barruel's *Memoirs*, which he read and reread 'swallowing with eager credulity the fictions and exaggerations of that readily believing, or readily inventing, author.'[15] Yet Shelley condemned the book in a letter to Elizabeth Hitchener (February 27 1812), declaring it to be 'half filled with the vilest and most unsupported falsehood.' In spite of this denunciation, he went on to recommend the *Memoirs* as 'a book worth reading.'[16] It is ironic to consider that his pursuit of rational liberty should have been inspired by Barruel's vilification of the Illuminati as a subversive organisation committed to the 'annihilation of every Empire, of all order, rank, distinction, property, and social tie.'[17]

Barruel deliberately distorts Weishaupt's ideals of world-wide reform, which were grounded in the principles of Rational Enlightenment. Mary Shelley's monster expressed the revolutionary fervour of the young Shelley, who declared: 'Indeed I think it is to the benefit of society to destroy the opinions which can annihilate the dearest of its ties ... *Adieu. écrasez l'infâme écrasez l'impie.*'[18] This quotation taken from Voltaire was identified by Barruel as the motto of the Illuminati. Shelley must have used this phrase to register his determination to adopt a course of Enlightened thinking by founding a secret society which would be analogous with Illuminism.

The influence of the philosophical anarchism of his father-in-law William Godwin meant that Shelley was Godwin's heir not only in the line of Rosicrucian fiction but also in his utopian vision of the 'Kingless continents sinless as Eden.'[19] Henry Crabb Robinson makes a distinction between the kind of anarchism preached by Godwin in his *Enquiry Concerning Political Justice* (1793) and the lawlessness popularly believed to have been propagated by the Illuminati. Robinson is particularly critical of the Illuminés for shrouding their objectives in secrecy: 'The great difference between Godwinism and Illuminatism consists in this that Godwin proudly rejects all temporising, he shows the distant End and would have his followers strive to attain it immediately.'[20] Paradoxically, the Illuminati, who professed to be the arch-enemies of such obscurantists as the Jesuits, had become, according to Robinson, 'an Antijesuitical Jesuitism.'[21] adopting not only the rhetoric of their opponents but virtually the same means and end. Gothic novelists had seized on this internal irony by portraying the secret tribunals of the Illuminati and the authorities of the Inquisition as one order of tyranny. Consequently the Illuminati, which had originated as a 'harbinger for the Enlightenment,' were now represented through fiction as an instrument of repression. In this way, the subversive image of the Illuminati provided a paradigm for the dialectical reversal of the Enlightenment movement which had transmogrified into its own opposite. The Terror of the French Revolution proved to be the most cogent example of how the 'Enlightenment behaves toward things as a dictator toward men.'[22]

For the middle classes, conspiracy theories sustained the myth that political irrationality had been brought about by a conscious agency. This paranoia was exploited by Gothic novelists such as the Marquis of Grosse. In his *Horrid Mysteries* (1796), a specimen of *Schauerromantik*, a band of desperate Illuminati strive for world dominion. The English translator of the novel claims in his preface:

> Secret Societies have, at all times, and in all civilised countries, either held out private advantages, or pretended to aim at the welfare of whole nations, in order to increase the number of their members. Amongst the former, the Rosycrucians, whose order was instituted in Germany in the latter end of the fifteenth century, and pretended to be in possession of the philosophers' stone, and of many more valuable arcana, were, by far, the most famous; and among the latter, the association known under the name of the Secret Tribunal, acquired the greatest celebrity.[23]

The mythologies of the Rosicrucians and Bavarian Illuminati, having acquired the dimensions of folklore, had carved out a permanent niche in the European popular imagination. Novelists had only to draw on those fictions already circulating in society, which were being amplified by politicians and historians. For instance, Disraeli seems to find it artistically satisfying to channel his political fears into his novel *Lothair* (1870). Elsewhere he blames the outbreak of the revolutions of 1848 and the social upheaval of the previous century on the secret societies:

> The origin of the secret societies that prevail in Europe is very remote. It is probable that they were originally confederations of conquered races organised in a great measure by the abrogated hierarchies. In Italy they have never ceased, although they have at times been obliged to take various forms; sometimes it was a literary academy, sometimes a charitable brotherhood; freemasonry was always a convenient guise. The Inquisition in its great day boasted that it had extirpated them in Spain, but their activity in that country after the first French revolution rather indicates a suspension of vitality than an extinction of life. The reformation gave them a great impulse in Germany, and towards the middle of the eighteenth century, they had not only spread in every portion of the north of that region but had crossed the Rhine.

> The two characteristics of these confederations, which now cover Europe like a network, are war against property and hatred of the Semitic revelation. These are the legacies of their founders; a proprietary despoiled and the servants of altars that have been overthrown. Alone, the secret societies can disturb, but they cannot control, Europe. Acting in unison with a great popular movement they may destroy society, as they did at the end of the last century.[24]

Not surprisingly, Thomas Love Peacock in his satire of the Gothic novel, *Nightmare Abbey* (1818), ridiculed the preoccupation of novelists with secret societies.

Nightmare Abbey

In *Nightmare Abbey*, Peacock caricatures Shelley's attraction towards politically subversive secret societies through the character of Scythrop:

> He now became troubled with the passion for reforming the world. He built many castles in the air, and peopled them with secret tribunals, and bands of illuminati, who were always the imaginary instruments of his projected regeneration of the human species. As he intended to institute a perfect republic, he invested himself with absolute sovereignty over these mystical dispensers of liberty.[25]

Peacock satirises Shelley's fascination with 'secret tribunals, and bands of illuminati' which were stock ingredients of the Gothic novel imported from Germany. Much of the poet's attraction to Gothic romance may be attributed to his reading of terror literature,[26] parodied by Peacock in chapter 3 of *Nightmare Abbey*. Here Marionetta, who is based on Shelley's first wife, Harriet Westbrook, accidentally comes across Scythrop rehearsing a role as the president of some imaginary secret tribunal. Realising that he has an audience, Scythrop recovers sufficiently from his embarrassment to invite Marionetta to act out some scenes with him from one of the tales of the German Illuminati, *Horrid Mysteries*. According to Hogg, Shelley would read aloud from this novel with 'rapturous enthusiasm.'[27] Peacock ridicules Shelley's fascination with the Gothic through his description of Scythrop sleeping with *Horrid Mysteries* under his pillow while dreaming of 'venerable eleutherarchs and ghastly confederates holding midnight conventions in subterranean caves.'[28] Scythrop has fancifully described himself as a 'transcendental eleutherarch,'[29] a term which T. J. Hogg uses in his novel *Alexy Haimatoff* (1813) for a ruler of a secret society. Scythrop has assumed this title in order to win the affections of another heroine, Stella, modelled on Shelley's second wife, Mary. Scythrop suspects Stella to be an Illuminée because she eulogises 'the sublime Spartacus Weishaupt' as the 'immortal founder of the sect of the Illuminati.'[30] Stella eventually confesses to Scythrop that she is fleeing from persecution. Since Scythrop has given her refuge he fears that he has now harboured an Illuminée in contravention of Lord Castlereagh's Aliens Act (1816), which offered little protection to political refugees. Scythrop believes Stella has been a victim of the witch-hunt against secret societies such as the Illuminati. In March 1785 the Elector of Bavaria, under pressure from the Jesuits, exiled all Masonic and Illuminist organisations, which forced Weishaupt to escape to Gotha. Scythrop has become so agitated by her history of persecution that he fears attracting the attention of the authorities himself. Consequently he takes the precaution of having a number of cells and recesses, sliding panels and secret passages built into the tower of Nightmare Abbey, where he can conceal himself should such an emergency arise. Peacock wryly comments that Scythrop has not resorted to such self-preservation for his own sake but for the greater benefit of mankind! Fortunately, Scythrop's foresight enables him to offer Stella the protection of his 'unknown apartments.'[31] In his description of these, Peacock parodies the Gothic settings to be found in so many novels of the period, since Scythrop's 'apartments' are merely inferior imitations of the caverns and subterranean passages frequented by bands of Illuminati.

Scythrop is particularly captivated by Stella because he believes that she must be one of the seven people who have bought a copy of a treatise he has written. He makes this assumption when Stella recognises him as the author of *Philosophical Gas; or, a Project for a General Illumination of the Human Mind.* Even though Scythrop has managed to sell only seven copies, he consoles himself with the solace of numerology, by reasoning that 'Seven is a mystical number, and the omen is good. Let me find the seven purchasers of my seven copies, and they shall be the seven golden candle-sticks with which I will illuminate the world.'[32] Scythrop assumes that Stella must be one of his golden candlesticks as one of the seven consumers of his *Philosophical Gas*. Scythrop's treatise is a parody of one of Shelley's pamphlets for reform, the most likely being his *Proposals for an Association of those Philanthropists who convinced of the inadequacy of the moral and political state of Ireland to produce benefits which are nevertheless attainable are willing to unite to accom-*

plish its regeneration (1812). Here, with reference to Barruel's *Memoirs,* Shelley expands on his earlier proposals to Leigh Hunt about founding a secret society. The *Proposals* for political reform were written in support of Catholic emancipation and for the repeal of the Union Act. Shelley's pamphlet, like Scythrop's *Philosophical Gas*, written to launch a grandiose world-wide campaign of philanthropy, which had been intended to illuminate the whole of mankind. In order to build up the membership of his society, Shelley invited readers of his pamphlet to communicate with him at a Dublin address, presumably in the first instance to attract radical Irish nationalists. Both Shelley and Scythrop hope that their readers would form a vanguard in order to enlighten the world.

Scythrop, wanting to revive a 'confederation of regenerators,'[33] cryptically conceals his revolutionary message in *Philosophical Gas,* where 'his meanings were carefully wrapt up in the monk's hood of transcendental technology.'[34] Peacock's oblique reference to the monastic setting of many Gothic novels alongside an allusion to Kant's transcendentalism draws attention to conflicting elements in Enlightenment thought. In *Nightmare Abbey,* Mr Flosky is based on Coleridge, who was a disciple of Kant. Scythrop is encouraged by Mr Flosky 'to pore over ponderous tomes of transcendental philosophy, which reconciled him to the labour of studying them by their mystical jargon and necromantic imagery.'[35] By comparing Kant's writings to magical jargon, Peacock satirically suggests that both are sources of mystification. He dismisses Kantians as members of an esoteric sect who may be compared to the initiates of a secret society, since Kant 'delivers his oracles in language which none but the initiated can comprehend.'[36] According to Peacock, these cryptic sources of wisdom express 'the views of those secret associations of illuminati, which were the terror of superstition and tyranny.'[37] Ironically, Peacock, by clubbing together Illuminist and quasi-Illuminist societies with Kant's transcendentalism and the Gothic literary tradition, undermines the aspirations of these esoteric organisations towards Rational Enlightenment.

Kant was a notable spokesman for the Enlightenment, as typified in his famous essay '*Was ist Aufklärung?*' ['What is Enlightenment?']. This was a reply to a question raised by J. F. Zollner, who was a member of a Berlin secret society founded in 1783, called the *Berliner Mittwochsgesellschaft* or 'Wednesday Society' and also known as the *Freunde der Aufklärung* or 'Friends of the Enlightenment.'[38] Although Kant himself was not a member of this secret society, he did sympathise with its objectives. For instance, the Horatian tag *Sapere aude* ['Dare to be wise'][39] which appears in Kant's essay became the watchword for the

Enlightenment movement and sums up the sentiments of Weishaupt, who asked the Godwinian question 'Why should it be impossible that the human race should attain to its highest perfection, the capacity to guide itself?'[40] Although Kant argues from a standpoint of pure reason, Sir William Drummond in his *Academical Questions* (1805) denounces him as one of the philosophers who places metaphysics 'upon infallible principles which they have obtained from intuition.'[41] Peacock, who makes oblique references to *Academical Questions* in *Nightmare Abbey,* must have realised that here Drummond had reinterpreted Kant's rationalist use of the term 'intuitive' to refer to its mystical sense.

Likewise, the aims of the secret societies had been transmogrified by Gothic novelists into a regression towards Medieval superstition. Such a bad press for the Illuminist organisations through the medium of Gothic literature must have gratified the opponents of these secret societies, who undoubtedly felt threatened by the prospect of widespread reform. The connection between the secret societies and the Gothic genre may have occurred to Peacock when he wrote to Shelley outlining his purpose in writing *Nightmare Abbey* as 'merely to bring to a sort of philosophical focus a few of the morbidities of modern literature, and to let in a little daylight on its atrabilious complexion.'[42]

It would have been interesting to have discovered whether or not Shelley had succumbed to the lure of the Gothic in his proposed novel *Hubert Cauvin,* where he intended to develop his ideas for a secret society. In his early terror novel, *Zastrozzi* (1810), Shelley comes near to portraying a degenerated image of the Illuminati in Gothic fiction through his hero Verezzi, who has become 'the victim of secret enemies.'[43] Through *St Irvyne,* Shelley advances the Gothic novel from its preoccupation with bands of subversive Illuminists to a rudimentary study of the Romantic anguish of the Rosicrucian hero. A. J. Hartley detects in *St Irvyne* an attempt to incorporate the social and political reform advocated by the Rosicrucian tradition:

> Though Gothic convention is paramount in *St Irvyne* it should be noted, however, that the Rosicrucian, like his creator, and in conformity with the aims of the Rosicrucian Society, is concerned with reform. The book abounds in references to conscience, decries selfishness, and closes on a note of admonition to remorse and repentance.[44]

In *St Irvyne,* Shelley's exploration of the metaphysics of the mortal immortal reveals how Rosicrucianism, like Illuminism, was capable of opening up new insights into the Romantic imagination.

St Irvyne: The Rosicrucian

Generally considered to be the better of Shelley's two early novels, *St Irvyne* has not been singled out otherwise for any merit, and as early reviews make abundantly clear, met with little critical success. A typical contemporary response which appeared in the *Anti-Jacobin Review and Magazine* denounced it as 'description run mad' with 'every wild expression' of the 'disordered imagination of the romance-writer.'[45] Later critics were just as dismissive of *St Irvyne*. Elizabeth Barrett Browning could scarcely believe Shelley to be the author of such 'boarding-school idiocy.'[46] William Michael Rossetti found the novel to be unintelligible to the sane reader,[47] while John Cordy Jeaffreson described it as a 'piece of lunacy' which had a conclusion that 'surpasses all human understanding.'[48] Andrew Lang went even further by claiming that *St Irvyne* proves that Shelley at Oxford was a donkey, and also demonstrates that 'we can never tell how a young wild ass may turn out.'[49] Modern critics have relegated *St Irvyne* along with *Zastrozzi* to the category of obscure and tedious fiction. Nevertheless, the novel has an intrinsic interest in terms of the Rosicrucian tradition, and particularly as a continuation of Godwin's *St Leon,* which Shelley claimed to have read shortly before writing *St Irvyne*. It may have been because of this that Shelley had felt obliged to apologise to Godwin for the defects in the novel by attributing them to a temporary state of 'intellectual sickliness and lethargy.'[50] Ellsworth Barnard, however, suggests that, far from shedding his sickness into books, Shelley's real intention had been to catch the eye of the public by pandering to current taste.[51] Shelley's eagerness for commercial success is apparent from his excited enquiry to his publisher Stockdale: 'Do you find that the public are captivated by the title-page of *St Irvyne*?'[52] If Shelley had been prepared to sacrifice literary quality for eye-catching sensationalism then Peacock's remark that 'this rage for novelty is the bane of literature' would also ring true for him. In Shelley's case, the 'bane of literature' or hankering after novelty is apparent from the subtitle, *The Rosicrucian*.[53] This, as well as the similarity of the main title to Godwin's *St Leon* (both are place-names) would suggest that Shelley had hoped to capitalise upon the success of his predecessor.

St Irvyne tells the story of Wolfstein, a young nobleman, who has joined a band of brigands. One of these is a man named Ginotti, a servant of the devil, who is in possession of the elixir of life. Ginotti, however, wants to relinquish his gift of perpetual life and pass on the secret to Wolfstein. But before this transaction takes place, Wolfstein becomes romantically involved with the beautiful Megalena, who has been captured by bandits. Wolfstein, aided by Ginotti, eventually escapes with her to Genoa. Shortly afterwards Megalena discovers that Wolfstein has become infatuated by the Lady Olympia. Enraged with jealousy, Megalena tries to persuade Wolfstein to murder her rival. Though he cannot bring himself to do this, Megalena is satisfied once she finds out that Olympia has conveniently committed suicide. But she does not savour her victory long, but dies mysteriously in the vaults of the church of St Irvyne. Before her death Wolfstein's sister, Eloise, has already replaced her as the central female character. Eloise's adventures take place as she accompanies her dying mother on a long journey. Eventually, she encounters a sinister stranger, Nempere, who sells her to an English nobleman, Mountford. At Mountford's house, Eloise falls in love with his friend, Fitzeustace. Subsequently, Nempere and Mountford quarrel, which leads to a duel in which the former is killed. Mountford is forced to flee to London in order to avoid the officers of justice, which leaves Eloise free to settle down with Fitzeustace. Meanwhile, Wolfstein arrives at St Irvyne's church, where he has arranged to meet Ginotti, who has promised to reveal the secret of immortality to him. But when the moment of blasphemy arrives Wolfstein finds that he is unable to renounce his creator. Consequently, Ginotti is reduced to a mouldering skeleton forced to endure all the horrors of an eternal existence in hell. Wolfstein also dies 'blackened in terrible convulsions,' though 'over him had the power of hell no influence.'[54]

Shelley's revelation in the last paragraph of the novel that Ginotti, in fact Nempere, considerably complicates the circumstances surrounding the Rosicrucian's death. The main problem now, of course, is that Ginotti-Nempere has died twice, once in a duel and again in the vaults of St Irvyne. Furthermore, Shelley makes no attempt to disguise the fact that he has passed from chapter 4 to chapter 7 in a short-cut for which, Carl Grabo dryly remarked, 'the reader is not ungrateful.'[55] Shelley had barely attempted to harmonise the contradictory plot of *St Irvyne*. Stockdale, who was justifiably mystified by the confused ending to the novel, received the following explanation from the author:

> Ginotti, as you will see did not die by Wolfstein's hand, but by the influence of that natural magic which when the secret was imparted to the latter, destroyed him. – Mountford, being a character of inferior import, I do not think it necessary to state the catastrophe of him, as at best it would be uninteresting. – Eloise and Fitzeustace, are married and happy I suppose, and Megalena dies by the same means as Wolfstein. – I do not myself see any other explanation that is required.[56]

Five days later, Shelley supplied a puzzled Stockdale with an explanation for the subtitle of the novel:

> What I mean as "Rosicrucian" is the elixir of eternal life which Ginotti has obtained. Mr Godwin's romance of *St Leon* turns upon that superstition ... I enveloped it in mystery for the greater excitement of interest, and on a re-examination, you will perceive that Mountford physically did kill Ginotti, which must appear from the latter's paleness.[57]

Here, Shelley acknowledges the influence of *St Leon* on *St Irvyne*. But he departs from Godwin by taking a far more retributionalist line in regard to the penalty for dabbling with the elixir of life. For this reason, Dorothy Scarborough's claim that Shelley's 'adaptation' of *St Leon* 'amounts to actual plagiarism'[58] is not entirely justifiable.

Shelley's approach to the Rosicrucian novel enabled him to indulge his love of mystery and his fascination with the subject of immortality. His attraction towards the mysterious is expressed in the aspirations of his Rosicrucian hero, Ginotti, which echo those of the young Shelley: 'From my earliest youth, before it was quenched by complete satiation, curiosity and a desire of unveiling the latent mysteries of nature was the passion by which all other emotions of my mind were intellectually organised.'[59]

This excerpt from Ginotti's life-story, which is being told to Wolfstein, traces his progress along the paths of forbidden knowledge towards the possession of the philosopher's stone and the attainment of the elixir of life. This is similar to Zampieri's speech to St Leon, which probably provided Shelley with a model for Ginotti's confession to Wolfstein. Like Godwin, Shelley does not divulge details of the magical formula and ritual of the elixir of life. Yet Shelley dwells more than Godwin upon the implications of immortality. In keeping with the *Fama,* Shelley condemns those whose 'wanderings of error'[60] have enticed them towards procuring the blasphemous *elixir vitæ.* *St Irvyne* ends with the warning that endless life may only be 'sought from Him who alone can give an eternity of happiness.'[61] This lesson has been gleaned from the heresies of Ginotti, who has secularised his immortality because, as he admits to Wolfstein: 'I feared, more that ever, now, to die; and, although I had no right to form hopes or expectations for longer life than is allotted to the rest of mortals, yet did I think it were possible to protract existence.'[62] Faced with the prospect of death, Ginotti submits himself to the powers of Hell which, in a vision, reveal to him the secret of eternal life.

As he confesses to Wolfstein: 'I ascertained the method by which *man* might exist for ever, and it was connected with my dream.'[63] Ginotti pares down the ontological problem of eternal life into two options: 'I must either dive into the recesses of futurity, or I must not, I cannot die. Will not this nature – will not the *matter* of which it is composed – exist to all eternity?'[64] Ginotti's wish to perpetuate his life is derived from a desire to retain the familiar rather than to obviate the oblivion of non-existence. In his essay, *On a Future State,* written in 1818, Shelley draws attention to the lure of life-extension:

> This desire to be for ever as we are; the reluctance to a violent and unexperienced change, which is common to all the animated and inanimate combinations of the universe, is, indeed, the secret persuasion which has given birth to the opinions of a future state.[65]

Ginotti's view of death as containing 'the recesses of futurity' rather than as a negation, points to Shelley's belief in a personal immortality. In a note to *Hellas* (1822), written towards the end of the poet's life, he again refers to death as 'that futurity towards which we are all impelled by an inextinguishable thirst for immortality.'[66] Ginotti is not choosing between immortality and the void but between two immortal states. Mary Shelley's short story, 'The Mortal Immortal,' which was inspired by Shelley, also makes this distinction between life-extension and spiritual immortality. The *elixir vitæ* gives rise to a dilemma which is expressed in *St Irvyne* through a structural irony. Ginotti, who inhabits a limbo of moral isolation, has feared death as an estrangement from life. Instead he finds that by perpetuating his existence he has become a stranger to himself and to society. By distancing himself from his kind, Ginotti reinforces his self-imposed solipsism and longs to pass on the secret and surrender to death, saying: 'To one man alone, Wolfstein, may I communicate this secret of immortal life: then must I forego *my* claim to it, – and oh! with what pleasure shall I forego it!'[67] Ginotti goes on to reveal: 'You, Wolfstein, have I singled out from the whole world to make the depository'[68] of the elixir. Wolfstein's reluctance to inherit the secret of eternal life forms part of the nightmarish struggle between himself and his alter-ego, Ginotti, which may be described as a psychomachy.[69] As Andy P. Antippas argues, the Gothic mode lends itself to this type of combat by representing a fragmented moral vision which manifests itself through adversaries who contend as emblems of good and evil. Shelley makes a direct connection between Ginotti and Nempere by identifying them as the same person. This relates to a *Doppelgänger,* the folklore belief that the image of the projected self was a harbinger of impending death.[70] Given Shelley's knowledge of German literature, it is possible that he adopted the motif in order to illustrate moral conflict. The Manichean struggle between Wolfstein and Ginotti may be viewed as a metaphor for the divided self, even of the lost soul. But it is more likely that Shelley was unconscious of any deep underlying meaning to these dualities, since he neglects to explore their allegorical significance. As James Rieger points out in *The Mutiny Within: The Heresies of Percy Bysshe Shelley*: 'The Jew's elixir does not point the same frightening moral as the Titan's stolen fire does because Shelley was not yet thinking symbolically.'[71]

Rieger also draws attention to Shelley's indifference over the contradictory plot of *St Irvyne*. Clearly plot was not a prime concern for him in this novel. He was far more interested in conjuring up a Gothic atmosphere with undertones of black magic. For instance, he hints at a demonic presence in the Miltonic epigraph to chapter 3:

> Whence, and what art thou, execrable shape,
> That darest, though grim and terrible advance
> Thy miscreated front athwart my way.[72]

This extract from *Paradise Lost,* which anticipates Mary Shelley's monster in *Frankenstein,* foreshadows the diabolical being who bargains for the possession of Ginotti's soul. Ginotti has agreed on this price in exchange for eternal life, but when he is dragged to the edge of the precipice by the creature who insists 'Say, art thou willing to be mine?'[73] he hesitates at the last moment. This supernatural being is a nexus for the Rosicrucian and Faustian traditions. Such Germanic influences do not appear in *St Leon*, where the secret of the philosopher's stone is traded independently of diabolical interference. In his novel, Shelley draws on the Faustian selling of a soul to a demonic being for forbidden knowledge. According to Peacock, Goethe's *Faust* was one of the works which took deepest root in Shelley's mind, having had the strongest influence on the formation of his characters.[74] Shelley's admiration of *Faust* is revealed in a letter to John Gisbourne:

> I have been reading over and over again *Faust* and always with sensations which no other composition excites. Perhaps all discontent with the less (to use a Platonic sophism) supposes the sense of a just claim to the greater and that we admirers of *Faust* are on the right road to Paradise.[75]

An inversion of this pattern may be seen in Wolfstein's death-wish made at the beginning of the novel, where he begs 'Oh, God! take my soul; why should I longer live?'[76] Wolfstein's wish is granted in the last chapter, where Ginotti for his blasphemy is 'borne on the pinions of hell's sulphurous whirlwind' to 'the frightful prince of error.'[77]

The Wandering Jew

Vessel of deathless wrath, a slave that feels
No proud exemption in the blighting curse
He bears, over the world wanders for ever.
Lone as incarnate death! O, that the dream
Of dark magician in his visioned cave,
Raking the cinders of a crucible
For life and power, even when his feeble hand
Shakes in its last decay, were the true law
Of this so lovely world!

Shelley[78]

The most famous predecessor of the Rosicrucian wanderer was the Wandering Jew,[79] who figures in at least four of Shelley's poems, *Ghasta* (1809-10),[80] *The Wandering Jew* (1822), *Queen Mab* (1813) and *Hellas* (1821). This particular specimen of Gothic immortal has much in common with the Rosicrucian wanderer.

The ancestry of the Wandering Jew may be traced back to Cain, who was condemned to wander the earth in atonement for his brother's murder:

> And now art thou cursed from the earth, which hath opened her mouth to receive thy brother's blood from thy hand; when thou tillest the ground, it shall not henceforth yield unto thee her strength; a fugitive and a vagabond shalt thou be in the earth .... And the Lord set a mark upon Cain, lest any finding him should kill him.[81]

The branding of Cain by some distinctive mark was later to characterise the Wandering Jew. This legacy was then passed on to the Rosicrucian wanderer in the form of a hypnotic glance. Peacock makes a connection between Cain and Rosicrucianism in 'a song from Mr Cypress' in *Nightmare Abbey:*

There is a fever of the spirit,
The brand of Cain's unresting doom,
Which in the lone dark souls that bear it
Glows like the lamp in Tullia's tomb:
Unlike that lamp, its subtle fire
Burns, blasts, consumes its cell, the heart,
Till, one by one, hope, joy, desire,
Like dreams of shadowy smoke depart.

When hope, love, life itself, are only
Dust-spectral memories – dead and cold –
The unfed fire burns bright and lonely,
Like that undying lamp of old:
And by that drear illumination,
Till time its clay-built home has rent,
Thought broods on feeling's desolation –
The soul is its own monument.[82]

Cain's brand is a metaphor for the fever of the spirit in 'lone dark souls,' which is compared to the lamp in Tullia's tomb. Allegedly, this sepulchral light was still burning in the tomb of Cicero's daughter Tullia when it was opened during the sixteenth century. This parallels the opening of Rosencreutz's tomb with its perpetual-burning lamp described by Eustace Budgell in his essay on the Rosicrucians in *The Spectator* (May 15, 1712). In the second verse of the song, Mr Cypress compares 'the unfed fire' burning 'bright and lonely' to 'that undying lamp of old,' which may be a reference to the Rosicrucian lamp. In the light of this, it is significant that Mr Hilary had already accused Mr Cypress of talking like a Rosicrucian.

Mr Cypress, whose name is evocative of funereal gloom, is a parody of Byron. Peacock's mention of 'Cain's unresting doom' in Mr Cypress's song echoes Byron's lines in *Childe Harold's Pilgrimage* (1812):

... life-abhorring gloom
Wrote on his faded brow curst Cain's unresting doom.[83]

Like Cain, the Wandering Jew has been condemned to 'unresting doom,' since he has been sentenced to wander the earth until the Second Coming of Christ. Although the legend is believed to have emerged from the events surrounding the Crucifixion, the actual identity of the Wandering Jew is complicated by a number of different versions of the tale. The most well known deals with Cartaphilus, Pontius Pilate's janitor, who surprisingly was not even Jewish. Cartaphilus is believed to have been punished by Christ after spurning him on his way to Calvary. Matthew predicted the penance Cartaphilus would pay for his blasphemy in the following pronouncement: 'Verily I say unto you, there be some standing here which shall not taste death till they see the Son of Man coming in his kingdom.'[84]

In other versions of the myth, this was also the penalty incurred by Caiaphas and Malchus, who were recorded in the gospels as guilty of striking Christ.[85] A more benevolent prototype for the Wandering Jew is John, who arouses the curiosity of Peter. For this he is reprimanded by Christ in a passage which Shelley uses as the epigraph to his poem *The Wandering Jew:*

> If I will that he tarry till I come, what is that to thee? Follow thou me. Then went this saying abroad among the brethren, that third disciple should not die; but if I will that he tarry till I come, what is that to thee?[86]

The earliest written account of the Wandering Jew appears in a monastic chronicle recorded in 1228 from the Monastery of St Albans by Roger of Wendover in *Flowers of History.* In his preface to *The Wandering Jew,* Shelley states that reference to the medieval monkish chronicles on the subject was currently in vogue. Nevertheless, he attempted to excuse his unscholarly approach to the subject by arguing that since his treatment of the Wandering Jew would only be 'in the form of a bare poem,' it would not be of 'sufficient consequence to authorise deep antiquarian researchers on the subject.'[87] By the sixteenth century, there were a number of different versions of the legend, which Baring-Gould relates in his *Curious Myths of the Middle Ages* (1866–8). As Shelley points out in the preface to his poem, *The Wandering Jew:*

> The subject of the following poem is an imaginary personage, noted for the various and contradictory traditions which have prevailed concerning him – The Wandering Jew. Many sage monkish writers have supported the authenticity of this fact, the reality of his existence.[88]

Such documentary accounts of the Wandering Jew cropped up during the seventeenth century when, for example, he was credited with Rosicrucian healing powers, as described in Peck's *History of Stamford* and Aubrey's *Miscellanies.*

The Wandering Jew also travelled under a number of different names. His most popular designation is 'Ahasuerus,' which was used by Shelley in *The Wandering Jew.* This name was established by the author of the anonymous pamphlet, *Kurtze Beschreibung und Erzehlung von einem juden mit Namen Ahasverus* (1602). The interest aroused by this publication led to a number of reprints, translations and adaptations of the *Kurtze Beschreibung.* Soon, English writers recognised the possibilities contained within the fable of the Wandering Jew and drew on the mythology accordingly. In 1640, Malone's portrait of the Wandering Jew as a fortune-teller typifies such irreverent approaches to the legend. But towards the end of the eighteenth century, the Romantic treatment of the Wandering Jew prevailed, as in Christian Schubart's *Der Ewige Jude* (1783). The literary use of the immortal Jew was pioneered on the continent by such distinguished writers as Goethe and Schiller.[89] A major contribution was made by Reichard, whose *Der Ewige Jude* (1785) forms part of the Wandering Jew chronicles which document the entire course of his wanderings throughout history. Certainly, the subject opened up unlimited possibilities for the picaresque novelist. But it was to be through the Gothic novel that Matthew Lewis effectively launched the Wandering Jew's career in English literature. The Jew appears in the subplot of *The Monk* which concerns Don Raymond and Agnes. While some believe him to have been an Arabian astrologer, others suspect him to be Doctor Faustus, who has been sent back to Germany, where this part of the story is set, by the devil. As Raymond's narrative reveals, the mysterious stranger provides several clues to his real identity. For example, he makes the following confession to Raymond:

> Fate obliges me to be constantly in movement; I am not permitted to pass more than a fortnight in the same place. I have no friend in the world, and, from the restlessness of my destiny, I never can acquire one. Fain would I lay down my miserable life, for I envy those who enjoy the quiet of the grave; but death eludes me, and flies from my embrace .... God has set his seal upon me, and all his creatures respect this fatal mark.[90]

This seal or mark is in fact the burning cross imprinted on his forehead, which is hidden by a velvet band. The reason for this is that the mark is a sign of the Almighty's vengeance and so instils terror into all who look upon it. The identity of the wanderer is revealed by Raymond's uncle, a cardinal, who 'had no doubt of this singular man's being the celebrated character known universally by name of The Wandering Jew.' [91]

It is likely that Shelley, who greatly admired *The Monk,* had gleaned Ginotti's mesmeric stare in *St Irvyne* from Lewis's *Wandering Jew.* An earlier example of the influence of *The Monk* appears in the *Original Poetry of Victor and Cazire*, written by Shelley and his sister Elizabeth between 1809-10.[92] One of the seventeen poems in the collection is 'Ghasta; or the Avenging Demon,' which is set in the Black Forest of Germany. The principal character is the Wandering Jew, even though he is not mentioned by name. His identity is revealed by the burning cross on his 'flaming brow' and the hypnotic power of his 'sparkling eye:'

> Mighty one I know thee now,
> Mightiest power of the sky,
> Know thee by thy flaming brow,
> Know thee by thy sparkling eye.[93]

The poem consists of a dialogue between a warrior and a mysterious stranger, who appears to be the Wandering Jew. The warrior enlists the help of the stranger to rescue him from the power of a sprite who is haunting him, for 'every night the spectre comes.'[94] Here, Shelley draws on Rosicrucian folklore, since the 'wandering sprite'[95] is an elemental being whose head is bound with 'lambent flame.'[96] Like Fouque's *Undine* (1811), 'Ghasta'[97] is a Rosicrucian romance telling of how mortals become bewitched by sprites and sylphs. In 'Ghasta' the warrior's dilemma is such that he invites his own death if he submits to the love of the sprite, who tells him:

> Now I claim thee as my love,
> Lay aside all chilling fear.
> My affection will I prove,
> Where sheeted ghosts and spectres are![98]

While Faust risked his soul for forbidden knowledge, the warrior has exposed himself to the powers of hell because of his love for a supernatural being:

> Haply I might ne'er have sank
> On pleasure's flow'ry, thorny bed.[99]

The stranger agrees to help the warrior, and with his necromantic powers summons up the demon Ghasta in order to seize the sprite. Here we have a curious meeting-point between the Wandering Jew and the Rosicrucian traditions. The consequence of this is that the Wandering Jew is triumphant in sending the sprite back to hell, but before the warrior has time to rejoice, the stranger requests that he looks at his forehead:

The warrior upwards turned his eyes,
Gazed upon the cross of fire,
There sat horror and surprise,
There sat God's eternal ire.[100]

Since the Jew is a blasphemer and a symbol of God's vengeance, he cannot be an instrument of good, thus the twist in the tale is that the warrior, after gazing on the burning cross, 'sank convulsed in death.'[101]

Shelley's most famous treatment of the Wandering Jew is in the poem of that name which he wrote in collaboration with his cousin, Thomas Medwin. Once again, it is highly probable that Lewis supplied him with the idea, especially since the poem was written around the same time as the poems of *Victor and Cazire*, though it was not published until after the poet's death in 1822. The authorship of individual stanzas of *The Wandering Jew* is problematic, as it is by no means clear how much Shelley actually wrote. In view of Shelley's life-long interest in the Wandering Jew, it is generally assumed that he supplied many of the ideas as well as the initial impetus for the work, even though Medwin is acknowledged to have contributed to its composition.[102] To complicate matters still further, the poem exists in two widely differing versions. The first of these appeared in the *Edinburgh Literary Journal* for 1829, while the second was printed in *Frazer's Magazine* in 1831.[103] The poem, as well as the 'Ahasuerus' section of *Queen Mab,*[104] is based on a prose translation of a German verse 'rhapsody' called *Ahasver* (1786) by Schubart.[105] Yet the circumstances surrounding Shelley's acquisition of this source material are rather puzzling, since we are faced with the problem of conflicting accounts. According to Shelley, the excerpt from *Ahasver,* which he quotes in a note to *Queen Mab,* is the translation of part of some German work, the title of which he claims 'I have vainly endeavoured to discover.'[106] Shelley goes on to inform his reader of how he had discovered this 'mysterious work' by saying 'I picked it up, dirty and torn, some years ago, in Lincoln's Inn Fields.'[107] One of the more sceptical reactions to this story is expressed by Hogg, who claims that Shelley's annotation is itself no more than an integral part of the fiction.[108] Furthermore, Hogg alleges that when Shelley claimed to have retrieved the work, he did not know a single word of German. In view of Hogg's reputation as an inaccurate reporter, such an allegation is by no means conclusive. Nonetheless, Hogg does indeed recognise that such a fable would add to the interest of the romance. This view is shared by Rieger, who suggests that Shelley was probably too embarrassed to admit that he had obtained a prose translation of Schubart's *Ahasver* extract from *Bell's Court and Fashionable Magazine.*[109]

Schubart describes the sufferings of the Wandering Jew, which begin when he refuses to give Christ rest on His way to Calvary. As a result, an angel of death condemns Ahasuerus to wander the earth. In order to perpetuate his wanderings, the angel unleashes a black demon to hound him from country to country. Two thousand years later, Ahasuerus recounts his miseries by reproaching the skulls of his long-dead family with the words, 'They *could die;* but! reprobate wretch alas! I cannot die!'[110] He goes on to lament how he has witnessed the cycles of mankind and complains about his thwarted suicide attempts, which have included provoking tyrants such as Nero and Mulay Ismail. But to Ahasuerus's dismay, even the executioner's hand cannot strangle him.[111] He also recollects how he jumped into Etna's crater, an attempt echoed by Shelley in *The Wandering Jew:*

Thrice happy had I found a grave
'Mid fierce combustion's tumults dire
'Mid oceans of volcanic fire,
Which whirl'd me in their sulphurous wave,
And scorched to a cinder my hated frame.
Parch'd up the blood within my veins,
And racks my breast with damming pains;
Then hurl'd me from the mountains's entrails dread ...
Have I 'scaped the bickering fire ...
And Etna's doom'd by fate to stand.
A monument of the Eternal's ire.[112]

There are many echoes of Ghasta in *The Wandering Jew*, such as the description of the fiery cross on the protagonist's forehead as 'a lambent flame.'[113] It may be significant that the flaming cross closely resembles the Rosicrucian symbol, the rose on the cross, which has Christian connotations. The image of Christ as the dying rose on the cross of humanity is relevant to the genesis of the legend of the Wandering Jew. It is also interesting to note that the hero of Shelley's poem reveals his mark of God's vengeance to Rosa, whose name may signify the rose of the cross:[114]

He raised his passion-quivering hand,
He loosed the grey encircling band,
A burning Cross was there;
Its colour was like to recent blood
Deep marked upon his brow it stood.
And spread a lambent glare.[115]

In this passage, the colour of the cross is compared to that of recent blood, which is indicative of the blood of Christ. The Wandering Jew, who in this version has been designated Paulo, discovers that after his blasphemy, Christ 'shed / His dews of poppy o'er my head.'[116] Here Paulo is anointed with drops of blood from the crucified Christ in a baptism of fire:

A burning cross illumed my brow,
I hid it with a fillet grey,
But could not hide the wasting woe
That wore my wildered soul away.
And ate my heart with living fire.
I knew it was the avenger's sway,
I felt it was the avenger's ire![117]

Even the devil is awed by the cross upon his head which gives Paulo control over the powers of hell:

To me is known the magic spell.
To summon e'en the Prince of Hell;
Awed by the Cross upon my head,
His fiends would obey my mandates dread,
To twilight change the blaze of noon,
And stain with spots of blood the moon –
But that an interposing hand
Restrains my potent arts, my else
Supreme command.[118]

These thaumaturgical arts possessed by the stranger in 'Ghasta' are also part of the magical apparatus of Lewis's *The Monk*. Shelley may have taken his description of a necromantic ceremony from Lewis's account of the magic circle in which the spirit of Beatrice the nun is summoned.[119] In canto 3 Paulo claims:

Oft I invoke the fiends of hell,
And summon each in dire array –
I know they dare not disobey
My stern, my powerful spell …
On death resolved – intent.
I marked a circle round my form;
'Bout me sacred reliques spread,
The relics of magicians dead,
And potent incantations read –
I waited their event.[120]

Here the Wandering Jew is described as possessing powers which are associated with the Rosicrucian sage. For example, this species of Gothic immortal is endowed not only with perpetual life, but also with necromantic powers. Like the Rosicrucian sage, the Wandering Jew is the author of his own misery and suffers the anguish of loneliness and exile:

> A burden on the face of earth,
> I cursed the mother who gave me birth;
> I cursed myself – my native land.
> Polluted by repeated crimes.
> I sought in distant foreign climes
> If change of country could bestow
> A transient respite from my woe.[121]

A distinct link between the Wandering Jew and the Rosicrucian is apparent from the fragments of the poem which serve as epigraphs in *St Irvyne*.[122]

Unfortunately Shelley never managed to get the entire poem published during his life-time, but he recycled the figure of the Jew in *Queen Mab* and *Hellas*. In the first of these poems, the poet uses Voltaire's famous catch-phrase for the Enlightenment, '*écrasez l'infâme.*' [123] According to Barruel, this expression signified the revolutionary fervour of the Illuminati, and so it attracted Shelley. The quotation from Voltaire sets the tone of the poem as an attack on governments, institutionalised religion and established morality. In *Queen Mab,* it is Ahasuerus who is 'mocked with the curse of immortality,'[124] and who has evolved into a Promethean figure determined to defy the Almighty tyrant who has cursed him. Like Milton's Lucifer, the Wandering Jew has long learned to prefer the freedom of Hell to the servitude of heaven. Even the red cross on his forehead, with its overtones of the Rosy Cross and Templarism, is now seen as a symbol of victory in mockery of peace. Once again, in *Hellas*, the burning cross is seen as an emblem of insurrection:

> While blazoned as on Heaven's immortal noon,
> The cross leads generations on.[125]

The insignia of fire on Ahasuerus's forehead, his brand of blasphemy, is symbolic of Prometheus's crime against the gods when he stole fire from the heavens. The Jew, a Promethean conqueror, is also represented as trampling on the thorns of death and shame, the circuit of Christ's kingship on earth. The prophecies of Ahasuerus herald the dawn of liberty in an apocalyptic age when 'the world's great age begins anew' and 'the golden years return.'[126]

An oriental counterpart to the Rosicrucian and the Wandering Jew is Sadak the Wanderer, who forms the main subject of an obscure poem which does not appear in standard editions of Shelley's poems. Davidson Cook came across the poem in *The Keepsake* for 1829 and reproduced it in *The Times Literary Supplement* (May 16, 1936).[127] According to Cook, the poem was inspired by James Ridley (1736-65), whose oriental tale 'Sadak and Kalasrade' appears in *Tales of the Genii* (1764). There seems to be little connection between the poem and the tale apart from the names of the main characters. 'Sadak and Kalasrade' is a love story punctuated by the supernatural interventions of Alla, a genii, a magic ring and a golden goblet. Shelley's poem *Sadak the Wanderer* has more echoes of his *Wandering Jew*. For example, Sadak appears to have the traditional hypnotic glance as indicated by the following:

> Look upon that wither'd brow,
> See the glance that burns below![128]

The narrator also urges the hero to 'dare the tomb / In the red volcano's womb,'[129] which is reminiscent of Ahasuerus's attempt to destroy himself by jumping into Etna's crater.

As we have seen, Shelley's preoccupation with wandering immortals is not confined to the Rosicrucian sage but extends to the tradition of the Wandering Jew. Occasionally the two traditions overlap, particularly when, as in *The Wandering Jew,* the hero is credited with several Rosicrucian attributes such as necromancy and power over the spirit-world. In *Queen Mab* and *Hellas,* the fiery cross on the Jew's forehead is transformed from a badge of shame into a symbol of revolution. This transition reflects the changing social role of secret societies such as the politically inspired Illuminist organisations which made manifest Rosicrucian idealism. The trials of Percy Shelley's Gothic immortal provide a blue-print for the portrait of the Romantic hero which Mary Shelley goes on to develop in her treatment of Rosicrucianism.

Notes

1. Thomas Love Peacock, *Nightmare Abbey* (1818), ed. Raymond Wright (Harmondsworth, 1979), p. 102.
2. See Carl Grabo, *The Magic Plant: The Growth of Shelley's Thought* (Chapel Hill, 1936), p. 3. For an account of Shelley's scientific ideas see Grabo, 'Electricity, the Spirit of the Earth, in Shelley's *Prometheus Unbound*,' *Philological Quarterly*, VII, 2 (April, 1927), pp. 133-50 and *A Newton among Poets – Shelley's Use of Science in Prometheus Unbound* (Chapel Hill, 1930).
3. *The Letters of Percy Bysshe Shelley*, ed. Frederick L. Jones (Oxford, 1964), I, p. 303.
4. For the influence of Darwin on Shelley's verse see Desmond King-Hele, *Shelley: His Thought and Work* (London, 1960), pp. 162-4.
5. Dowden, *The Life of Percy Bysshe Shelley* (London, 1969), p. 13.
6. Loc. cit.
7. Thomas Jefferson Hogg, *The Life of Percy Bysshe Shelley and Edward John Tralawny* (London, 1933), I, p. 58.
8. Shelley, *Letters*, ed. Jones, I, p. 54.
9. Shelley, *The Complete Works of Percy Bysshe Shelley*, ed. Roger Ingpen and Walter Edwin Peck (London, 1965), II, p. 61.
10. Walter Scott, *Waverley, or, 'Tis Sixty Years Since* (London, 1910), p. 64.
11. See Shelley, *Works*, ed. Ingpen and Peck, VI, pp. 155-71. Paul Dawson suggested to me that Shelley probably associated the Assassins with the Essenes.
12. *Secret Societies*, ed. Mackenzie, p. 170. See also Nesta H. Webster, *Secret Societies and Subversive Movements* (London, 1964), pp. 196–268.
13. Shelley, *Letters*, ed. Jones, I, p. 54. See Richard Holmes, *Shelley the Pursuit* (London, 1974), pp. 52-3. Although the Illuminati was a model, Shelley's proposed society had relatively limited aims. See Paul Dawson, *The Unacknowledged Legislator: Shelley and Politics* (London, 1980), pp. 157 ff.
14. Shelley, *Letters*, ed. Jones, I, p. 54.
15. Hogg, *The Life of Shelley*, I, p. 376.
16. Shelley, *Letters*, ed. Jones, I, p. 264. See James Rieger, *The Mutiny Within: The Heresies of Percy Bysshe Shelley* (New York, 1967), pp. 62-8.
17. Abbé Barruel, *Memoirs Illustrating the History of Jacobinism*, trans. Robert Clifford (London, 1797), IV, p. 584. See Walter Edwin Peck, 'Shelley and the Abbé Barruel,' *Publications of the Modern Language Association of America*, XXXVI (1921), pp. 347-53 and M. H. Dodds, 'Shelley's Use of Abbé Barruel's Work on Secret Societies,' *Notes and Queries*, CXIII (1917) p. 196.
18. Shelley, *Letters*, ed. Jones, I, pp. 27-9.
19. A. L. Morton, *The English Utopia* (London, 1978), p. 154.
20. Crabb Robinson in *Germany 1800–1805: Extracts from his Correspondence*, ed. Edith T. Morley (London, 1929), p. 51.
21. Loc. cit. Weishaupt modelled the organisational aspects of the Illuminati on the Jesuits who had educated him.
22. Adorno and Horkheimer, *Dialectic of Enlightenment*, p. 9.
23. Marquis of Grosse, *Horrid Mysteries* (1796), trans. P. Will, 2 vols (London, 1927), p. xxi.
24. Benjamin Disraeli, *Lord George Bentinck, A Political Biography* (London, 1852), pp. 553-4.
25. Peacock, *Nightmare Abbey*, p. 47.
26. See Kenneth Neill Cameron, *The Young Shelley: Genesis of a Radical* (London, 1951), p. 29.
27. Hogg, *The Life of Shelley*, I, p. 376.

28. Peacock, *Nightmare Abbey*, p. 47.
29. Ibid., p. 92.
30. Ibid., p. 94.
31. Ibid., p. 92.
32. Ibid., p. 48.
33. Loc. cit.
34. Loc. cit.
35. Ibid., p. 46.
36. Ibid., p. 47.
37. Loc. cit.
38. See *The Age of Enlightenment*, ed. Eliot and Stern, pp. 249-55.
39. Ibid., p. 250.
40. *Secret Societies*, ed. Mackenzie, p. 170.
41. William Drummond, *Academical Questions* (London, 1805), p. 352.
42. Quoted by Raymond Wright in Peacock, *Nightmare Abbey*, pp. 17-18.
43. Shelley, *Zastrozzi: A Romance* and *St Irvyne or The Rosicrucian* (New York, 1977), p. 3.
44. Ibid., VI.
45. Newman Ivey White, *The Unextinguished Hearth: Shelley and His Contemporary Critics* (North Carolina, 1938), p. 36.
46. Sylvia Norman, *Flight of the Skylark: The Development of Shelley's Reputation* (London, 1954), p. 162.
47. William Michael Rossetti, *A Memoir of Shelley* (London, 1886), p. 19.
48. John Cordy Jeaffreson, *The Real Shelley: New Views of the Poet's Life* (London, 1885), I, p. 160.
49. Edmund Blunden, *Shelley: A Life Story* (London, 1948), p. 44.
50. Shelley, *Letters*, ed. Jones I, p. 266.
51. See Ellsworth Barnard, *Shelley's Religion* (Minnesota, 1937) p. 20
52. Shelley, *Letters*, ed. Jones, I, p. 40.
53. Peacock, *Nightmare Abbey*, p. 62.
54. Shelley, *St Irvyne*, p. 219.
55. Carl Grabo, *The Magic Plant: The Growth of Shelley's Thought*, p. 16.
56. Shelley, *Letters*, ed. Jones, I, p. 20.
57. Ibid., I, p. 21.
58. Dorothy Scarborough, *The Supernatural in Modern English Literature* (London, 1917), p. 17.
59. Shelley, *St Irvyne*, p. 198
60. Ibid., p. 220.
61. Loc. cit.
62. Ibid., pp. 199–200.
63. Ibid., p. 203.
64. Ibid., p. 199.
65. Shelley, *Works*, ed. Ingpen and Peck, VI, p. 209.
66. Ibid., III, p. 56.
67. Shelley, *St Irvyne*, p. 203.
68. Ibid., p. 155.
69. See Andy P. Antippas, 'The Structure of Shelley's *St Irvyne*: Parallelism and the Gothic Mode of Evil,' *Tulane Studies in English*, XVIII (1970), p. 67.
70. See Margaret Loftus Ranald and Ralph Arthur Ranald, 'Shelley's Magus Zoroaster and the Image of the *Doppelgänger*,' *Modern Language Notes*, LXXVI (January, 1961), pp. 7-12.
71. Rieger, *The Mutiny Within*, p. 61.
72. *St Irvyne*, p. 146.

73. Ibid., p. 203.
74. Thomas Love Peacock, *The Life of Percy Bysshe Shelley* (London, 1933), II, p. 328.
75. Shelley, *Letters*, ed. Jones, II, p. 406.
76. *St Irvyne*, p. 116.
77. Ibid., p. 219.
78. Shelley, *Works*, ed. Ingpen and Peck, I, p. 196.
79. See Katherine M. Briggs, 'Legends of Lilith and the Wandering Jew,' *Folklore*, 92, ii (1981), pp. 132-40 and George K. Anderson, 'The Legend of the Wandering Jew,' *Books at Brown*, XIX (May, 1963), pp. 143-159 and Joseph Gaer, *The Wandering Jew* (New York, 1961).
80. 'Ghasta' means 'guest' which refers to the visitor from the spirit-world. This also contradicts Hogg's claim that Shelley did not know a single word of German at the time.
81. *Genesis*, IV: 10-15.
82. Peacock, *Nightmare Abbey*, p. 104.
83. Byron, *Poetical Works*, ed. Page and Jump, p. 193.
84. *Matthew*, XVI: 28.
85. For Caiaphas see *John*, XVIII, 22 and for Malchus see *John*, XVII.
86. John, XXI: 22 This extract about the Wandering Jew is also used in the subtitle of George Croly's novel, *Salathiel or, Tarry-now-till-I-Come* (1829). Shelley uses a slightly different version in the epigraph, 'If I will that he tarry till I come, what is that to thee? Follow thou me.' See *The Wandering Jew* in Shelley, *Works*, ed. Ingpen and Peck, IV, preface, p. 347.
87. Shelley, *The Wandering Jew*, preface.
88. Ibid., IV, p. 347.
89. See Johann Wolfgang Goethe, *'Fragment' on The Wandering Jew* (1774) and Johann Christoph Friedrich Von Schiller, *Geisterseher* (1789). Here the Wandering Jew is an Armenian disguised as a Russian officer.
90. See Matthew Lewis, *The Monk* (London, 1974), p. 136.
91. Ibid., pp. 142-3.
92. Shelley and Mary met Matthew 'Monk' Lewis. See A. B. Young, 'Shelley and M. G. Lewis,' *Modern Language Review*, I (1906), pp. 322-4.
93. Shelley, *Works*, ed. Ingpen and Peck, I, p. 31.
94. Ibid., I, p. 29.
95. Ibid., I, p. 31.
96. Ibid., I, p. 27.
97. It is unlikely that Shelley had read this work in manuscript before he wrote 'Ghasta' though he may have drawn upon the Paracelsian material which had inspired Fouque. See *The Oxford Companion to English Literature*, ed. Paul Harvey, revised ed. (Oxford, 1975), p. 845.
98. Shelley, *Works*, ed. Ingpen and Peck, I, p. 28.
99. Loc cit.
100. Ibid., p. 32.
101. Loc cit.
102. After the appearance of the poem in *Frazer's Magazine* for July 4, 1831, Medwin claimed that he had contributed six or seven cantos of the poem of which four were exclusively his own. Furthermore, in Medwin's *Life of Shelley* (1847) he appears to have used quotations from *The Wandering Jew* taken from *Frazer's* version of the poem.
103. Four cantos of the poem along with Shelley's preface and dedication appeared in the *Edinburgh Literary Journal* (nos 33 and 34, June 27 and July 4, 1829). An-

other version of these cantos without the preface and dedication were printed in *Frazer's Magazine* with Mrs Shelley's permission.

104. See Shelley, *Works* ed. Ingpen and Peck, I, pp. 115–20.

105. See Christian Friedrich Daniel Schubart, *Ahasver* (1786).

106. Shelley, 'Notes to Queen Mab,' in *Works*, ed Ingpen and Peck, I, p. 151.

107. Loc. cit.

108. Hogg, *The Life of Shelley*, I, p. 122.

109. See Rieger, *The Mutiny Within*, p. 52.

110. Shelley, 'Notes to "Queen Mab,"' in *Works*, ed. Ingpen and Peck, I, p. 152.

111. Ibid., I, p. 151.

112. Shelley, *Works*, 33, IV, p. 377.

113. Ibid., IV, p. 366.

114. Shelley may also have derived the name from Charlotte Dacre's pseudonym 'Rosa Matilda' which she uses in *Zofloya the Moor* (1806) a novel which, according to Edith Birkhead in *The Tale of Terror* (p. 122) influenced *St Irvyne*. Rieger in *The Mutiny Within*, p. 62 suggests that Shelley's Rosa resembles Sarah in *The Monk* whose escape from a convent coincided with the blooming of a mystic rose. Rieger also points out that Shelley may have modelled his Rosa on Lewis's Matilda who attracts Ambrosia while she is disguised as the young monk, Rosario.

115. Shelley, *Works*, Ingpen and Peck, IV, p. 377.

116. Ibid., pp. 371-2.

117. Ibid., p. 373.

118. Ibid., p. 377.

119. See Lewis, *The Monk*, p. 138.

120. Shelley, *Works*, IV, p. 379.

121. Ibid., IV, pp. 373-4.

122. Canto II, lines 94, 102-10 forms the epigraph for chapter VIII of *St Irvyne* and canto III, lines 212 for chapter X.

123. This is translated as 'Crush the monster!' from *Queen Mab* in Shelley, *Works*, III, p. 26.

124. Ibid., II, p. 24.

125. Ibid., III, p. 26.

126. Ibid., III, p. 52.

127. See Davidson Cook, '*Sadak the Wanderer*: An Unknown Shelley Poem,' *Times Literary Supplement*, no. 1789, May 16 1936.

128. Appendix I.

129. Loc. cit.

4

Mary Shelley and the Mortal Immortal

> immortal mortals, mortal immortals , living their death and dying their life.
>
> Heraclitus [1]

Naming the parts of the assembled title, Mary Wollstonecraft Godwin Shelley, signposts the three major influences playing on her life and work: namely that unholy trinity of Shelleyan aesthetics, Wollstonecraftian feminism and Godwinian radicalism, which ironically produced a daughter of the Enlightenment as ideologically hybrid and disparate as the very creature pieced together by Victor Frankenstein. Invoking such an irresistible parallel is not to comply with Aristotle's equation of the female with the monstrous, but instead to give resonance to this amalgam of conflicting elements destined to propagate both the unexpected and the incongruous.

Examples of such abound as in Mary Shelley's creative urge to beget monsters, which clashed with her adherence to a model of feminine propriety. Likewise, her unwillingness to inculcate the radical feminism of her mother, Mary Wollstonecraft, is offset by her apparent deployment of a feminist critique of science in *Frankenstein* (1818). The Gothic Rosicrucian ingredients of this novel, the legacy of her father Godwin are, for want of a more appropriate metaphor, cross-fertilised by the Romanticism of, amongst others, her husband, Percy Shelley who, according to some critics, provided the author with a model for the monster, even though its hideous appearance is anathema to Romantic aesthetics. An affront to the rationality of scientific developments taking place during the eighteenth century, the novel is dedicated nonetheless to the Enlightenment philosopher Godwin. De Quincey is quick to point out a family resemblance by remarking that 'Most people felt of Mr Godwin ... the same alienation and horror as of a ghoul, or a bloodless vampyre [*sic*] or the monster created by Frankenstein.'[2] Aside from the obvious familial connections conflating the discordant elements in Mary Shelley's life and art, a measure of kinship may be realised by way of a Rosicrucian reading of her novels and short stories.

Most of Mary Shelley's short stories appeared in *The Keepsake*, one of the most popular nineteenth-century periodicals. The first collection was published in 1891 by Richard Garnett, who claimed: 'in these little tales [Mary Shelley] is her perfect self, and the reader will find not only the entertainment of interesting fiction, but a fair picture of the mind ... of a lonely, thwarted, misunderstood woman, who could seldom do herself justice, and whose precise place in the contemporary constellation of genius remains to be determined'.[3] The autobiographical element in much of her writings should not be over-stressed at the expense of understating her reliance on external sources, since she sought to maintain a distance between her life and art, being aware that:

> merely copying from our own hearts will no more form a first-rate work of art, than will the most exquisite representation of mountains, water, wood, and glorious clouds, form a good painting, if none of the rules of grouping or colouring are followed.[4]

Having inherited these 'rules' of composition from her father, it is likely that she was inspired by *St Leon,* which she read in 1815, to experiment in Rosicrucian fiction, which in *Frankenstein*, *The Last Man*, and 'The Mortal Immortal' she advances towards Romanticism.

The Mortal Immortal

Mary Shelley's most overtly Rosicrucian piece of fiction is the short story 'The Mortal Immortal,' set around Winzy, a young man who accidentally stumbles on the twin secrets of immortality and perpetual youth. According to Charles E. Robinson, Mary Shelley uses the supernatural as a device with which to instigate a study in character.[5] As it turns out, the popularity of the story owes less to her characterisation than to the occult motif concerning the hero's acquisition of the elixir of life. This potion has been manufactured by the alchemist Cornelius Agrippa, whose portrayal in 'The Mortal Immortal' provides a legendary framework for the tale's evocation of Renaissance occultism. The year after Mary published her short story, Godwin's *Lives of the Necromancers* (1834) appeared, containing a short biography of Agrippa.[6] It is likely that Mary's interest in the magician, which dates back to 1816, may have been rekindled by her father's researches.

Cornelius Agrippa was most renowned for his influential textbook on Renaissance occult philosophy. His particular blend of Hermetic-Cabalism made a valuable contribution to Rosicrucian thought, as pointed out by Yates in *The Rosicrucian Enlightenment:*

> the Rosicrucian was one fully in the stream of the Renaissance Hermetic-Cabalistic tradition, but distinguished from the earlier phases of the movement by his addition of alchemy to his interests. This did not alter the basic adherence of the Rosicrucians to the scheme of "occult philosophy" as laid down by Cornelius Agrippa.[7]

In *Frankenstein*, Mary Shelley shows how the writings of Agrippa exert a powerful influence on the mind of the young Victor, thereby indirectly leading him to create his monster. Victor describes how he first became acquainted with Agrippa's work:

> I chanced to find a volume of the works of Cornelius Agrippa. I opened it with apathy; the theory which he attempts to demonstrate, and the wonderful facts which he relates soon changed this feeling into enthusiasm. A new light seemed to dawn upon my mind.[8]

In 'The Mortal Immortal' Agrippa plays an active role as one of the three main characters.

The story opens with an account of Winzy's apprenticeship to Agrippa. After returning from temporary leave, Winzy discovers that all the other apprentices have fled because of some sinister occurrence. Apparently one of the apprentices has disobediently tried to raise the 'foul fiend,' which has subsequently destroyed him. According to Winzy, this led to notoriety for his employer since now 'all the world has heard of Cornelius Agrippa.'[9] Like the others, he also deserts his former master, who is now unable to continue his work on the *Opus Magnum* alone. Agrippa needs assistants to observe the results of his experiments and to attend to his ever-burning fires, the alchemical equivalent of the Rosicrucian perpetually-burning lamp. Without such co-operation, he cannot bring his task to completion. Even the dark spirits mock Agrippa's plight and 'laughed at him for not being able to retain a single mortal in his service.'[10] He is unable to bribe Winzy back into his service with a purse of gold. At first understandably hesitant in entering into the employment of such a notorious necromancer, Winzy is persuaded eventually by Bertha into conquering his fears on account of his poverty as she argues; 'You pretend to love and, you fear to face the Devil for my sake!'[11] After a year as the sorcerer's apprentice, Winzy is rather disenchanted when he reflects that 'In spite of the most painful vigilance, I had never detected the trace of a cloven foot; nor was the studious silence of our abode ever disturbed by demonic howls'[12] and so he dismisses the past as a scandal invented by superstitious minds. Now he is determined to assist Agrippa, who has reached a critical point in his experiments.

Unlike Godwin and Shelley, Mary Shelley is far more explicit about the magico-chemical processes involved in the search for the philosopher's stone, possibly drawing on Humphrey Davy's knowledge of alchemical transmutation during one of his visits to Godwin's house.[13] In 'The Mortal Immortal' Mary refers specifically to the red and white mercury from whose reunion the ultimate perfection is achieved and the philosopher's stone obtained. According to alchemical literature, the appearance of a white liquid in the compound signified the second stage of the Great Work. In the language of alchemy, the Red King or Sulphur of the Wise then appears out of the womb of his mother and sister, Isis or mercury, *Rosa Alba,* the White Rose. In the story, Agrippa asks Winzy to observe a crucial stage in the *Opus Magnum* which yields up the *elixir vitæ*: 'Look at that glass vessel. The liquid it contains is of a soft rose-colour: the moment it begins to change its hue, awaken me … First, it will turn white, and then emit golden flashes.'[14] Agrippa, by deceiving Winzy into believing that the phial contains nothing more than a cure for love, rather than an antidote for death, hopes thereby to ensure that his assistant will not drink the potion himself. Unfortunately, this deception has the opposite effect on Winzy, who can no longer endure the pangs of unrequited passion and so drinks the elixir in order to rid himself of his infatuation. Instead, 'the celestial potion'[15] has the immediate effect of revitalising him, which, ironically, enables him to win Bertha's love. After marrying her, he eventually becomes prosperous enough to leave his employment. Agrippa continues to be his close friend even though Winzy destroyed the experiment which was the culmination of his life's work. Winzy nevertheless recalls with gratitude that he owes his present happiness to the magician for having procured 'that delicious draught of a divine elixir.'[16]

Throughout the story, Mary Shelley paints a touching picture of Agrippa as the dignified philosopher whose stoicism directed towards a single goal is tempered by the knowledge of his own human vanity. It is not until Agrippa is dying that he informs Winzy that he has unwittingly drunk the immortal elixir. At first Winzy believes his former master, but later dismisses the possibility as ludicrous. He goes on to defend the recently deceased Agrippa and his tarnished reputation as a magician:

> I loved him as a man – I respected him as a sage – but I derided the notion that he could command the powers of darkness and laughed at the superstitious fears with which he was regarded by the vulgar. He was a wise philosopher, but had no acquaintance with any spirits but those clad in flesh and blood.[17]

Winzy has greatly underestimated Agrippa's occult powers, for as time passes it turns out that his ensuing rejuvenation not only gained Bertha's undying love but also eternal life. Mary Shelley provides a playful variation on the Faustian theme of a hero consumed by the desire for forbidden knowledge and power, since Winzy is initially unaware that he has drunk the *elixir vitæ*. Once his immortality is recognised, his wife Bertha insists that he pass the secret on to her. But since Winzy does not possess the formula for the elixir, Bertha is unable to join him in his immortality. This episode may be seen as a parody of Genesis, where Adam asks God for a companion. Likewise, in *Frankenstein* the monster, craving for companionship, pleads with Victor to create for him a female being with whom he can share his eternal existence.

Having outlived all his companions, Winzy diagnoses himself as being desirous of death, yet never dying – a mortal immortal. This is the inescapable dilemma for the Rosicrucian hero. Lemming-like, these wandering immortals resolutely throw themselves into the craters of active volcanoes, in the path of avalanches, offer themselves as targets in the front line of battle and beckon the eye of the hurricane to consume them. But alas all fails: even poison, fire, pestilence and deadly friends prove to be ineffectual. Robbed of the self-determination of the suicide, these defeated kamikazes are doomed to live for ever. A modern version of this may be found in Martin Amis's *Einstein's Monsters* (1986), where the disconsolate immortal, so determined to end his life, even lies in the epicentre of a nuclear explosion only to find that his embrace with Armageddon leaves him with nothing more than a gigantic hangover! But Winzy admits to being still a relatively young immortal compared to the eighteen centuries endured by veterans like the Wandering Jew, and is not yet willing to accept defeat.

After three centuries Winzy, now weary of his longevity, resolves to terminate his protracted existence, saying:

> I shall adopt more resolute means, and, by scattering and annihilating the atoms that compose my frame, set at liberty the life imprisoned within, and so cruelly pre-

> vented from soaring from this dim earth to a sphere more congenial to its immortal existence.[18]

William A. Walling finds this an 'incongruous ending,'[19] which for Bradford Booth illustrates one of the chief weaknesses of the annual's stories by encouraging authors 'to force the plot for a complete novel into a dozen or a score of pages.'[20] Yet the short story format provides a refreshing break from the almost endless sagas about wandering immortals. But as the opening lines suggest, Winzy has barely started on his career as an immortal in comparison with others:

> July 16, 1833.
> – This is a memorable anniversary for me; on it I complete my three hundred and twenty-third year!
> The Wandering Jew? – certainly not. More than eighteen centuries have passed over his head. In comparison with him, I am a very young immortal.[21]

Mary Shelley distinguishes her mortal immortal from the Wandering Jew and the Seven Sleepers of Ephesus, who are victims of an enchantment. Throughout the tale a juxtaposition between the comic and the sinister is maintained. Even the hero's name, Winzy, with its humorous overtones of a 'whimsical' character is overshadowed by its resemblance to the Scottish word 'winze' meaning 'curse.'[22] Like St Leon, Winzy reflects upon the misery of being doomed to an immortal existence and resorts to narrating his life-story in an attempt 'to pass some hours of a long eternity.'[23] In this way he echoes the endless refrain of the immortal being with the lament 'but, oh! the weight of never-ending time – the tedious passage of the still-succeeding hours!'[24]

In her description of Winzy's torments, Mary Shelley must have drawn upon her own loneliness and despair following her husband's death. Often the tone of her *Journal* matches the mood of her hero's darker moments. Mary Shelley appears to have transmitted her own preoccupation with the passing of time to her mortal immortal, who sometimes tries 'to imagine by what rule the infinite may be divided.'[25] In her *Journal*, she complains 'Time rolls on, and what does it bring? … Months change their names, years their cyphers.'[26] Like St Leon, who complains that he is forced to endure 'months, years, cycles, centuries,'[27] she experiences the purgatorial timelessness of the mortal immortal but without the consolation of perpetual youth. She observes signs of age, saying: 'My brow is sadly entrenched, the blossom of youth faded. My mind gathers wrinkles.'[28] By enshrining the memory of Shelley as her 'lovely boy,'[29] Mary Shelley may well have identified herself with the ageing Bertha who co-exists with the ever-youthful Winzy. In desperation, Bertha, tired of being mistaken for his mother, persuades Winzy to wear a grey wig, while she tries to imagine wrinkles in his face and decrepitude in his walk. Finally Bertha convinces herself that Winzy's apparent youth is a disease which prevents him from ever joining the 'Nestors'[30] of the village. It is indeed tempting to view Winzy as a Shelleyan figure who haunts the author as a vision of perpetual youth and symbol of immortal genius.

'Valerius: The Reanimated Roman' and 'Roger Dodsworth: The Reanimated Englishman'

Mary Shelley's interest in reanimation arose from her curiosity about how individuals from the remote past would behave if transported into the present day. She was drawn to reconsider the boundaries between life and death in her story 'Valerius' through the reanimated Roman, whose 'semblance was that of life, yet he belonged to the dead.'[31] Like the Rosicrucian wanderer, Valerius is severed from his own time and history, having lost all meaning to life. His reanimation has brought about a mechanical awakening which leaves his spiritual self dormant. An analogy of this may be seen in the rebirth of a physical body without its soul. Valerius has no desire to continue his alienated existence and so prepares himself for death, now that he is 'a being cut off from our world: the links that had bound him to it had been snapped many ages before'[32] and, unless they can be joined together again, he will soon perish.

In order to preserve his sense of life-preserving historical continuity, Valerius is taken on a tour of the ruins of Ancient Rome based on Mary Shelley's visit in 1819 and more recent reading of Gibbon's *Decline and Fall of the Roman Empire* (1776-88). Valerius, having recovered his own sense of history rediscovers a purpose to his existence. The reanimated individual and the immortal wanderer are metaphors for the continuity between past and present which is essential for the well-being of any country or society.

'Roger Dodsworth: The Reanimated Englishman' is a variation on this theme. The story was based on a hoax regarding the revival of a seventeenth-century Englishman. Reported first on June 28, 1826 in the *Journal du Commerce de Lyon*, the sensation was publicised in at least six British newspapers.[33] Widely discussed for the next four months, the phenomenon was debated by William Cobbett, Thomas Moore and even Roger Dodsworth himself! Mary Shelley introduces her story with a newspaper report which describes how Dr Hotham of Northumberland dug out from under an avalanche on Mount St Gothard in Italy 'a human being whose animation had been suspended by the action of the frost.'[34] In 'Roger Dodsworth' she discusses the latest theories of suspended animation:

> Animation (I believe physiologists agree) can as easily be suspended for an hundred or two years, as for as many seconds. A body hermetically sealed up by the frost, is of necessity preserved in its pristine entireness. That which is totally secluded from the action of external agency, can neither have any thing added to nor taken away from it: no decay can take place, for something can never become nothing; under the influence of that state of being which we call death, change but not annihilation removes from our sight the corporeal atoms; the earth receives sustenance from them, the air is fed by them, each element takes its own, thus seizing forcible repayment of what it had lent.[35]

There are similarities between Roger Dodsworth 'the dead alive'[36] and the Rosicrucian adept, since both are able to recall first-hand details of the remote past. The description of Dodsworth's clothes in resembling those depicted in a Van Dyck portrait is rather like Godwin's account in *St Leon* of the similarity between the attire of a Rosicrucian and the dress of the subject of a portrait by Titian painted one hundred and fifty years earlier. In 'Roger Dodsworth,' Mary Shelley makes a humorous reference to her father when she explains that Dodsworth has preserved not only himself but also some documents which provide important information for Godwin, who now has been obliged to suspend 'for the sake of such authentic information the history of the Commonwealth he had just begun.'[37] Mary wryly suggests that Dr Hotham should erect a tablet over Dodsworth's twice-buried remains, inscribed:

To the memory of R. Dodsworth,
An Englishman,
Born April 1, 1617; Died July 16, 1826;
Aged 209.[38]

It may be significant that Dodsworth was born on 'April Fools' Day'! Mary taunts the hoaxers responsible for the Dodsworth fraud by insisting that he reveal himself to those who are sceptical about his resuscitation, entreating him to 'no longer to bury himself in obscurity.'[39] Mary also ridicules the venerated Antiquarian Society which intended making a bid for Dodsworth's antique clothes. Dodsworth, who is himself an antiquarian, finds that on being transported to the future he is able to look back on his own age from a vantage point of nearly two hundred years.

Dodsworth's reanimation mimics the Rosicrucians' power of necromancy. In the story, Mary Shelley refers to a number of necromantic theories such as Virgil's account in book six of the *Æneid* of how every thousand years the dead return to life. She amuses herself with the idea that if 'the witch, memory, were in a freak, to cause all the present generation to recollect that some ten centuries back they had been somebody else,'[40] a great deal of injustice and hypocrisy would be exposed. Mary Shelley is in favour of the type of novel which would document the experiences of an individual throughout the cycles of world history 'if philosophical novels were in fashion, we conceive an excellent one might be written on the development of the same mind in various stations, in different periods of the world's history.'[41]

The hero of the Rosicrucian novel has the opportunity to experience this historical continuity. Tragedy arises when the individual denies his own sense of history and allows himself to be reduced to the kind of atomistic state of being which is delineated in Hume's theories of causality. Such a possibility does not deter Mary Shelley from suggesting that transmigration would furnish an 'instructive school for kings and statesmen.'[42]

'Transformation' and 'The Evil Eye'

The 'Transformation' (1830) is a necromantic mystery dealing with transmigration. The hero, Guido, agrees to exchange his handsome body for that of a deformed dwarf in return for a treasure chest. Mary Shelley probably derived the idea for this from Byron's unfinished drama, *The Deformed Transformed* (1824), which she transcribed in 1822-3. In Byron's drama the transaction is reversed, since the hunchbacked Arnold donates his deformed body to a stranger who haunts him as an *alter ego*. The *Doppelgänger* in Mary's 'Transformation' turns out to be a kind of demonic guardian angel who, having returned Guido's body to him after the allotted three days, has shown him 'an excess of fiendly pride.'[43] The story, which concludes with Guido's spiritual transformation, departs from the model of Faust in that it is the body and not the soul which is forfeit in a diabolical bargain. Perversely the dwarf denounces Guido as a cousin of Lucifer who: 'hast fallen through thy pride; and, though bright as the son of Morning, thou art ready to give up thy good looks ... and thy well-being, rather than submit thee to the tyranny of good.'[44] Guido is susceptible to the dwarf's mesmeric powers and mastery of the elements, and notes that 'he did gain a kind of influence over me, which I could not master .... His supernatural powers, made him an oracle in my eyes.'[45]

Mesmeric powers were popular attributes for Gothic villains, as in *St Irvyne* and in Mary Shelley's short story, 'The Evil Eye' (1829) where the main character, Dmitri, is an Albanian wanderer who is feared and respected by his comrades:

> men trembled before his glance, women and children exclaimed in terror, 'The Evil Eye!' The opinion became prevalent – he shared it himself – he gloried in the dread privilege; and when his victim shivered and withered beneath the mortal influence, the fiendish laugh with which he hailed this demonstration of his power, struck with worse dismay the failing heart of the fascinated person.[46]

The supernatural device of the evil eye heightens the drama of a story which, like so many of Mary Shelley's tales, is bound up with passion and intrigue. Her writing was in demand by the editors of the *Keepsake*, which was selling up to fifteen thousand copies within a few months. Mary Shelley, along with other contributors to the journal, exerted a considerable influence on the development of the short story, although it is clear that she needed more space to develop more fully the literary techniques which were most congenial to her talent.[47] Indeed, it was through the form of the novel and particularly *Frankenstein* that Mary Shelley found the scope to develop the Rosicrucian themes relating to the wanderer, immortality and the occult.

Frankenstein

> There are things born in the twilight
> hours more monstrous than nightmares.
>
> Byron[48]

In *Frankenstein,* Victor and his monstrous creation form between them another version of the Rosicrucian hero who has transcended death via the forbidden byways of magic and science. As a metonymy for alienation, the Rosicrucian who has been deserted by death is left lonely and isolated. In *Frankenstein*, there is displacement in this respect since it is the monster who by proxy, pays the penalty for Victor's pursuit of the philosopher's stone.

Critics were prompt to identify the author of *Frankenstein* as a disciple of Godwin.[49] Walter Scott noted in a review that *Frankenstein* with its emphasis upon alchemy and the elixir of life is a novel written on similar lines to *St Leon*:

> In this latter work, assuming the possibility of the transmutation of metals and of the *elixir vitæ*, the author has deduced, in the course of his narrative, the probable consequences of the possession of such secrets upon the fortunes and mind of him who might enjoy them. *Frankenstein* is a novel upon the same plan as *St Leon*.[50]

Through Frankenstein's monster, Mary Shelley created a metaphor for terror which captured the popular imagination. Indeed, *Frankenstein* had been designed as the kind of horror story that would 'curdle the blood, and quicken the beatings of the heart.'[51] *Frankenstein,* which has been summarily classified by literary critics as Gothic horror, science-fiction and even birth-myth, is really a fictional hybrid.[52] Radu Florescu in his *In Search of Frankenstein*, suggests that Mary's monster is more a child of the alchemists than of the scientists.[53] But, in terms of the Rosicrucian novel, it is not essential to separate these distinctions since the dialogue between magic and science was also an important feature of the tradition of the Rosy Cross.[54]

Frankenstein had originated as Mary Shelley's contribution to a ghost-story contest which had been proposed by Byron during the Shelleys' stay at Villa Diodati on June 16 1816. A rival competitor, John Polidori, Byron's physician, composed a tale called *The Vampire* (1819) which revamps the stock Rosicrucian plot.[55] The story is about a mysterious Byronic stranger, Lord Ruthven, whose hypnotic powers enable him to consume his way through existence by drinking the blood of young women in order artificially to prolong his life. The vampire is iconic of the parasitic nature of the mortal immortal who steals a life-span to which he is not entitled. Franco Moretti in 'The Dialectic of Fear' sees Frankenstein's monster and the vampire as metaphors for the terrors lurking in bourgeois society.[56] Polidori's vampire is a feudal aristocrat who with hindsight may be seen as symbolising capitalist exploitation by living off the life-force of the workers. Frankenstein's monster has the characteristics of both worker and product, having been negated and alienated by capitalist society. The dialectic between Victor and the monster may be posited along the lines of Marx's four types of alienation, the first of which concerns mankind's alienation from the product of his labour. Moretti argues that the monster incarnates the dialectic of estranged labour which is described by Marx: 'The more formed the product the more deformed the worker, the more civilised the product, the more barbaric the worker, the more powerful the work, the more powerless becomes the worker, the more cultured the work, the more philistine the worker becomes and more of a slave to nature.'[57] The grotesque appearance of the monster may also be seen in terms of this analogy, since the product of alienated labour is beauty for the master but deformity for the worker, 'it produces culture, but also imbecility and cretinism for the worker.'[58] The monster has been designed as a man yet turns out to be the antithesis of anything human. It is an artificial creation which is also a gross distortion of nature. Like Marx's proletariat, the monster has been denied a name and an individuality. His identity is an extension of his master's property for he is known as the Frankenstein monster, since he belongs to his creator.

The interchangeability of owner and owned is a parody of the relationship between creator and created. Mary Shelley draws attention to the blasphemy implicit in such mimesis by saying 'supremely frightful would be the effect of any human endeavour to mock the stupendous mechanism of the Creator of the world.'[59] Yet she herself self-consciously participates in the creative process, mimicking part of the Genesis creation myth by conceding that literary invention does not emerge from the void but is formed out of chaos. Her authorial creativity is a continuation of the creation of the universe since she helps to populate the world of the imagination. But it is through the darker consciousness of nightmare and terror that on the night of the story-telling contest she witnesses in her 'acute mental vision'[60] the 'pale student of unhallowed arts kneeling beside the thing he had put together'[61] which contains the genesis of *Frankenstein.*

The story concerns Victor Frankenstein, a Genevan student, who constructs a monstrous creature which he is able to bring to life. The monster is modelled on a human being yet is so loathsome in appearance that it inspires horror in all who see it. Cast out from human society, the monster blames his creator for his unhappiness. In order to alleviate the monster's suffering and loneliness, Victor consents to build for him a female companion with whom he can share his exile. Then, haunted by the possibility that the progeny of these artificial beings would be a line of immortal monsters or 'race of devils,'[62] Victor destroys the creature's mate. In revenge for this, the monster murders Frankenstein's bride,

Elizabeth. Determined to destroy his creation, Frankenstein pursues the creature to the Arctic regions but dies in the attempt. The relationship between master and servant has been dialectically reversed during their power struggle since the monster claims his creator as his last victim before departing into the icy wastes to take his own life.

The Rosicrucian Cavern

In 1831 when Mary Shelley came to revise *Frankenstein*, her 'hideous progeny'[63] she tried to answer the question, 'How I, then a young girl, came to think of, and to dilate upon, so very hideous an idea?'[64] A visual source of inspiration may have come from the paintings and engravings of Henry Fuseli, who frequently dined at Godwin's house until 1813. Fuseli's paintings, *The Nightmare* (1781) and *Incubus Leaving Two Sleeping Women* (1810) are evocative of the waking dream described in her preface (1831).[65] Peter Tomory, however, in his critical biography of Fuseli, suggests that Mary may have seen his painting, *The Rosicrucian Cavern*, which was exhibited at the Royal Academy in 1804.[66] Engraved by William Sharp for *The Spectator*, it illustrates an earlier essay by Eustace Budgell on the opening of the tomb of Rosicrucius, 'the founder of the Rosicrucian Sect' whose 'Disciples still pretend to new Discoveries, which they are never to Communicate to the rest of mankind.'[67] Budgell relates how a man digging near Rosicrucius's burial place finds a small door which he opens:

> He was immediately surprised by a sudden Blaze of Light, and discovered a very fair Vault. At the upper end of it was a Statue of a Man in Armour sitting by a Table, and leaning on his Left Arm. He held a Truncheon in his Right-Hand, and had a Lamp burning before him. The Man had no sooner set one Foot within the Vault, than the Statue erecting itself from its leaning Posture, stood bolt upright; and upon the Fellow's advancing another Step, lifted up the Truncheon in its Right Hand. The Man still ventured a third Step, when the Statue with a furious Blow broke the Lamp into a thousand Pieces, and left his Guest in a sudden darkness.[68]

The neighbouring people soon solve this Pygmalion mystery when they arrive at the sepulchre. A mechanical statue guarding the tomb and primed to attack intruders turns out to be no more than a piece of vicious clockwork. In retrospect, it may also be seen as a distant relative of the clunking, bolted cinematic version of the monster:

> the Statue, which was made of Brass, was nothing more than a piece of Clock-work; that the Floor of the Vault was all loose, and underlaid with several Springs, which upon any Man's entring [sic], naturally produced that which had happened.[69]

Fuseli's visualisation of this mechanical marvel and Percy Shelley's enthusiasm for the current vogue for automata may have sparked off Mary Shelley's imagination.[70] Percy Shelley is regarded as the model for Victor Frankenstein, who in turn has been inspired by Albertus Magnus (1206-80), renowned for the invention of a talking brass man. Godwin, in his *Lives of the Necromancers*, describes how over a period of thirty years Magnus built this metal man, which he used as a servant since it was able to make complex calculations, carry out instructions and communicate verbally.[71] According to Godwin, St Thomas Aquinas, a pupil of Albertus, had become so irritated by the continual speech of the mechanical man that he smashed it to pieces with a hammer. Some sources claim that the automaton was really created out of flesh and blood though the traditional account maintains that it was made out of brass. Magnus's mechanical man may have inspired Fuseli with the idea for his *Rosicrucian Cavern*. This painting would have made a particularly vivid impression upon Mary Shelley in view of the unhappy love-affair which had taken place between the artist and her mother, Mary Wollstonecraft.

Castle Frankenstein and Alchemist Dippel

It may be argued that the title of the novel has Rosicrucian connections if we accept that it was named after Castle Frankenstein, the home supposedly of Johann Konrad Dippel, a brother of the Rosy Cross. The tentative connection between Dippel and the Frankenstein legend, while awaiting historiographical confirmation nevertheless, serves to aid and abet the mystique of the novel. Parallels between Victor and the eighteenth-century alchemist Dippel are much in evidence: both were body snatchers drawn to the quest for the philosopher's stone and elixir of life. More compelling still, Dippel even used to sign his name 'Frankenstein,' and in common with Victor one of his sports was to plunder graves for the purposes of furthering experiments in the artificial creation of life; an activity which in the eyes of the authorities hardly compensated for the blasphemy of exhuming the dead! Dippel's necromantic interests led him to suppose that it was possible to reanimate a cadaver through the infusion of a life-spirit. His researches into the elixir of life suggested to him that blood as opposed to other vital body fluids held the life-giving properties he sought. His distillation of blood and then bones which were liquidised and conducted through iron tubes conjure up the crude mechanics of a scene from Victor's laboratory. The end product, known as Dippel's Oil, far from being the panacea it was heralded, served most effectively as a nervous system stimulant, doubtless able to expel the most persistent opium dream. But this chemical compound was eclipsed by yet another formula which Dippel offered to disclose to the local landowner, Landgrave of Hesse, in exchange for Castle Frankenstein:

> The most humble undersigned asks of His Princely Highness to permit him to receive and to buy as a FEUDUM BONUM for himself and his brothers and sisters along with their offspring of both the masculine and the feminine sex, who are his responsibility in this matter, the free and titled property and the castle Frankenstein situated at the beginning of Bergstrasse, along with all dependants, subjects and judicial rights which belonged to the property before it was sold to the princely house of Hesse-Darmstadt.
>
> For this he promises to cede to His Princely Highness an ARCANUM CHYMICUM which easily, with little labour and no dangerous work, and with the help of three to four persons, should yield at least as much revenue, all expenses deducted, as the total sum would be if the property were sold according to the ordinary assessment. I am saying that it will bring in at least as much: for the results will show that it can bring in much more.[72]

Hesse could scarcely refuse such a magnanimous offer on learning that the secret was either that of transmuting base metals into gold or the distillation of the elixir of life. It may well have been the latter, for in a pamphlet of 1733, the Rosicrucian divulged that he had discovered the secret of prolonging his own life up to the age of 135. But unfortunately, Dippel died a year after making the claim! The mysterious circumstances surrounding his death indicate that he might have been poisoned. Like Winzy's experiment, the elixir may not have had the desired effect. Local gossip that Dippel had been killed by the devil for breaking a pact furnishes a fitting epitaph for a character whose Faustian career would have provided any of the Rosicrucian novelists with a worthy prototype.

Franklin and Frankenstein

The title of the novel may also have been derived from the first syllable of the surname of Benjamin Franklin, who had been delving into the secrets of life and death. In a letter to his colleague, Dr Barbeau-Dubourg, Franklin commented:

> Your observations on the causes of death and the experiments which you propose for recalling to life those who appear to be killed by lightning, demonstrate equally your sagacity and your humanity. It appears that the doctrines of life and death in general are yet but little understood.[73]

Franklin's experiments with electricity and lightning had prompted Condorcet to hail him as a 'Modern Prometheus' which appears as the sub-title of Mary Shelley's novel.[74] In the story, Alphonse Frankenstein is responsible for stimulating his son Victor's interest in science by carrying out a scientific investigation based on Franklin's experiment with the kite and the key.[75] Since Mary and Shelley had such a great admiration for Franklin, it is possible that the title of the novel is a compound of the first syllable of Franklin's name and the last syllable of the name of Shelley's Rosicrucian hero, Wolfstein from his own Gothic monstrosity.[76] The blend between science and magic is expressed through the heterozygous title of the novel. This magico-scientific infusion is laced into the poetry of Erasmus Darwin, who refers to Franklin in Promethean terms in *The Botanic Garden* (1789-91):

> You led your Franklin to your glazed retreats,
> Your air-built castles, and your silken seats;
> Bade his bold arm invade the lower sky
> And seize the triple lightnings, as they fly,
> O'er the young sage your mystic, mantle spread,
> And wreath'd the crown electric round his head.[77]

The Botanic Garden and Female Monstrosity

The influence of Darwin upon *Frankenstein* is undeniable. His biographer Desmond King-Hele claims that 'Darwin stands, then, as a father-figure over this first and most famous work of science.'[78] In her preface, Mary Shelley describes a conversation between Byron and Shelley relating to Darwin's experiments with artificial life. This may have triggered off the waking dream which sparked off her nightmare:

> Many and long were the conversations between Lord Byron and Shelley, to which I was a devout but nearly silent listener. During one of these, various philosophical doctrines were discussed, and among others the nature of the principle of life, and whether there was any probability of its ever being discovered and communicated. They talked of the experiments of Dr Darwin (I speak not of what the doctor really did, or said that he did, but, as more to my purpose, of what was then spoken of as having been done by him), who preserved a piece of vermicelli in a glass case till by some extraordinary means it began to move with voluntary motion. Not thus, after all, would life be given. Perhaps a corpse would be reanimated; galvanism had given token of such things: perhaps the component parts of a creature might be manufactured, brought together, and endued with vital warmth.[79]

Attempting to authenticate the foundations of her fiction, Mary Shelley calls upon the authority of Darwin to confirm that reanimation was 'not of impossible occurrence.'[80]

Darwin's biological interests are evident from his poems, *Zoonomia or the Laws of Organic Life* (1794-6), described as the 'most original book ever written by man,'[81] *The Temple of Nature* (1804) and *The Botanic Garden* (1791). Shelley had read these books[82] and communicated his enthusiasm for Darwin's poetry to Mary. A less well known Darwinian source for the monster may be found in *The Botanic Garden*, which contains a description of the creation of a monstrous being. It is based on a mythological superstructure of the Rosicrucian spirit-world which Darwin claims to have derived from Francis Bacon:

> The Rosicrucian doctrine of Gnomes, Sylphs, Nymphs, and Salamanders, was thought to afford a proper machinery for a Botanic poem; as it is probable, that they were originally the names of hieroglyphic figures representing the elements or of Genii presiding over their operations. The fairies of more modern days seem to have been derived from them, and to have inherited their powers.[83]

According to Peter Tomory, Darwin regarded the Rosicrucian spirits as vital symbols of physiological and chemical processes.[84] The presence of these life-giving forces is known to the 'Adept' of 'Hermetic art'[85] referred to by Darwin in the poem. He goes on to describe a monstrous being 'castled on ice,'[86] which puts us in mind of the image of the Frankenstein monster cast out on the Arctic wastes. In *The Botanic Garden*, the first faltering steps of Mary Shelley's creation seem to be almost anticipated:

> IMMORTAL LIFE, her hand extending, courts
> The lingering form, his tottering step supports,
> Leads on to Pluto's realms the dreary way,
> And gives him trembling to Elysian day.[87]

Like Frankenstein's monster, Darwin's creature inspires terror in all who see it:

> His mass enormous to the affrighted South;
> Spreads o'er the shuddering line his shadowy limbs,
> And Frost and Famine follow as he swims.[88]

Darwin's monster is eventually redeemed and hailed by nations as the 'Monarch of the Air.' The sylphs have been instructed by the Goddess of Botany how to bring about this change:

> Sylphs! round his cloud-built couch your band array,
> And mould the monster to your gentle sway
> Charm with soft tones, with tender touches check,
> Bend to your golden yoke his willing neck
> With silver curb his yielding teeth restraint.[89]

In *The Botanic Garden*, Darwin explores his interest in the artificial production of life through the allegory and myth of the Rosicrucian tradition.

In his other botanic poem, *Zoonomia*, Darwin had noted that environmental conditions could mould monstrosities. Possibly as a response to this, Mary Shelley shows how environment rather than heredity is responsible for poisoning the mental, spiritual and psychic faculties of the Frankenstein monster. Darwin's theory of generation, founded on the belief that gender and other genetic inheritances are determined by the mind of the male parent, may also have significance in relation to the Frankenstein creation.

Victor Frankenstein is the architect of an immortality which is independent of woman. Usurping the female reproductive role, he symbolically slays the goddess. The monster, though literally of woman born, is a dire warning of the dangers of solitary paternal propagation. As a grim parable of Lockean empiricism, it is fed on a diet of primarily patriarchal sense impressions. Maternal deprivation accelerates mental and physical degeneration, moral and spiritual decline. Mary Shelley debunks the masculine myth that woman was born of man by portraying the offspring of a male mother as a monster. Frankenstein's Luciferian folly of pride and failure of the imagination is posited on the belief that men, basking in the illusion of the dispassionate objectivity of so-called scientific rationality rather than relying on the workings of nature, can produce a higher form of life than that brought about by sexual reproduction and nurturing by the female. Although professing to shy away from polemic, Mary Shelley challenges the historically pervasive and culturally validated polarization of rational science with masculinity which marginalizes instinctual nature and feminity. Her own procreation of fictional monstrosities amplifying the monstrous consequences of male narcissism, shows the scientist striving to subjugate nature and denying the value of domestic relations – – a matter which had aroused Godwin's attention in *St Leon*.

Anne Mellor develops this argument by showing how Mary Shelley deploys a feminist critique of science predicated on the way in which scientific developments sometimes employ metaphor and imagery. Virile male science pitted against a passive and subdued nature for the purposes of violation and penetration was a predominant image of the Scientific Revolution. This is the imperative uttered in *Frankenstein* when Professor Waldman urges the young Victor to adhere to the example of those scientists who penetrate into the recesses of nature, and show how she works in her hiding places. Mellor cites Bacon's famous injunction: 'I am come in very truth leading to you Nature with all her children to bind her to your service and make her your slave.'[90] Regarded generally as the father of the scientific method, Bacon does not here explicate his role merely in the prose of paternity but instead resorts to the highly charged language of the slave trader.

The Rosicrucian tradition may have attracted Mary Shelley as an ideological alternative to this bifurcation of magic and science and binary opposition between male and female. The Rosicrucian Invisible College had been outlawed, presumably because of its refusal to locate science, magic and nature, male and female within incommensurable paradigms. The central symbolism, the rose on the cross, is a representation of the unity of the male and female compounding the name of the legendary founder, Christian Rosencreutz. The androgyny of this system of symbolism grounded in the iconography of alchemy may be suspect to present day thinking, since androgynous compromises invariably end up by privileging the male and as such do not offer a satisfactory alternative to the gendering of male science and female nature.[91] Nevertheless, the marrying of the male and female principles celebrated in the Hermetic allegory, *The Chemical Wedding*, accepted generally as the third Rosicrucian manifesto, may well have appealed to Mary Shelley as preferable to the denial of the feminine, as in the case of Victor Frankenstein's experiments.

The public way in which she defines herself through her fiction belies her projected private image of docility and submission, when we consider such denunciations of her novel as William Beckford's verdict that it was 'perhaps, the foulest toadstool that has yet sprung up from the reeking dunghill of the present times.'[92] The idea of a woman conjuring up sacrilegious visions of the grotesque and gargantuan desire of the mad scientist defied patriarchal precepts governing constructs of femininity. Beckford's pronouncement that *Frankenstein* was the Gothic novel's most 'hideous progeny' would have been endorsed by those who regarded it as a monstrosity penned by a woman. Less threatening were the kind produced by men, even in the case of the Jacobin monster, which proved to be a far more political animal than that which Mary Shelley had created.

The Illuminati and the Monster, Jacobin

The founder of the Illuminati, Adam Weishaupt, claimed that the brotherhood had derived their rituals from the Eleusinian Mysteries, one of the ancient mystery religions which provided Darwin with the machinery for his *Temple of Nature.* This poem is an exposition of the Great Chain of Being and an initiation into the 'mysteries' of nature. According to Darwin:

> In the Eleusinian Mysteries the philosophy of the works of Nature, with the origin and progress of society, are believed to have been taught by allegoric scenery explained by the Hierophant to the initiated, which gave rise to the machinery of the following poem.[93]

Like the Rosicrucians, the Illuminists were intent upon world reform through mystical illumination. Their campaign attracted the attention of the authorities, who began to persecute members of the organisation. The witch-hunts of the 1790s generated an atmosphere of political paranoia during which conspiracy theories propagated. The most radical example of this was the accusation made by the Abbé Barruel in his *Memoirs, Illustrating the History of Jacobinism* (1797-8), and Robinson's *Proofs of a Conspiracy against all the Religions and Governments of Europe* (1798), that the Illuminati had instigated the French Revolution.

Irwin Primer suggests that Darwin's *Temple of Nature* is a guarded reply to the harassment of the Illuminati by Robinson and Barruel. The association between magic and political subversion may be illustrated by the frontispiece to the poem, which is a painting by Fuseli depicting the unveiling of the goddess Nature. Primer believes that this classical pose acquires political connotations in the revolutionary context of anti-clericalism and nature-worship. In *Frankenstein,* Victor admits that philosophy had partly unveiled the face of Nature, 'but her immortal lineaments were still a wonder and a mystery.'[94] Primer suggests that Robinson may have had Darwin's poetry in mind when he launched the following attack:

> Ingenious or designing men of letters have attempted to show that some of the ancient mysteries were useful to mankind, containing rational doctrines of natural religion. This was the strong hold of Weishaupt, and he quotes the Eleusinian, the Pythagorean, and other mysteries .... But, like the Illuminati, they [the Dionysians] tagged to the secrets of Masonry the secret of drunkenness and debauchery ... but they too were Illuminatores [sic], and thought it their duty to overset the State, and were themselves overset.[95]

Robinson's views were shared by Barruel, whose *Memoirs* had been read by both Mary and Shelley. As mentioned earlier, Barruel regarded the secret societies as agents for political change, and attributed the origin of the French Revolution to the Illuminati of Ingoldstadt and the Freemasons, alleging that the Illuminés 'conspiring against Christianity, and with the Sophisters who, with the Occult Masons, conspired against both Christianity and Kings.'[96] Barruel goes on to claim that it was the coalition of 'the adepts of impiety, of the adepts of rebellion and the adepts of anarchy' which gave birth to the 'monster called Jacobin.'[97] Barruel makes extensive use of this parent-child metaphor in his account of the Jacobin monster terrorising Europe. Lee Sterrenburg suggests that Mary Shelley had Barruel's *Memoirs* in mind when she composed *Frankenstein.*[98] An extension of the birth-myth genesis for the novel is Barruel's contention that the monster Jacobin was conceived by the Illuminati at the University of Ingoldstadt, the place where Victor not only studied but also produced the monster. The disruption caused by Victor's creation has similarities with the Illuminists' strategy of destroying the social, political and religious institutions which enchain the individual. This may be seen as a parody of the Second Coming causing domestic as well as political havoc. The analogy between the monster and the French Revolution may be explored further in terms of Barruel's rhetoric: 'The French Revolution has been a true child of its parent sect; its crimes have been its filial duty; those black deeds and atrocious acts the natural consequences of the principles and systems that gave it birth.'[99]

The monster mirrors Rousseau's belief that liberty may be achieved by the destruction of institutions. The Illuminati had adopted an anarchistic programme demanding the overthrow of monarchs and existing institutions in a welter of world reform. As a metaphor for this revolutionary fervour, Mary Shelley's monster epitomises the attempted dissolution of the most fundamental social unit, the family. The Illuminati, as portrayed through the Gothic novel, insisted that their members dissolve domestic ties in order to devote themselves entirely to the revolutionary cause. In *Frankenstein*, Victor's single-minded pursuit of his nefarious activities means that he neglects his duties to his family. Later he becomes aware of the dangers inherent in such an unhealthy absorption in his work, saying:

> If the study to which you apply yourself has a tendency to weaken your affections, and to destroy your taste for those simple pleasures in which no alloy can possibly mix, then that study is certainly unlawful that is to say, not befitting the human mind.[100]

Victor goes on to argue that if man had retained the 'tranquillity of his domestic affections'[101] then empires would not have risen to enslave nations and great civilisations would not have been destroyed.

The potential of the monster as a catalyst for revolution is where it may most noticeably be identified with Percy Shelley. Victor is generally believed to have been modelled on Shelley, yet the darker side of his character is expressed in the torments of the monster, who resolves to annihilate the ties of domestic affection: 'Indeed I think it is to the benefit of society to destroy the opinions which can annihilate the dearest of its ties … *Adieu – écrasez l'infâme écrasez l'impie*.'[102] Barruel cites the words above by Voltaire as the catch-phrase of the Illuminati. Shelley identified with Illuminism by adopting their political code for his projected secret society mentioned earlier. He believed the Illuminati to be a mouthpiece for 'rational liberty'[103] yet Barruel's account of the organisation as an instrument of mass destruction prefigures the monster's oaths of vengeance against mankind: 'Oh how I wish I were the Antichrist, that it were mine to crush the Demon, to hurl him to his native Hell never to rise again.'[104] Shelley's romantic agonising may be seen in the creature's monologue, which expresses its desire to wreak senseless destruction as an antidote to its own misery:

> Cursed, cursed creator! Why do I live? Why, in that instant, did I not extinguish the spark of existence which you had so wantonly bestowed? I know not; despair had not yet taken possession of me; my feelings were those of rage and revenge. I could with pleasure have destroyed the cottage and its inhabitants, and have glutted myself with their shrieks and misery.[105]

Instead of inflicting suffering upon the innocent, the monster wanders into the woods where he howls in anguish like a wild beast, wanting to tear up the trees around him. He feels as though he has a hell within him and compares himself to the arch-fiend. After having rescued a young girl from drowning, he is rewarded for his good deed by being shot by her companion. As his sense of injustice grows, he senses that he has no other choice than to wage 'everlasting war against the species'[106] of mankind. Godwin, whose utopianism would have attracted him to this Rosicrucian vision of radical, social, political and spiritual reform became the target of the young Percy Shelley's outrage against the human race:

> Do not talk of forgiveness again to me, for my blood boils in my veins, and my gall rises against all that bears the human form, when I think of what I, their benefactor and ardent lover, have endured of enmity and contempt from you and from all mankind.[107]

This invective is mirrored in the monster's anger as he calls for anarchic destruction and wholesale destruction.

The Unhallowed Arts

In view of Percy Shelley's occultist interests and graveyard pursuits, it is tempting to read in him a model for Victor Frankenstein. Mary Shelley's use of Shelley as a model for her scientist is evident from the early stages of the novel which trace the development of the hero's interests in magic and science. During his formative years Victor is attracted to the occult, particularly through the writings of Cornelius Agrippa, which his father, Alphonse, dismisses as 'sad trash.'[108] Undeterred, Victor obtains Agrippa's complete works as well as the writings of Paracelsus and Albertus Magnus. These authors contributed towards the Rosicrucian tradition, and inspire Victor to search for the secret of eternal life, which he records as follows:

> I entered with the greatest diligence into the search of the philosopher's stone and the elixir of life. But the latter obtained my most undivided attention: wealth was an inferior object, but what glory would attend the discovery, if I could banish disease from the human frame, and render man invulnerable to any but a violent death![109]

Both Shelley and Victor have visions of raising ghosts and devils. But eventually Victor's mentors, Agrippa, Albertus Magnus and Paracelsus, whom he describes as 'the lords of my imagination,'[110] are supplanted by the gods of science. This transition is paralleled in the life of Shelley for, as Thomas Jefferson Hogg recalled, the pale atheist while at Oxford purchased 'treatises on magic and witchcraft, as well as those modern ones detailing the miracles of electricity and galvanism.'[111]

In the novel, Victor becomes a student of science at the University of Ingolstadt, where his professor, M. Krempe, condemns Agrippa, Magnus and Paracelsus when telling Victor that he has 'exchanged the discoveries of recent enquirers for the dreams of forgotten alchymists.'[112] Yet Victor is discontented with the narrow definition of modern science which dictates that 'metals cannot be transmuted, and that the elixir of life is a chimera.' [113] Victor realises that 'it was very different when the masters of the science sought immortality and power,'[114] for now he must 'exchange chimeras of boundless grandeur for realities of little worth.'[115] His reluctance to do this prompts him to seek out another adviser, M. Waldman, who assures him that modern science is founded upon the work of the occultists who devised the taxonomies of natural philosophy. Victor's decision to embrace all branches of science is in keeping with the tradition of the Rosicrucian magician-scientist. In addition to his interests in magic, Victor studies branches of natural philosophy, including chemistry, anatomy, physiology and experimental science. After a period of intense research he discovers that he is capable of 'bestowing animation upon lifeless matter.'[116]

This discovery has the effect of making Victor feel re-animated like the Arabian on the fourth voyage of Sinbad, who has been buried with the dead whose passage to life had been guided by a 'glimmering, and seemingly ineffectual light.'[117] With his newly-acquired knowledge, Victor decides to try and create a human being. The details of this operation have the flavour of a necromantic activity since Victor has to make clandestine visits to the local graveyard in order to learn from the dead the secrets of life. Determined to pursue 'nature to her hiding places,'[118] he conducts several unsavoury experiments for the purpose of animating his 'lifeless clay.'[119] With 'profane fingers,'[120] Victor scavenges the charnel-house for bones for his 'work-shop of filthy creation.'[121] At last he unearths the secrets of the grave so that he can give life to the being he has constructed. But to his horror he realises that he has bestowed life on a grotesque creature. D. H. Lawrence was later to note that the ideal being was created by man and so was the supreme monster.

The monster reasons with his creator that he ought to be another Adam, but instead he finds himself to be worse off than the fallen angel. At least Lucifer, unlike the monster, was not lonely or isolated, since he had his entourage from Hell for companionship. The creation of the monster is a mockery of the second Fall of mankind, which Bacon had argued ought to have been the legacy of the Rosicrucian seeker. Frankenstein has gone beyond the search for the *elixir vitæ* to the discovery of the creation of life itself. This blasphemy may be viewed as an abuse of the Rose and Cross, since a spiritually unprepared individual has taken upon himself the responsibility of tampering with the mysteries of life and death. As a result, the teachings of the Rosicrucian manifestos have been once again violated.

Rosicrucian Romanticism

> The bride of time no more, I wed eternity –
> She is immortal
>
> Mary Shelley[122]

Mary Shelley continued to develop her Romantic treatment of themes relating to the Rosicrucian seeker through three later novels, *Valperga or The Life and Adventures of Castruccio, Prince of Lucca* (1823), *Falkner* (1837) and *The Last Man* (1826). Her second novel, *Valperga* is a departure from the world of the supernatural, since it sets out to highlight the dangers arising from the Napoleonic ideal. Mary Shelley spoke out directly against Napoleon in her study of the *Most Eminent Literary and Scientific Men of Italy, Spain and Portugal* (1835-7).[123] Her anxiety lest England, like France, should succumb to despotism was conveyed in a letter to Maria Gisbourne written shortly before she started writing *Valperga* in 1820. The novel was produced partly in response to those fears, and is in many ways an attempt to resurrect the monster Jacobin from the pages of *Frankenstein.*

The novel is about Castruccio, who, after freeing his native Lucca from tyranny becomes instead its tyrant. His betrothed, Euthanasia, is opposed to his rule, since she embraces the spirit of republicanism. The plot is complicated further by the love of Beatrice of Ferrara for Castruccio. Beatrice, who is blinded by religious delusions, finally takes henbane and dies in a delirium after being seduced by Castruccio. Her undying belief in the triumphant power of evil is confirmed by Castruccio's corruption and moral decline, which leads to the drowning of Euthanasia at the end of the story. In *Valperga*, Mary Shelley equates moral with political decay, sharing Percy Shelley's vision of spiritual regeneration and socio-political reform. By now, he had cast aside the Abbé Barruel for his own vision of political change as expressed in such works as *The Mask of Anarchy* (1819) and *A Philosophical View of Reform* (1819).

Ostensibly, *Valperga* is a study of tyranny which attempts to examine the corrupting influence of power, both political and supernatural. Part of the quest for forbidden knowledge promises the prospect of illicit power. Castruccio's ambition to elevate himself above humanity is prompted by his desire for fame, since he asks 'Is it not fame that makes men gods?'[124] Likewise the Rosicrucian is discontented with the state of mortality and seeks instead the stature of a god. St Leon ranks himself with the gods after taking the *elixir vitæ* while Victor Frankenstein mimics the Creator through his experiments with artificial life. Like the Rosicrucian, Castruccio becomes consumed by narcissism, becoming everything to himself while his creed seems to contain no articles of faith, only the end and aim of his ambition. Beatrice attempts to gain power over Castruccio and seeks out the help of the witch, Fior di Mandragola, who has occult powers associated with the Rosicrucians. For example, she boasts of her power over the spirit-world by saying: 'I rule the spirits, and do not serve them: what can angels do more?'[125] Mandragola explains to Beatrice that true power lies in the realm of that other self which: 'at one time lies within you, and anon wanders at will over the boundless universe, [which] is a pure and immediate emanation of the divinity, and, as such, commands all creatures, be they earthly or ethereal.'[126]

As astral and sublunary wanderers, Mary Shelley's characters endure the intense loneliness of the Rosicrucian outcast. Beatrice's narrative consists of an account of her wanderings through which she hopes to discover her true destiny, saying 'Alone! alone! I travelled on day after day, in short but wearisome journeys, and I felt the pain of utter and forced solitude.'[127] Euthanasia's isolation is perpetuated by her existence as a solitary hermitess, which is broken by intermittent wanderings. Towards the end of the novel, Castruccio himself turns into a persecuted wanderer who 'wanders about the world a proscribed and helpless thing, hooted from the palace of kings, excommunicated from churches.'[128] Indeed he experiences much of the degradation suffered by Godwin's Rosicrucian hero, St Leon. For like the Rosicrucian wanderer, whose unnatural existence lends itself to a cycle of life-in-death, Castruccio's presence in human society is likened to the existence of a corpse within a living body.

In Mary Shelley's final novel *Falkner,* the Rosicrucian wanderer is transformed into the Romantic seeker. Instead of searching for the material possession of the elixir, Falkner embarks on a purely metaphysical quest for youth. He is described in terms not dissimilar to those used for the wandering adept:

> There was something in the stranger that at once arrested attention – a freedom, and a command of manner – self-possession joined to energy .... You could not doubt at the instant of seeing him, that many singular, perhaps tragical, incidents were attached to his history.[129]

Falkner has been harbouring a misplaced sense of guilt ever since he has wrongly blamed himself for the accidental death of the mother of his child-companion, Elizabeth. A self-imposed exile from the moral order, 'his will was his law; the limits of his physical strength were the only barriers to his wildest wanderings.'[130] Like the Rosicrucian who is compelled to wander even after obtaining the elixir of life, Falkner finds that he wanders 'with the speed of a misery that strove to escape from itself.'[131] Falkner believes himself to be isolated from the rest of society, which he regards as a secret organisation from which he is excluded: 'He could not among strangers at once discern the points to admire, and make himself the companion of the intelligent and good, through a sort of Freemasonry some spirits possess.'[132] Falkner's sole companion is the child Elizabeth, who is symbolic of the elixir. Through her Falkner eventually absolves himself of his guilt by purifying himself in a kind of spiritual alchemy.

Mary Shelley's third novel, *The Last Man*, is an inversion of the Rosicrucian dilemma in that her hero by becoming a second Adam suffers the loneliness of a mortal immortal. The novel is a record of the emotional upheaval in her life following the death of Byron in 1824. In her *Journa*l she records that now Byron 'had become one of the people of the grave – that miserable conclave to which the beings I best loved belong.'[133] His loss, occurring two years after Shelley's drowning, had prompted Mary Shelley to describe herself as 'The Last Man.'[134] The novel is a dramatisation of this desolation.

The story, which is set in a republican England, concerns Lionel Verney, whose narrative opens around the year 2073. Verney and his sister, Perdita, are orphans who are the descendants of a line of nobility. Perdita eventually marries the politically ambitious Lord Raymond, a military hero who eventually becomes the Lord Protector of England. Raymond becomes disillusioned with high office and resigns so that he can return to active service. In pursuit of military honours, Raymond leaves England for Greece and then Turkey followed by Lionel and Perdita. Here, where 'Death had become Lord of Constantinople,'[135] Raymond dies of the plague. The remainder of the novel plots the inexorable advance of the pestilence which wipes out the world's human population leaving only eighty survivors at Dijon. Gradually this number is depleted to three, until finally one individual remains: Lionel, who thus becomes 'Verney – the LAST MAN.'[136]

The concept of the last man was not an original idea. Elizabeth Nitchie tries to account for the poor reception of Mary Shelley's *Last Man* by suggesting that 'Perhaps the public had had a surfeit of Last Men.'[137] Byron had already dealt with this theme in his *Darkness* (1816), followed by Thomas Campbell's *Last Man* in 1824.[138] The reviewer for *Blackwood's Edinburgh Magazine* had given the accolade of all last men to Thomas Hood's contribution from his *Whims and Oddities*, announcing this as 'worth fifty of Byron's darkness (a mere daub) a hundred and fifty of Campbell's *Last Man* and five hundred of Mrs Shelley's abortion.'[139] Even the twenty-first century setting of Mary's *Last Man* was not innovatory, since an anonymous novel, *The Last Man, or Omegarus and Syderia*, advertised as 'a romance in futurity'[140] had appeared as early as 1806.

Mary Shelley opens her story on a prophetic note with an account of how she discovers the 'gloomy cavern of the Cumæan Sibyl' during her visit to Italy. Inside the cave, she comes across the Sibylline leaves, parchments which were inscribed with the writings of many languages including ancient Chaldee, Egyptian hieroglyphics and even modern English and Italian. According to the author, *The Last Man* is a transcription from these ancient prophecies:

> I present the public with my latest discoveries in the slight Sibylline pages. Scattered and unconnected as they were, I have been obliged to add links, and model the work into a consistent form. But the main sub-

> stance rests on the truths contained in these poetic rhapsodies, and the divine intuition which the Cumæan damsel obtained from heaven.[141]

The sibyl is a distant relative of the Rosicrucian wanderer who after having been granted eternal life by Apollo, forgot to ask for perpetual youth. And so she longs for death. The Rosicrucian's death-wish is prompted more by the infinite torments of an unnaturally extended life-span than by the never-ending ravages of age.

Through his illusion of immortality, Verney experiences the anguish of the mortal immortal. As a survivor of the plague, he enters into the consciousness of an immortal being, since 'time is no more, for I have stepped within the threshold of eternity.'[142] Verney believes that he has become one of the living dead who, like the Rosicrucian adept, has cheated the course of nature by prolonging his life to outlive his contemporaries. Before the pestilence destroys his remaining two companions, Verney urges, 'let us exist no more in this living death, but die that we may live!'[143] Desirous to die, so far he has been unable to escape his *Todestraum* or dream of death, but continues to survive. Unable to face the brutal reality around him, he escapes into the 'creative powers of the imagination,'[144] allowing himself to be 'soothed by the sublime fictions it presented.'[145] The sibyl has found a measure of consolation from the prospects of unending life in her sacred task of oracle. But the powers of prophecy are denied Verney because there can no longer be any future for the human race. He realises that even the immortality of the nation-state is a myth, since the belief that 'man remains, while we the individuals pass away'[146] is negated by the death of humanity.

Now Verney like a newly created Adam must live out his allotted span utterly alone:

> Shall I wake, and speak to none, pass the interminable hours, my soul, is landed in the world, a solitary point, surrounded by vacuum .... Great God! Would it one day be this? One day all extinct, save myself, should I walk the earth alone?[147]

Verney shares the tormented consciousness of the Rosicrucian wanderer even though he declares 'I am not immortal; and the thread of my history might be spun out to the limits of my existence.'[148] Though his mortality is stressed, the reader may feel that the last man is following the tortuous footsteps of St Leon rather than those of a Robinson Crusoe who is alone on a desert island of the world.

MARY SHELLEY AND THE MORTAL IMMORTAL

The literary tradition of the Rosy Cross enabled Mary Shelley to proclaim the importance of the domestic affections as espoused by her parents as well as to explore the ontological theme of mortal immortality, the enduring premise of her work. By way of a Rosicrucian hermeneutic, she was able to foreground the plight of the mortal immortal as an allegory of the tormented self-consciousness of creative genius countenanced by its own tragic despair. The spiritual odyssey of the Rosicrucian wanderer had perilously over-loaded existing Gothic structures; hence its shift towards the spaces of Romanticism. Her fiction effectively freed the Rosicrucian preoccupation with immortality from Godwin's Enlightenment materialism and Percy Shelley's Germanic melodrama, thus allowing it to take its rightful place within the Romantic imagination.

Notes

1. Quoted by G. S. Kirk and J. E. Raven, *The Presocratic Philosophers* (London, 1957), p. 210.
2. *The Collected Works of Thomas De Quincey*, ed. David Masson, 16 vols (Edinburgh, 1880), III, p. 25.
3. *Tales and Stories by Mary Wollstonecraft Shelley*, ed. Richard Garnett (London, 1891), p. xi.
4. Review of *Cloudesley* in *Blackwood's Edinburgh Magazine*, 27 (May, 1830), p. 712.
5. See *Collected Tales and Stories*, ed. Charles E. Robinson (London, 1976), p. 390.
6. See Godwin, *Lives of the Necromancers*, pp. 322-9. For a survey of the wider impact of Godwin upon Mary Shelley's work see Katherine Richardson Powers, 'The Influence of William Godwin on the Novels of Mary Shelley,' unpublished Ph.D. thesis (University of Tennessee, August, 1972).
7. Yates, *The Rosicrucian Enlightenment*, p. 264.
8. Mary Shelley, *Frankenstein or The Modern Prometheus*, ed. James Rieger (New York, 1974), p. 32. This text, which reproduces the 1818 edition, will be referred to throughout unless stated otherwise.
9. Shelley, *Collected Tales and Stories*, p. 219.
10. Ibid., p. 220.
11. Loc. cit.
12. Ibid., p. 221.
13. See Harold Hartley, *Humphrey Davy* (Yorkshire, 1972), p. 91. Here reference is made to Davy's study of the early alchemists which he discusses in the introduction to his *Elements of Chemical Philosophy*. Mary Shelley records in her *Journal* that she started reading this work on October 28, 1816 at the same time as she was writing *Frankenstein*. Significantly, Davy had been universally acclaimed for a lecture delivered in 1806 for a paper 'On the chemical effects of Electricity.'
14. Shelley, *Collected Tales and Stories*, p. 222.
15. Ibid., p. 224.
16. Loc. cit.
17. Ibid., p. 226.
18. Ibid., p. 230.
19. William A. Walling, *Mary Shelley* (New York, 1972), p. 115.
20. Bradford A. Booth, 'The Pole: A Story by Claire Clairmont,' *English Literary History*, V (1938), 69 n.
21. Shelley, *Collected Tales and Stories*, p. 219.
22. Ibid., p. 390.
23. Ibid., p. 219.
24. Loc. cit.
25. Ibid., p. 229.
26. *Mary Shelley's Journal*, ed. Frederick L. Jones (Norman, 1947), p. 196.
27. Godwin, *St Leon*, p. 163.
28. *Mary Shelley's Journal*, ed. Jones, p. 196.
29. Ibid., p. 195.
30. Shelley, *Collected Tales and Stories*, p. 227.
31. Ibid., p. 343.

32. Ibid., p. 340.
33. See Charles E. Robinson, 'Mary Shelley and the Roger Dodsworth hoax,' *Keats-Shelley Journal*, 24 (1975), pp. 20-8.
34. Shelley, *Collected Tales and Stories*, p. 43. Here Mary Shelley returns to the scenes of ice and snow towards the end of *Frankenstein* where the monster survives the frozen wastes.
35. Ibid., p. 44.
36. Ibid., p. 50.
37. Ibid., p. 43.
38. Ibid., p. 50.
39. Ibid., p. 49.
40. Loc. cit.
41. Loc. cit.
42. Loc. cit.
43. Ibid., p. 121.
44. Ibid., p. 128.
45. Loc. cit.
46. Ibid., p. 101.
47. See Walling, *Mary Shelley*, p. 115.
48. See Donald F. Glut, *The Frankenstein Legend: A Tribute to Mary Shelley and Boris Karloff* (New Jersey, 1973), p. 7.
49. See the *Quarterly Review*, XVIII (March, 1818), p. 382.
50. Walter Scott's review of *Frankenstein* appears in *Blackwood's Edinburgh Magazine*, XII, II (March, 1818), p. 614.
51. Shelley, *Frankenstein*, p. 226.
52. For a compendium of critical interpretations see *The Endurance of Frankenstein: Essays on Mary Shelley's Novel*, ed. George Levine and U. C. Knoepflmacher (London, 1979).
53. See Radu Florescu, *In Search of Frankenstein* (London, 1975), p. 234.
54. See Marie Roberts, 'Science, Magic and Masonry: Swift, the Error of Death and the Limits of Reason' in *Secret Texts: The Literature of Secret Societies*, ed. Marie Roberts and Hugh Ormsby-Lennon (forthcoming).
55. Henry Colburn published *The Vampire* as Byron's work in *New Monthly Magazine* (April, 1819). Rieger reproduces the tale in Appendix C of his edition of *Frankenstein*, pp. 266-87.
56. See Franco Moretti, 'The Dialectic of Fear', *New Left Review*, 136 (1982), pp. 67-87.
57. Karl Marx, *Early Texts*, ed. David McLellan (Oxford, 1972), p. 136.
58. Loc. cit.
59. Shelley, *Frankenstein*, p. 228.
60. Ibid., pp. 227–8.
61. Ibid., p. 228.
62. Ibid., p. 163.
63. Ibid., p. 229.
64. Ibid., p. 222. In his survey of sources of *Frankenstein*, B. R. Pollin treats Rosicrucianism as an 'obvious derivation.' See 'Philosophical and Literary Sources of Frankenstein,' *Comparative Literature*, 17 (Spring, 1965), p. 100.
65. Both Fuseli and Erasmus Darwin were interested in theories relating to an electric or nervous fluid which was believed to be similar to the 'magnetic fluid' of

animal magnetism. In *The Nightmare*, the oracular Pythoness, Laura, writhes under the pressure of a leering incubus. Fuseli graphically illustrates the principles of terror later experienced by Mary Shelley which has been described as:

> A strange and unexpected event awakens the mind and keeps it on the stretch: and where the agency of invisible beings is introduced ... of "forms unseen mightier far that we," our imagination darting forth explores with rapture the new world which is laid open to its powers. Passion and fancy co-operating elevate the soul to its highest pitch, and the pain of terror is lost in amazement.

Quoted by Peter Tomory in *The Life and Art of Henry Fuseli* (London, 1972), p. 72.

66. See ibid., pp. 204–5.
67. See *The Spectator*, May 15 1712, 379, ed. Bond, III, p. 425.
68. Loc. cit.
69. Loc. cit.
70. See Florescu, *In Search of Frankenstein*, pp. 230-4.
71. See Godwin, *Lives of the Necromancers*, p. 261.
72. Quoted by Florescu, *In Search of Frankenstein*, p. 86, taken from *The History of Johann Konrad Dippel in the Theological Period of his Life* (Darmstadt, 1908), p. 183.
73. Gruman, 'A History of Ideas about the Prolongation of Life,' p. 84
74. Loc. cit.
75. See Shelley, *Frankenstein*, p. 35.
76. '*Stein*' is German for 'stone', which may be an allusion to the philosopher's stone. It is possible that Mary Shelley had derived the title *Frankenstein* from the names Frankheim and Falkenstein used in Matthew Lewis's *Tales*, which she had read in 1815.
77. Erasmus Darwin, *The Botanic Garden* (London, 1789-91), pp. 37-8. Darwin's knowledge of electricity is revealed in a learned appendix to the poem.
78. Desmond King-Hele, *Erasmus Darwin* (London, 1963), p. 143.
79. Mary Shelley, *Frankenstein*, p. 227.
80. Ibid., p. 6.
81. Florescu, *In Search of Frankenstein*, p. 218.
82. See Carl Grabo, *A Newton among Poets* (Chapel Hill, 1930), pp. 59-166.
83. Darwin, *The Botanic Garden*, vii.
84. See Tomory, *The Life and Art of Henry Fuseli*, p. 166.
85. Darwin, *The Botanic Garden*, p. 48.
86. Ibid., p. 187.
87. Ibid., p. 88.
88. Ibid., p. 188.
89. Ibid., p. 189.
90. Quoted by Anne K. Mellor, '*Frankenstein:* A Feminist Critique of Science,' *One Culture: Essays in Science and Literature*, ed. George Levine (London, 1987), pp. 305.
91. Androgyny is discredited by Daniel A. Harris in 'Androgyny: The Sexist Myth in Disguise,' *Women's Studies*, 2 (1974), pp. 171-84 and Cynthia Secor in 'Androgyny: An Early Reappraisal,' *Women's Studies*, 2 (1974), pp. 161-9.

William Veeder looks at androgyny in *Mary Shelley and Frankenstein: The Fate of Androgyny* (London, 1986).

92. Howard B. Gotlieb, *William Beckford of Fonthill* (New Haven, 1960), p. 61.
93. Darwin, *The Temple of Nature or The Origin of Society: a poem with Philosophical Notes* (London, 1803), preface.
94. This is taken from the 1831 edition, Shelley, *Frankenstein*, p. 238.
95. Irwin Primer, 'Erasmus Darwin's *Temple of Nature*, Progress, Evolution, and the Eleusinian Mysteries,' pp. 74-5.
96. Barruel, *Memoirs Illustrating the History of Jacobinism*, I, xxii-xxiii.
97. Ibid., II, p. 479.
98. See Lee Sterrenburg, 'Mary Shelley's Monster: Politics and Psyche in *Frankenstein*' in *The Endurance of Frankenstein*, ed. Levine and Knoepflmacher, p. 157.
99. Barruel, *Memoirs Illustrating the History of Jacobinsism*, III, p. 414.
100. Shelley, *Frankenstein*, p. 51.
101. Loc.cit.
102. Shelley, *Letters*, ed. Jones, I, pp. 27-9.
103. Ibid., p. 34.
104. Ibid., I, p. 35.
105. Shelley, *Frankenstein*, p. 132.
106. Ibid., p. 133.
107. Hogg, *Life*, I, p. 459.
108. Chris Baldick points out that Shelley is portrayed more clearly in the character of Henry Clerval. See *In Frankenstein's Shadow: Myth, Monstrosity and Nineteenth-Century Writing* (Oxford , 1987), p. 36.
109. Shelley, *Frankenstein*, p. 35. David Ketterer argues that:

    > symbolically, the transformation of lead into gold betokens the transmutation of the alchemist from a physical to a presumably eternal spiritual state. To a degree, then, *Frankenstein* is posing a false dichotomy. No less than the elixir of life, the philosopher's stone promises immortality. The effect is to blur the equation between immortality and transcendence.

    Frankenstein's Creation: The Book, The Monster, and Human Reality (University of Victoria, Canada, 1979), p. 83.
110. Shelley, *Frankenstein*, p. 35
111. Hogg, *Life of Shelley*, I, p. 36.
112. This is taken from the 1831 text, Shelley, *Frankenstein*, p. 241.
113. Ibid., p. 42.
114. Ibid., p. 41.
115. *Three Gothic Novels*, ed. Peter Fairclough (Harmondsworth, 1974), p. 306.
116. Shelley, *Frankenstein*, p. 47.
117. Ibid., p. 48.
118. Ibid., p. 49.
119. Loc. cit.
120. Ibid., p. 50.
121. Loc. cit.
122. Quoted by Elizabeth Nitchie, *Mary Shelley: Author of Frankenstein* (New Brunswick, 1953), p. 199.

123. See Mary Shelley, *Lives of the Most Eminent Literary and Scientific Men of Italy, Spain and Portugal* (1835-7).
124. Mary Shelley, *Valperga or The Life and Adventures of Castruccio, Prince of Lucca*, 3 vols (London, 1823), I, p. 54. This analogy is evident from the epigraph of *Frankenstein* taken from Milton's *Paradise Lost*:

    Did I request thee, Maker, from my clay
    To mould me man? Did I solicit thee
    From darkness to promote me?

125. Shelley, *Valperga*, p. 4.
126. Ibid., p. 133.
127. Ibid., p. 78.
128. Ibid., p. 48.
129. Shelley, *Falkner: A Novel* (London, 1837), pp. 36-8.
130. Ibid., p. 159.
131. Ibid., p. 60.
132. Ibid., p. 88.
133. Shelley, *Journal*, ed. Jones, p. 193.
134. Loc. cit.
135. Shelley, *The Last Man* (London, 1826), ed. Hugh J. Luke, Jr (Lincoln, 1965), p. 139.
136. Ibid., p. 342.
137. See Nitchie, *Mary Shelley*, p. 152.
138. Loc. cit.
139. Loc. cit.
140. Loc. cit.
141. *The Last Man*, pp. 3-4.
142. Ibid., p. 135.
143. Ibid., p. 301.
144. Ibid., p. 145.
145. Loc. cit.
146. Ibid., p. 165.
147. Ibid., p. 327.
148. Ibid., p. 173.

Plate 1: Goya, *The Sleep of Reason Produces Monsters* (1799)

Plate 2: Doré, *The Wandering Jew* (1867)

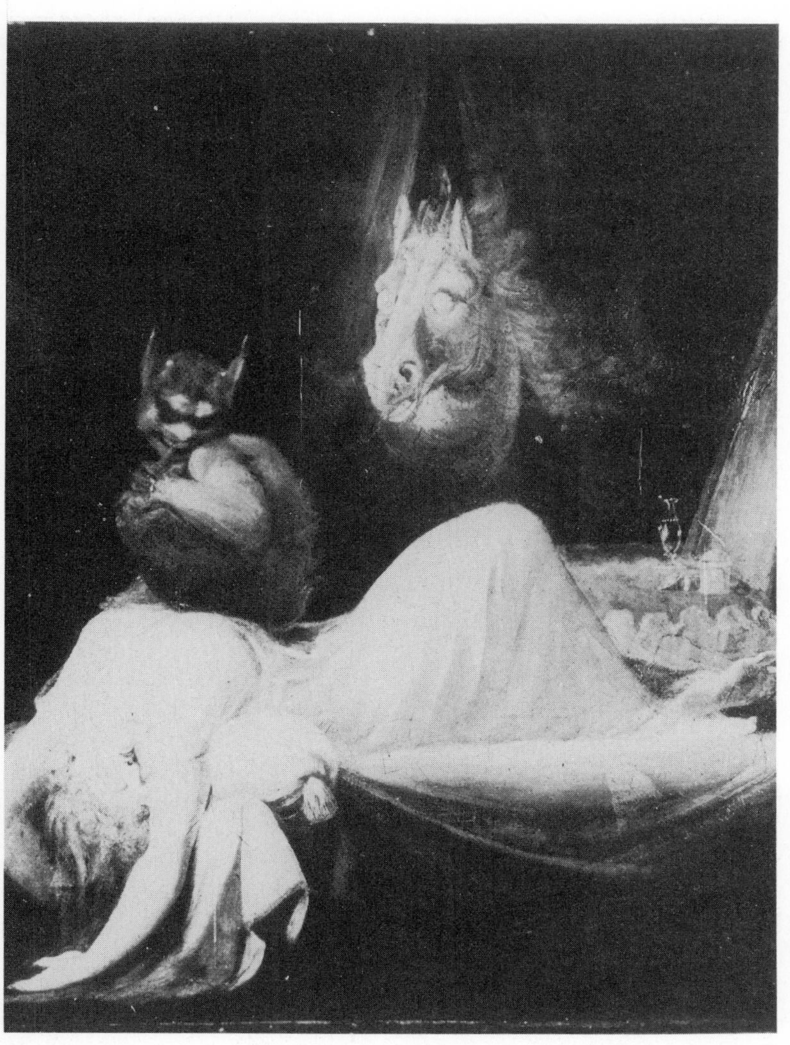

Plate 3: Fuseli, *The Nightmare* (1781)

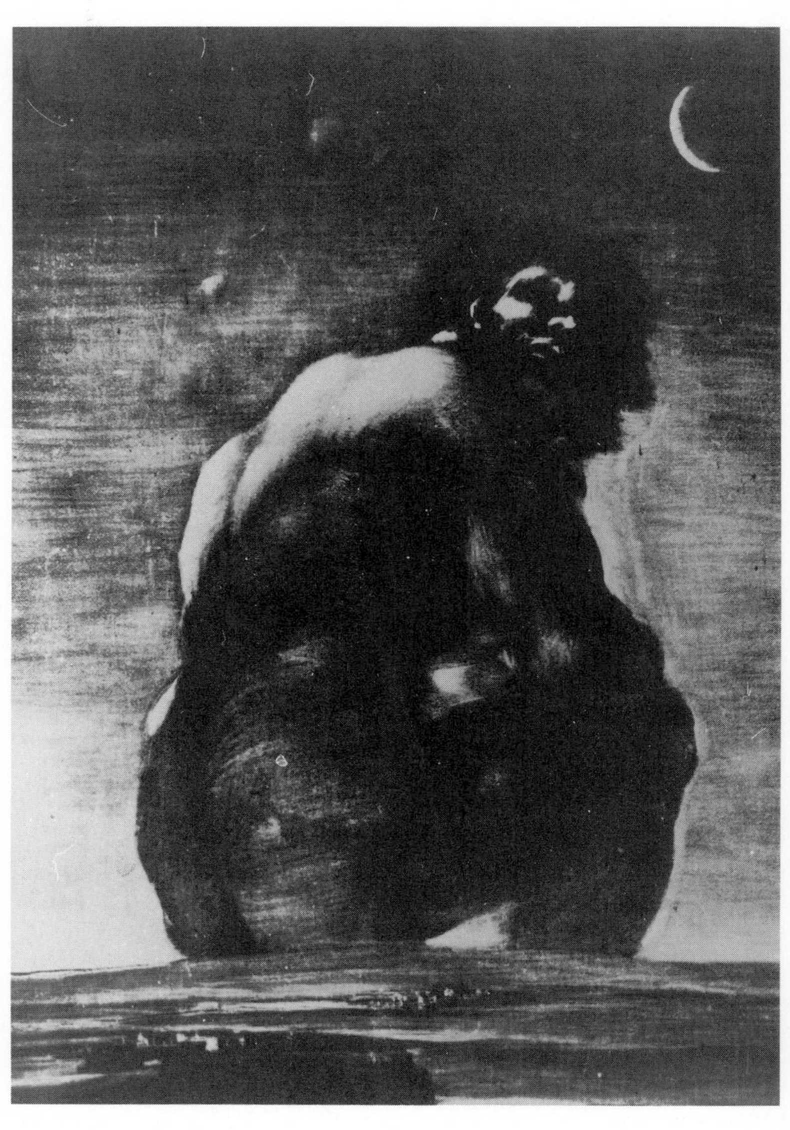

Plate 4: Goya, *The Colossus* (1810-1817)

5

Maturin and the Rosicrucian Heresy

> If I possess any talent, it is that of darkening the gloomy, and of deepening the sad; of painting life in extremes, and representing those struggles of passion when the soul trembles on the verge of the unlawful and the unhallowed.
>
> Maturin [1]

Charles Robert Maturin is chiefly renowned as the author of the Gothic masterpiece, *Melmoth the Wanderer*[2] (1820). With its echoes of Faust and the Wandering Jew, Melmoth advances the Rosicrucian novel into the realms of theological controversy.

Maturin's interest in the Rosicrucian wanderer must have been stoked by his professional involvements in the supernatural in general. As a Gothic novelist Maturin had a vested interest in the occult, while his vocation as a preacher in the Established Church of Ireland fuelled his morbid fascination for 'the unlawful and the unhallowed.' Dale Kramer suggests that Maturin had suffered from a psychological imbalance which could only find satisfaction in the extravagances of the Gothic mode.[3] Yet when we consider the nature of Maturin's sermons these alone could have provided him with much raw material for his novels. In his hell-fire sermons Maturin would often dwell upon the horrific details of physical suffering. Not hesitating to remind his parishioners of their own mortality through lurid descriptions of putrefaction, he betrayed his macabre interest in the process of bodily decay. Indeed Lowry Nelson in 'Night Thoughts on the Gothic Novel' partly ascribed the rise of the tale of terror to the growing ranks of graveyard enthusiasts.[4] Maturin also used the pulpit as a platform for his bitter opposition towards Catholicism,[5] perhaps in retaliation for the Catholic Church's persecution of his French ancestor who was eventually imprisoned in the Bastille for twenty-six years. This episode, which Maturin claims as part of his anti-papist inheritance, contributed towards his 'mania concerning Catholic cruelty.'[6]

In Dublin circles Maturin was noted for such eccentricities as his interest in the Albigenses or Cathars, heretical sects associated by historians with the Knights Templar[7] whose descendents were believed to have been the Rosicrucians. Maturin's experience as a preacher would have been invaluable for his Gothic novels *The Albigenses* (1824) and *Melmoth the Wanderer*, which are case-histories of those who transgress God's eternal laws.

Fatal Revenge: A Gothic Melodrama

In his first novel, *Fatal Revenge*, which may be regarded as a blue-print for *Melmoth the Wanderer*, Maturin 'attempted to explore the ground forbidden to man,'[8] which involved tracing the 'fear arising from objects of invisible terror' to 'a high and obvious source.' By rationalising supernatural happenings into the villainous behaviour of a malevolent character[9] Maturin adopts the Gothic techniques as practised by Ann Radcliffe. *Fatal Revenge* also foreshadows the Rosicrucianism which is developed later in *Melmoth the Wanderer*. According to Birkhead, the plot of *Fatal Revenge* will cause many readers to 'wander, bewildered, baffled, and distracted through labyrinth mazes.'[10] The action is dominated by a revenge motif, as the title suggests: it was selected by the publisher in preference to Maturin's own choice, *The Family of Montorio*.[11]

Parricide is the starting point for the intrigue when two sons, Annibal and Ippolito, are manipulated by the scheming monk Schemoli,[12] into murdering their father as part of the monk's private vendetta against the family of Montorio. It turns out that Schemoli is really Count Orazio Montorio, who, twenty years earlier, was deceived by his brother into believing that his wife, Erminia di Amaldi, had been unfaithful to him. This revelation provoked Orazio into murdering his wife's alleged lover, the Cavalier Verdoni, an act which indirectly leads to her death. On learning that both Erminia and Verdoni were innocent of any adulterous relationship, Orazio plots revenge against his brother, whose jealousy prompted the initial deception. The deaths of Orazio's two sons determine the course of his revenge, namely that his brother Montorio, must be killed by his own two sons. Orazio is instrumental in superimposing a quasi-supernaturalism onto this Gothic scenario. Though Maturin employs the occasional occult device at various stages of the novel, the main interest is in the illusions created by Orazio, who poses as an agent of supernatural forces.[13] He achieves this deception by simulating his own death. By destroying his true identity, he is able to assume the disguise of Schemoli the monk. From this point onwards, *Fatal Revenge* exhibits the characteristics of an Illuminati novel. The two brothers Annibal and Ippolito, believe themselves to be hounded by an invisible terror from which they can never escape. Orazio manages to persuade them that spiritual forces have predetermined the premature death of their father as part of some demonic will. This is revealed to them by a mysterious stranger who is, of course, Orazio. After a highly complicated plot, Orazio discovers that the death of his own sons had been merely a false rumour propagated by Montorio who, now stricken with guilt, confesses this to his brother. Though it is too late to avert the murder of Montorio, Orazio confesses his wrongdoings and dies of natural causes shortly before his execution is due to take place.

Apart from exploding the psychotic paranoiac machinations of Orazio, Maturin has also created a prototype for Melmoth from within this Gothic paradigm. As Niilo Idman points out in his critical biography of Maturin, Schemoli's mysterious and unexpected entrances are traits which have descended to the Wanderer, with the proviso that the supernatural qualities of the latter are real 'and need not be explained as some utterly incredible, and merely human attainments.'[14] Even though Orazio is not an immortal, this is not always apparent to those who are persecuted by him, like Annibal, who marvels:

> I have seen a departed spirit, an inhabitant of those regions which are invisible to man; I cannot resist the evidence of his appearance and ministry. He prompts me to a crime, revolting to nature and fatal to my own life, reputation, and perhaps immortal interests.[15]

Annibal misinterprets Orazio's attempt to incite him to parricide mainly because he believes his tormentor to be an inhabitant of another world who thus must possess super-human powers. Convinced that there can be no escape from such a fiend 'whom no power can chase from his prey – whom no exorcist can subdue,' Annibal confesses to Filippo, his servant: 'He is not dead, poison cannot kill him; he crosses my path when I move, he lurks in my chamber when I sit, he pervades all the elements, and whispers audibly in my ear even when their senses are closed.'[16] In this speech Orazio is portrayed as possessing death-defying Rosicrucian powers. Accordingly Annibal, who is susceptible to superstition, fears that even the farthest distance can offer no protection, and his only hope of resistance lies in scepticism. Under the influence of Orazio, Annibal comes close to committing parricide, believing that:

> should he pursue me where I am flying I feel I have no further resource, no remaining powers of defence ... it will then be no longer possible to resist. Far be that day from me, oh heaven! In my present state, my misery is solitary and incommunicable; I have no associate, I can have none; for unimaginable distress there is no sympathy.[17]

Annibal's anguish is one which is commonly experienced by the Rosicrucian wanderer. Like Orazio, he is a prisoner of his own consciousness and worries that if he attempts to confide in a close friend or relative then he would be dismissed as a madman or visionary.[18] Caught in this dilemma, he feels that he has no option but to obey Orazio, whom 'he had every reason to believe had power of commission not to be disobeyed.'[19] Here is a curious twist to the Faustian pact, since Annibal has nothing to gain from the murder of his father. It is not until volume 4 that he resolves to turn the contact with the mysterious being to his advantage and begs for forbidden knowledge in order to plumb the secrets of another world, saying 'I would hazard life itself ... to look on them.'[20] But Orazio, disguised as a phantom, pleads with him, telling him of his miseries:

> Mortal perverse and fond, you would not throw away life to feed on unhallowed curiosity; and you listen, without emotion, to a spirit in despair that cries to you for remission and rest from the pit where there is no water.[21]

This would seem to be a convincing piece of play-acting, for at this stage in the story the reader is as yet unaware that the phantom is a hoax. The deception is perpetuated by the stranger or apparition's claim that he must reiterate his sufferings in this way: 'For every night my tale must be told perhaps by other voices than mine.'[22] Such a confession was often tantamount in the Rosicrucian novel to imparting secrets such as that of the elixir of life or the philosopher's stone. The narration of Zampieri's life-story is the preamble to his revelation of the secrets of immortality to St Leon in Godwin's novel, which had been read by Maturin.

Orazio is not the purest pedigree of a Gothic immortal since his magical attributes are merely illusionary. Nevertheless Devendra P. Varma in *The Gothic Flame* classifies Orazio or Schemoli as a Gothic villain 'whose ways lie in darkness and whose strength originates far beyond mortal thought.'[23] This is the typology of the terrible 'superman' who is also 'the immortal outcast, a masterful, vaunting villain, his spirit unbroken even in defeat.' Varma goes on to state 'He is the Rosicrucian, the Alchemist staking his very life on some dark hope, and behind him is all the mystery of Cabbala, Freemasonry, Medieval Satanism.'[24] Orazio reveals himself to be a student of the occult who has wandered the earth in search of magical powers. His quest, which lasts for fifteen years, sets out to prove the existence of superstition so that he can master the technique of how it may be manipulated by 'art and terror.'

Orazio's pilgrimage for occult knowledge has taken him through Turkey, Syria, Persia, Arabia, Egypt and Sicily. This is a variation on the itinerary of Rosencreutz, who journeys through Arabia and Africa. During his travels, Orazio assumes a number of different identities, such as a Grecian conjurer and a magian worshipper of fire. Persuaded of the superiority of Eastern adepti, Orazio urges practitioners of western magic to bow down before the wands of Oriental and African magi, convinced that: 'Among the vulgar I was a conjurer, but among the adepts only a novice; nor in truth could I well be more, had I been versed in all the dark wisdom of Europe, Rosicrucian or Sully's, or Nostradamus, or Albertus Magnus.'[25]

Despite his scepticism regarding the existence of occult powers, Orazio identifies with the triumph of the Rosicrucian adept who has conquered death and mortality: 'I felt myself superior to Kings, and all the mighty ones of the earth — "What is their power?" said I, internally, "it lasts for a few hours, and worms, like themselves, tremble beneath it."'[26] The Rosicrucian hero invariably making this comparison between worldly and supernatural powers over life and death comes to the conclusion that the treasure which no earthly wealth can buy is the *elixir vitæ* which gives the possessor a power over life and death surpassing that of kings. According to the *Fama*, Rosencreutz acquires a treasure 'surpassing that of Kings and Emperors.'[27] Orazio, basking in a psychical megalomania, lays claim to power over the elementals and spirits of the dead:

> Dependent on me is the state of beings, whose substance is indissoluble, and whose duration is eternal. To solicit my aid, the laws of heaven are changed and the veil of the temple of eternity rent in twain. I can fix in passivity, or bind down in torment, beings who could, if they were let loose, scatter and ravish the system and elements in which I live and I can do this, by powers exclusively entrusted to me, and for a period beyond that of my own life, perhaps that of mankind.[28]

Seduced by this vision of spiritual anarchy, Orazio imagines that he possesses an immortal power which he claims extends 'for a period beyond that of my own life, perhaps that of mankind.'[29] Like Melmoth, he is determined to terrorise a mortal victim who would feel powerless against the tyranny of supernatural forces. To Annibal, Orazio, who must seem to be analogous to the devil, announces that 'the eternal will has wedded me to you:'

> I may haunt you in more terrible shape – I may speak to you in a voice that resembles the seething sides of the lake that burneth with fire and brimstone; your reason may desert you in the struggle but I must pursue you till my body and soul are at peace.[30]

According to Varma, Orazio the tempter is 'a new mintage of the Satan portrayed by Milton in *Paradise Lost*.'[31] As the pulpit language of the passage above suggests, the preacher in Maturin was always ready to guide the novelist's pen. Orazio is punished not just by an untimely death but also by a sense of the futility of his lust for revenge:

> Oh! that midnight darkness of the soul in which it seeks for something whose loss has carried away every sense but one of utter and desolate privation; in which it traverses leagues in motion and worlds in thought, without consciousness of reality, yet with a dread of pausing. I had nothing to seek, nothing to recover; the whole world could not restore me an atom, could not show me again a glimpse of what I had been or lost.[32]

The problem for the Rosicrucian hero is restated here for once the quest for immortality has been accomplished then all meaning to life can vanish. If life is seen as a continuous process towards a goal, then the adept's predicament must be that of a living death. So, ironically, the *elixir vitæ* accelerates the *tædium vitæ*.

Maturin does not hesitate to condemn occult pursuits. In *Fatal Revenge* a group of wizards are punished for carrying out a necromantic ceremony involving the reanimation of a corpse. This was a nefarious activity associated with the Rosicrucian fraternity, whose alleged control over the spirit world furnished them with the means of resurrecting the dead. The ritual is interrupted by the eruption of a volcano which freezes the sorcerers in time and space just at the moment when the corpse is expected to stir into life:

> They remained fixed around a magic fire they had raised, each in the very form and attitude in which punishment overtook them, melted into the walls of the vast temple of magic, where they were assembled, and which was now a cavern in that inward region.[33]

The never-ending fire, in which the body had lain unconsumed for 2,000 years is evocative of the perpetual-burning lamp found in the tomb of Rosencreutz, whose body has also been preserved. According to the *Fama*, the Rosicrucian brethren exhume the corpse of their founder, finding it to be 'a fair and worthy body, whole and unconsumed.'[34]

The perpetual-burning lamp and Orazio's persona as a supernatural wanderer are Rosicrucian ingredients which enhance the novel's Gothic atmosphere. H. W. Piper and A. Norman Jeffares, however, regard *Fatal Revenge* as an important distillation of Irish nationalism and romanticism.[35] In *The Milesian Chief* (1811) and *The Wild Irish Boy* (1808) patriotism is regarded increasingly as one manifestation of the process of spiritual and self-awareness associated with the Romantic movement. Unlike *Fatal Revenge*, *Melmoth*, Maturin's most Gothic creation, is transmogrified into a *tour de force* of Romantic consciousness expressed through the convention of the Rosicrucian novel. Leven M. Dawson claims that Maturin's attack in *Melmoth* on exclusive reliance on rational modes of apprehending makes contact with what is most valuable in Romanticism.[36] The concerns of the Romantic movement had many features in common with the preoccupations of the tradition of the Rosy Cross.

Heresies of the Immortal

The heretical nature of the mortal immortal bears a family resemblance to the rebellious consciousness of the Romantic hero. In his sermons Maturin scorns the man who defies the divine laws to make his own imagination or passions the test for orthodoxy or 'oracle of truth.'[37] But the greatest danger of all he senses as coming from the individual who not only perverts 'some solitary and misconstrued text' but also sets up a system in relation to subjects upon which the Scriptures preserve 'an impenetrable silence.'[38]

Maturin takes up this theme in a number of his novels including *The Albigenses*,[39] where the persecution of a heretical sect is dramatised. One of the characters, Lord Courtenaye, is tempted into pursuing forbidden knowledge on being persuaded that this would be judged a god-like sin worthy of an angel not quite fallen. An astrologer advising

Courtenaye to experiment in astrology as opposed to more sinister forms of divination says 'even if our system err, is it not better to err with us' since

> If man will rend asunder the veil that wraps futurity, if he will know that which Heaven will not have known, let him seek it at least where the temptation may be a balance against the offence, as the fruit of Eden might be a palliation for the fall; — let him read the vast volume of the planetary skies, alive with glory and instinct with knowledge; — not the blood-scrawled leaves of dead men's skin where sorcery traces the dooms of hell.[40]

The Fall of man from a state of grace was one of Maturin's most cherished texts for his sermon, allowing him to warn his congregation of the hazards involved in seeking 'forbidden knowledge,' which he condemned as 'the last and most awful delusion in which a man can be plunged by the proud and insane wilfulness of his own understanding.'[41] This is an apt description of the Rosicrucian wanderer who also commits the sin of pride.

In Maturin's *Women; or Pour et Contre* (1818) the heroine, Zaire Dalmatiani, warns her friend Madam St Mawr of the kind of mortal immortal who is later refined into Melmoth:

> that terrible sensation so common in the imagination of the Irish, of a being whom we believe not to be alive, yet knowing not to be dead – who holds a kind of hovering intermediate existence between both worlds, and combines the passions of human existence with the power of a spirit, all produced in me a species of indefinite feeling towards this awful being, that neither reason or change of situation has ever been able to remove.[42]

This would indicate that the idea for Melmoth already existed in the local popular imagination to which Maturin was particularly susceptible.[43] Zaire attempts to rationalise the 'superstition' by speculating:

> Perhaps the cause of such wild imagery exists in the very nature of the human mind, and its unknown relation to futurity. We have never trod the confines of

> human existence with feet that felt the landmark of the boundaries of the future world we know still less.[44]

Because of the mysteries which surround death and the after-life, Zaire surmises that 'we are therefore compelled to admit the existence of beings, whose state, partaking of both [life and death] can at least be arrayed in the images borrowed from one [life], while the rest of its shadowy existence fades away in the inpermeable gloom of the other [death].'[45] Maturin refers to the being who exists between the states of life and death in the following dialogue from his successful play, *Bertram: or The Castle of Aldobrand* (1817):

> CLOTILDA What hath been with thee?
>
> IMOGEN Something dark that hovered deliriously
> Upon the confines of unmingling worlds
> In dread for life, for death too sternly definite,
> Something the thought doth try in vain to follow,
> Through mist and twilight.[46]

Here Imogen is registering the presence of an evil spirit who has haunted her wedding to Aldobrand taking the form of a ministering demon mocking the solemnity of the robed priest, thus anticipating Imogen's own levity towards her nuptial vows in her adultery with Bertram. In this play, Maturin times the supernatural happenings just before a character is tempted into breaking a moral law. For instance, Bertram murders Aldobrand after an encounter with 'a dark knight of the forest' who has awakened his latent thoughts of evil. The material presence of this Satanic being was deleted from the original manuscript by Scott and Byron on the grounds that it presented problems of staging. But considering that the plausibility of the action was already strained by the improbability of the plot, such well-meaning precautions to preserve the realism of the drama scarcely seemed worthwhile. In *Bertram* the hero is punished for his wrong-doings damned as one of the living-dead 'Till sense of life dissolved away within me' [47] and banished with his companion:

> The only tenants of a blasted world
> Dispeopled for my punishment, and charged
> Into a penal orb of desolation.[48]

This sense of isolation is experienced by the Rosicrucian wanderer as part of his punishment for blasphemy. Now that Bertram has arrived at this point of self-realisation, he makes a figurative return from the dead remarking, 'I am amazed to see ye living men.'[49]

In more literal terms, such a return from the dead or even the prolongation of a natural life-span is a heresy which Maturin explores in *Melmoth*. He condemns Melmoth for extending his life, yet he does not disapprove of the premature curtailment of life through suicide or euthanasia. Maturin claims that the Bible does not condemn suicide, which he describes as the most enviable type of departure from life on earth. In *Melmoth* he refers to euthanasia as 'blessed' and as 'a kind of passing with a light and lofty step from a narrow entry to a spacious and glorious apartment, without ever feeling ... the dark and rugged threshold that lies between.'[50] The circumstances surrounding the clergyman's death are suspicious, for it was rumoured that he deliberately took an excess amount of the wrong medicine. If this is true then it is significant that Maturin should die after completing a novel about a sect which approved of suicide, deeming it to be in accordance with the purification rather than the destruction of Christianity. According to Hoffman Nickerson, the Albigenses condoned suicide as a sacred act and 'above all others most pleasing to God.'[51] Why Maturin should be sympathetic towards suicide and euthanasia and yet condemn those who strive to prolong their lives beyond the natural span remains unanswered.

In his physio-theological poem, *The Universe* (1821), Maturin indicates that death ratifies the natural, moral and social order since 'all that is human fleeteth' and 'nought endures / Beneath the firmament.'[52] He also contemplates how on Judgement Day, the summoned spirits will travel 'on their earthless way / Into the dreams of death.'[53] The creature, like Melmoth, who defies the natural order and may be found 'talking with the things / Immortal as itself' becomes for Maturin

> A chance-born parentage from earth itself
> An uncreated monster of the deep
> Whose birth no being witnesses.[54]

Melmoth is a Promethean figure who by defying his Creator and the laws of nature abuses the message of the manifestos. As such he provides Maturin with a case-history through which to explore the Rosicrucian heresy. In this Gothic novel, Maturin highlights the universality of the Melmoth-myth by enabling his hero to act as a vehicle for human self-consciousness.

MATURIN AND THE ROSICRUCIAN HERESY

Melmoth the Wanderer

Alive again? Then show me where he is,
I'll give a thousand pounds to look upon him

Shakespeare, *Henry VI, Part 2*, iii, 3
(quoted by Maturin)[55]

According to Maturin, the idea for *Melmoth* came from the following passage in one of his sermons:

> At this moment is there one of us present, however we may have departed from the Lord, disobeyed his will, and disregarded his word – is there one of us who would, at this moment, accept all that man could bestow, or earth afford, to resign the hope of his salvation? – No, there is not one – not such a fool on earth, were the enemy of mankind to traverse it with the offer.[56]

It must have occurred to Maturin that the chance of life-extension could prove to be a greater temptation for the individual than he implies above. Thus it is this contingency which is explored throughout his 'sermon-in-fiction,'[57] *Melmoth the Wanderer*. In this novel Maturin draws attention to the power of sermons by citing the example of the puritanical weaver who has been driven mad by a single sermon delivered by the celebrated preacher Hugh Peters.[58] Both preacher and Gothic novelist deploy a discourse of disquiet. Maturin's private horror is that he may be one who, after 'preaching in a conventicle with distinguished success,' finds that 'towards twilight his visions were more gloomy and at midnight his blasphemies became more horrible.'[59] Such a dichotomy sums up the popular view of the dual personality which enabled Maturin to take on the role of Calvinist cleric by day and writer of tales of terror by night. As Alethea Hayter suggests, the nocturnal side of Maturin allowed his subterranean fears and hatreds to emerge in order to transform the fictions he planned during the day.[60] Maturin certainly recognised the perils involved in oscillating between the light of reason and the darkness of the imagination, for as he points out in *Melmoth*: 'There are some criminals of the imagination whom if we could plunge into the *oubliettes* of its magnificent but lightly-based fabric, its lord would reign more happy.'[61] Melmoth himself may be regarded as a criminal of the imagination, since he has sold his soul so that he could prolong his life. This life-extension could then be transferred to anyone who would be willing to make the same diabolical transaction. Thus the main interest of the novel is built up around Melmoth's search for such an individual, whom Maturin described earlier in his sermon as a 'fool on earth.'

The pursuit motif provides Maturin with a format which has the flexibility of a picaresque novel. *Melmoth*'s 'Chinese-box' arrangement would suggest that it had been conceived as a series of tales rather than as a centralised novel. A critic for the *Quarterly Review* states that even though the effect of these interpolated tales should be that of fine workmanship they are instead 'involved and entangled in a clumsy confusion which disgraces the artist, and puzzles the observer.'[62] In his preface, Maturin defends this intricate structure by claiming that 'I had made the misery of conventional life depend less on the startling adventures one meets with in romances, than on that irritating series of petty torments which constitutes the misery of life in general.'[63] In his analysis of the theme and structure of *Melmoth*, Jack Null sees Maturin's disjunction of the chronology and unity of the book as part of a deliberate process to fragment the reader's perception of the world of the novel.[64] This technique may also be intended to convey the characters' moral disorientation and spiritual entanglements brought about by Melmoth's persecutions.

Melmoth created for Maturin by far the greatest sensation of all his novels. It also proved to be an economic success, earning for him around five hundred pounds. Yet it received a mixed reception at the hands of the critics. Scott hailed Maturin as now worthy of taking the 'headship of the School of Terror,'[65] but the *Edinburgh Review* expressed the hope that he would soon abandon 'this new apotheosis of the old Raw-head-and-bloody-bones.'[66] Here the critic expanded on this metaphor to chastise Maturin for his 'Golgotha' style of writing as well as his zest for such horrors as cannibalism, all of which he denounced as a sacrifice of genius in the temple of false taste. John Wilson Croker, writing in *The Quarterly Review*, was just as damning in his assessment of Melmoth. According to Croker, in comparison with *Melmoth the Wanderer* Lewis's *Monk* appeared 'decent,' Polidori's *Vampire* seemed 'amiable' and Mary Shelley's *Frankenstein*, 'natural.'[67] Most of the adverse criticism of the novel was levelled at Maturin's treatment of suffering, which prompted the *New Monthly Review* to describe him as a connoisseur in agony. Maturin was even described in the *Edinburgh Magazine and Literary Miscellany* as revelling in the plight of the tormented:

> the reverend author appears to our imagination like some vulcan of the anvil, assiduously labouring and forging shackles, bolts and instruments of torture with

> this difference, that with the poor mechanic it was not his matter of choice whereas Mr Maturin with all the flowery paths of fiction open to him, has preferred this tortuous and gloomy one.[68]

Blackwood referred to the chaos of Maturin's absurdities, but nevertheless conceded that he was capable of true poetry and 'walks almost without a rival, dead or living, in many of the darkest, but at the same time the most majestic circles of romance.'[69] The mention of 'circles' above may be a response to the convolutions of the plot. Certainly the critic for the *Quarterly Review* resolved not to waste his time 'in endeavouring to unravel the tissue of stories which occupy these four volumes.'[70] Despite this reviewer's discouraging reaction, an attempt will be made here to outline the narrative.

Melmoth is made up of three tales concerning the characters Stanton, the Spaniard and the Parricide, followed by the 'Tale of the Indians,' 'Guzman's Family' and the 'Lovers' Tale.' These separate episodes focus upon Melmoth's persecutions contained within a frame-narrative which concerns John Melmoth. At the beginning of the novel, set in 1816, John, who is a student at Trinity College, Dublin, has been summoned to his uncle's death-bed. As the heir to the estate, young Melmoth is given instructions to destroy a painting of an ancestor as well as to destroy an old manuscript. The painting, which John had seen earlier, turns out to be a portrait of John Melmoth which was painted in 1646. Young Melmoth's uncle, who was reputed to be 'the last man on earth to be superstitious,'[71] assures his nephew that the subject of the painting is still alive and that he himself is dying of fright. In the preface to *St Leon*, as mentioned earlier, Godwin recounts a similar tale concerning a painting by Titian. Before his death, John Melmoth warns his future heir that he too will see the living original of the portrait. This prophecy is soon fulfilled, for, as the old man lies dying, a mysterious stranger enters the room bearing an uncanny resemblance to the painting of John Melmoth. Even though young Melmoth is prepared to dismiss this as a coincidence, he is nonetheless determined to satisfy himself that his uncle is neither insane nor prone to superstitious imaginings. Therefore he enquires amongst the servants about this family legend. Eventually he is told by the sibylline Biddy Brannigan of a persistent rumour concerning a seventeenth-century ancestor who was still 'without a hair on his head changed, or a muscle in his frame contracted.'[72] Apparently, his spasmodic appearances heralded the deaths of members of the family whom he haunted in their dying hour.[73]

At the beginning of the novel, young Melmoth is told that the key to the mystery of the portrait is contained within the manuscript which his uncle had ordered him to destroy. Melmoth decides to read the document, which contains six Gothic tales written by an Englishman, John Stanton. The first story is the 'Tale of Stanton' set in 1677, which follows out a story-within-a-story pattern with Stanton listening to an old woman's account of Melmoth as a guest at a wedding feast. In this account may be found echoes of Coleridge's *Rime of the Ancient Mariner* (1798), particularly since the mariner in the poem is noted for a hypnotic stare,[74] a characteristic of Melmoth when intent upon effusing 'a most fearful and preternatural lustre.'[75] The now sinister atmosphere at the wedding prompts Father Olavida to ask 'Who is among us? — Who?'[76] Olavida then proceeds, in the spirit of 'prophetic denunciation,'[77] to try and identify the mysterious stranger. Some of his guesses seem to allude to other famous wanderers and suggest that Maturin's version of the Rosicrucian hero is a synthesis of a number of other Gothic immortals and blasted sinners. For Olavida, Melmoth is Cain-like and ungodly, leaving behind him the fiery foot-prints of Hell: 'Where he treads, the earth is parched.'[78] His Satanic presence inhibits the priest's sacred task to utter a blessing because of the infernal vapours he exhales: 'where he breathes, the air is fire!'[79] Finally, Melmoth's typology may be extended to the Wandering Jew, for both accursed beings have a glance like lightning. Speculation ends (at least on one score) when by suddenly dropping dead, the priest obligingly confirms Melmoth's unsavoury reputation as a harbinger of death.

After hearing this doom-laden story, Stanton is warned that Melmoth also seeks out vulnerable individuals who have been struck by tragedy or disaster. Predictably Stanton's terror eventually leads to his confinement in a madhouse, where Melmoth bargains with him to exchange his soul for prolonged life. The diabolical transaction is contingent upon the exercise of free will and moral responsibility, for as Stanton's persecutor points out: 'with the loss of reason (and reason cannot long be retained in this place), you lose also the hope of immortality.'[80] The manuscript concludes with Stanton leaving the asylum having successfully resisted Melmoth's offer.

Having finished reading Stanton's tale, John Melmoth decides to comply with his uncle's wishes and burns both the manuscript and portrait. The second story, 'Tale of the Spaniard', tells of a monk, Monçada, who confides to the authorities that he is being tormented by a mysterious being. Not surprisingly Monçada is accused of conversing with the devil. The most effective way of dealing with this problem was to burn alive the possessed and afflicted monk. Most sensibly, he tries to escape, using the monastery's subterranean passages where he hallucinates hearing the anthems of demons howling 'on that awful verge where life and eternity mingle.'[81] When the escape attempt fails, Monçada is captured by the Inquisition, and his subsequent imprisonment neatly provides Maturin with a convenient interlude for the narration of the parricide's tale.

This time the victim is a mortal version of Melmoth who claims to have sold his soul to Satan and his minions in order to carry out their demonic works. Even though the parricide declares 'I have no religion, I believe in no God, I repeat no creed,' like Schemoli he has 'that superstition of fear and [of] futurity, that seeks its wild and hopeless mitigation in the sufferings of others when our own are exhausted.'[82] The parricide's belief that this is the best theology – since it is hostile to all human beings – recalls Maturin's dire warnings against those who set up their own creed.[83] The parricide anticipates the appearance of Melmoth, who visits Monçada while he is a prisoner of the Inquisition. Monçada manages to resist Melmoth's offer resolutely even though he has been condemned as a heretic to be burnt alive at an *auto da fé*. Remarkably Monçada manages to avert his ordeal in an escape attempt which resembles that of Godwin's St Leon.

Monçada finds refuge in a Jewish household by hiding in a secret passage beneath the house, where he discovers the aged Jew Adonijah. Like Melmoth, Adonijah has sought for forbidden knowledge, saying 'like our fathers in the wilderness, I despised angel's food and lusted after forbidden meats, even the meats of the Egyptian sorcerers.'[84] Ironically his punishment consists of unlimited life-extension. As he says to Monçada, 'my presumption was rebuked as thou seest: – childless, wifeless, friendless, at the last period of an existence prolonged beyond the bounds of nature.'[85] Surrounded by the skeletons of Melmoth's victims, Adonijah's fate is to record their stories. Littered around him are parchments and charts which appear to be scrawled with human blood. Ironically, his death has to be earned. Only when he has completed this task will he be allowed to die, in a perverse parody of Melmoth's quest for a willing victim who will agree to perpetual life in exchange for his soul. Monçada, whom he has chosen as his scribe, translates from the Greek the next three stories, which testify to Melmoth's failure to find a successor.

The first of these is the 'Tale of the Indians,' set in 1680, which describes Melmoth's discovery of an island in the Indian Ocean whose sole inhabitant is Immalee, an innocent European girl. On her island paradise she is also the epitome of Rousseau's ideal of the noble primitive. Here the state of nature represents a microcosmic recreation of the world before the Fall, being synonymous with Immalee's spiritual and moral purity. For a while, Melmoth forgets that he is the Cain of the moral world while he shares with Immalee the beauties of the idyllic isle.[86] As Maturin points out, 'at our first transgression, nature expels us, as it did our first parents from her paradise for ever.'[87] The imagery of Eden aptly expresses Immalee's transition from innocence to experience as Melmoth tells her of the evils of the outside world. Maturin describes this learning process as a painful initiation. Now that Immalee has sampled the Tree of Knowledge, she finds the fruit 'bitter to her taste.'[88] Indeed in the 'Lovers' Tale' the first state of love is likened to mankind before the Fall 'inhaling the odours of paradise' and 'enjoying the communion of the Deity.'[89] Nevertheless, Melmoth the tempter persuades Immalee to marry him three years later when the couple reach Spain, the country of Immalee's birth. By binding himself to Melmoth, Immalee risks sharing in his damnation. The ceremony is enacted in a ruined Gothic chapel where Immalee notices that the hand that binds them in marriage 'was as cold as that of death.'[90] Robert Kiely draws attention to this death imagery as indicative of how Immalee's life is eventually to become 'a series of dull and repetitive vows to death'[91] which culminate in her own death and that of Melmoth's child. Paradoxically she is described as the bride of death when her bridegroom is, in fact, the possessor of perpetual life. But the imagery of death in this context refers to the extinction of Melmoth's spiritual salvation.

Interpolated within this story is the 'Tale of Guzman's Family' which is set prior to 1676. This account of the poverty of a family may be autobiographical. Nevertheless, the description of how the eldest son is driven to selling his own blood to a surgeon in order to buy food for the starving family was probably taken from Polidori's tale of an immortal, *The Vampire* (1819).[92] Yet despite such grinding poverty, the father of the family manages to resist Melmoth's offer.[93]

The story of Walberg's family is followed by 'The Lover's Tale' set in the 1660s, which describes how once again Melmoth fails to secure a victim. Following the 'Lovers' Tale' the 'Tale of the Indians' is resumed with an account of the death of Immalee, who in Spain is known as Isidora. But just before Monçada tells young Melmoth more tales about his ancestor, the Wanderer himself arrives to announce that his own end has come. Melmoth then ages rapidly in a *Faust*-like ending to the novel. His final words are a warning to John Melmoth and Monçada: 'remember your lives will be the forfeit of your desperate curiosity. For the same stake I risked more than life – and lost it! – Be warned – retire!'[94]

Maturin regarded the Rosicrucian quest for the philosopher's stone and elixir of life as akin to madness. For Melmoth love is experienced as the joy of madness like Maturin's hero Connal in *The Milesian Chief*, who reflects on the relationship between desire and lunacy:

> my long night will be without a ray, but not without a dream: on my desolate rock the light of your image will visit me, as the moon does the cell of the maniac, it brings madness with it, but it brings the joy of madness too.[95]

Melmoth's madness is the purely mechanistic form of reason which eradicates irrational fears of extinction by extinguishing death itself. Hence Melmoth lives out the Rosicrucian tradition prefigured by Cornelius Agrippa, who insisted that individuals could surmount death through the power of the intellect. By transcending mortality, Agrippa believed that humanity could be elevated to god-like proportions. Theologically, the acquisition of the philosopher's stone and the elixir of life represented considerable autonomy from God's eternal laws.

The heresy implicit in Melmoth's defiance of his creator parallels Faust's attempt to regain the dominion lost through the Fall. Agrippa claimed that Adam by his 'original sin' lost power over nature which the magus regains through the conquest of death. The Christian and Rosicrucian patterns of redemption may be seen in the following analogies. First, Adam by eating the forbidden fruit of the Tree of Knowledge precipitated the necessity for the divine redemption of the Crucifixion and Resurrection. Similarly the adept who drinks the elixir of life having had access to the philosopher's stone must then seek out salvation in his own extended existence. For one of the characters in Melmoth, who is described as an apprentice of Satan, exculpation may be achieved through the guilt and suffering of others. As he tells one of his victims, Alonza Monçada, 'I have literally worked out my salvation by your fear and trembling.'[96] For the adept who has stepped outside the confines of his own mortality, there can be no Day of Judgement upon which he may exonerate himself for his sins. Since the symbolic effect of the Fall must be reversed in his own protracted lifetime, the adept is forced into a limbo of endless boredom within which there is no foreseeable goal. As a result the concept of 'life's journey' becomes a living metaphor for the mortal immortal who is compelled to wander in compensation for this displacement.

The question arises at the end of the novel whether or not Melmoth emerges triumphant. On one level, he has failed to secure a victim who would agree to his terms. Indeed when Melmoth reaches the end of his earthly existence, he has no option but to admit: 'No one has ever exchanged destinies with Melmoth the Wanderer. *I have traversed the world in the search, and no one to gain that world, would lose his own soul!*'[97] This failure is perhaps even more abject when we consider that he has been given superhuman powers to help him in his task:

> It has been reported of me, that I obtained from the enemy of souls a range of existence beyond the period allotted to mortality – a power to pass over space without disturbance or delay, and visit remote regions with the swiftness of thought – to encounter tempests without the *hope* of their blasting me, and penetrate into dungeons, whose bolts were as flax and tow at my touch. It has been said that this power was accorded to me, that I might be enabled to tempt wretches in their fearful hour of extremity, with the promise of deliverance and immunity, on condition of their exchanging situations with me.[98]

In the universal rejection of Melmoth's proposition lies Maturin's triumph over the Rosicrucian heresy. Even Melmoth is forced to admit that his failure 'bears attestation to a truth uttered by the lips of one I may not name, and echoed by every human heart in the habitable world.'[99] This admission proves Maturin's premise, set out in his sermon, that no individual would accept 'all that man could bestow, or earth afford'[100] if it meant that he had to resign the hope of his salvation, even if the 'enemy of mankind' were to traverse the world with such an offer.

'The Enemy of Mankind'

The problem which now emerges is that since Melmoth has failed so miserably in his task of converting others to commit the Rosicrucian heresy then how was he accredited with the title 'enemy of mankind?' In a discussion with a nobleman, Don Francisco di Aliaga, who is the father of Immalee, Melmoth argues that all men are sinners and at one time or another have acted as agents of Satan. He challenges Don Francisco:

> dare you say you have not been an agent of Satan? I tell you, whenever you indulge one brutal passion, one sordid desire, one impure imagination – whenever you uttered one word that wrung the heart, or embittered the spirit of your fellow-creature – whenever you made

> that hour pass in pain to whose flight you might have lent wings of down ... whenever you have done this, you have been ten times more an agent of the enemy of mankind than all the wretches whom terror, enfeebled nerves, or visionary credulity, has forced into the confession of an incredible compact with the author of evil, and whose confession has consigned them to flames much more substantial than those the imagination of their persecutors pictured them doomed to for an eternity of suffering.[101]

Although Melmoth himself has been guilty of many of the crimes against mankind listed above, he argues that the problem of evil should not be blamed upon the 'enemy of mankind.' Melmoth recognises that diametrical oppositions between good and evil are fallacies perpetuated by such misnomers as 'enemy of mankind.' He protests 'Alas! how absurdly is that title bestowed on the great angelic chief, – the morning star fallen from its sphere!'[102] Melmoth goes on to ask, 'What enemy has man so deadly as himself?' From this he concludes that if man were to ask on whom should be bestowed the title 'enemy of mankind' then 'let him smite his bosom, and his heart will answer, – Bestow it here!'[103]

As well as contending that he cannot be the 'enemy of mankind,' Melmoth argues that he does not deserve eternal damnation, and towards the end of the novel seeks to exonerate himself from any moral blame for the prolongation of his own existence by asking 'if all that fear has invented, and credulity believed of me be true, to what does it amount?'[104] Melmoth fears that since his crimes have been enacted beyond a mortal time-scale then so might his punishment. Using a retributionalist model of justice, Melmoth seeks to discriminate between act and intention. Although undoubtedly guilty in intention, Melmoth emphasises: 'I have been on earth a terror, but not an evil to its inhabitants. None can participate in my destiny but with his own consent – none have consented – none can be involved in its tremendous penalties, but by participation.'[105] It is indeed ironic that the 'enemy of mankind' should prove to have been so ineffectual. As the critic for the *Quarterly Review* jested, Melmoth was a failure as a devil, doing less damage in several lifetimes than a clever mortal could have done in one.[106] Edgar Allan Poe in a letter prefacing his *Poems* (1831) complained that Melmoth 'labours indefatigably through three octavo volumes, to accomplish the destruction of one or two souls, while any common devil would have demolished one or two thousand.'[107] For as Melmoth argues, his crimes have been no more than those which could have been committed by a mortal, and therefore were not deserving of eternal punishment. In reasoning thus, Melmoth reveals that the only crime carried out by the 'enemy of mankind' has been directed against himself. Hence he makes the plea that the penalty should be in just proportion to the crime. This undermines the fundamental assumption accompanying the Fall of man into Original Sin: that the human race had to pay the forfeit for the sin of Adam. Melmoth is emphatic that in this respect he is not another Adam, and so argues that:

> I alone must sustain the penalty. If I have put forth my hand, and eaten of the fruit of the interdicted tree, am I not driven from the presence of God and the region of paradise, and sent to wander amid worlds of barrenness and curse for ever and ever?[108]

The problem in determining the extent of Melmoth's moral responsibility is two-fold. First, he must take the blame for act and intention, since there is no external tempter (as in the case of Adam) with whom to share the responsibility. In this respect Melmoth is both Faust and Mephistopheles. Second, there is the problem of predestination. To a certain extent Melmoth has determined his own destiny by making it dependent upon his quest to find a successor. As Judith Wilt points out in *Ghosts of the Gothic*,

> in a thousand years Melmoth would not willingly resign his mortal existence; his eternal defeat in that chosen quest for another like himself is the term of his existence, and he has chosen it knowingly so that he can stay forever in mortality.[109]

This testifies to Melmoth's cunning since he realises that even though this quest has been futile, it would provide him with the excuse he needs in order to prolong his earthly existence. Since there was never any need to prove the truth of the proposition in Maturin's sermons, he scores a minor victory for himself.

Melmoth's ultimate destiny may be related to Calvinist notions of predestination. One incident in the novel highlights the madness of a Calvinist preacher, a supra-lapsarian who denounces sublapsarians in the belief that the Fall of man was predestined by God. His split personality caricatures the popular image of Maturin mentioned earlier: 'in proportion as his morning exercises are intense, vivid, and eloquent, his nightly blasphemies are outrageous and horrible.'[110] According to Melmoth, the preacher believes that his own redemptive creed is retaliating against him and so he grapples with the iron posts of his bed, and says that he is 'rooting out the cross from the very foundations of Calvary.'[111] Apart from the preacher there is another madman in the asylum who has been driven mad by a sermon. He obsessively repeats the five points of Calvinism, which include the doctrines of the total depravity of man and the predestined election to heaven or reprobation to hell for every individual.

Melmoth himself may be seen as a victim of a Calvinist universe, since the failure of his quest has been pre-ordained by God. As Melmoth admits towards the end of the novel, this is the 'truth uttered by the lips of one I may not name.'[112] Melmoth's conduct on earth also conforms to the notion of the total depravity of man. But since, as he claims, all men are the agents of Satan, then the quest to corrupt humanity is evidently a pointless exercise. There is also little doubt, in accordance with Calvinist creed, that Melmoth's fate has been pre-determined, since he states enigmatically, 'the secret of my destiny rests with myself.' Though taken up by demons in the final stages of the novel, his ultimate destination is uncertain. For instance, witnesses are unable to distinguish whether or not Melmoth's dying screams are 'shrieks of supplication, or the yell of blasphemy.'[113]

This eschatological problem arises in the 'Tale of the Indians,' where the dying Immalee confides to the priest administering the last rites her fear that Melmoth will follow her to the grave. The priest assures her that this could not happen since she is destined for heaven, as 'wreaths of palms are weaving for you in paradise.'[114] But the urgency of Immalee's question is understandable when we consider that Melmoth has forced his company upon her in the island utopia which the priest has obliquely associated with paradise. In addition to this, Melmoth experiences with Immalee a sensation like that of his master when he visited paradise reminiscent of Satan's contemplation of Adam and Eve in the Garden of Eden in Milton's *Paradise Lost.* Immalee may also be recalling how Satan found his way into Eden and how Lucifer had once resided in heaven when she puts to the priest a question about paradise: 'Will he be there?'[115]

Melmoth identifies with Lucifer and Adam when he explains that his crime has properties which are both angelic and mortal: 'mine was the great angelic sin – pride and intellectual glorying! It was the first mortal sin – a boundless aspiration after forbidden knowledge!'[116] Melmoth's hankering after forbidden knowledge is a continuation of the curse of Adam, while his pride may be seen as Luciferian. Yet sadly his only real crime is in attaching such paramount importance to life itself. This greed to live is perhaps less reprehensible than Faust's craving for occult wisdom or Adam's indomitable curiosity which led him to plunder the secrets of the Tree of Knowledge of Good and Evil. For at least some of Melmoth's existence, life must have been more precious to him than it could have been for those who so persistently refused his offer of immortality. The inevitability that this entails the loss of his immortal soul represents the kind of spiritual surrender encapsulated in Maturin's paradoxical concept of Melmoth as a hero of submission[117] who is prepared to sacrifice his salvation or 'eternal rest,' having reached the point when:

> we resign the hope of immortality for the hope of a profound repose, — when we demand from the harassings of fate, "rest, rest" and no more, — when the soul and body faint together and all we ask of God or man is to let us sleep.[118]

The anomaly of the term 'hero of submission' sums up the contradictory elements inherent in Melmoth's character. His heroism is evident from his willingness to brave the unknown, yet at the same time he is willing to submit to the pre-ordained fate of eternal damnation. Monçada recognises in Melmoth a heroism which is harnessed by guilt. He acknowledges that Melmoth exhibits criminal tendencies but he believes that his crime emits a kind of heroic immunity, particularly since premature knowledge in life is always to be purchased by guilt. Monçada admits to dreading Melmoth as a demon, yet he invokes him as a god. The heroic in Melmoth may also be seen in his attempt to work out his own salvation, an autonomous act which is in accordance with the Rosicrucian precepts. Hypothetically, if Melmoth had secured a victim who would accept his pact then he could have brought about his own redemption. Yet Melmoth's triumph is achieved through the control he exerts over his own destiny. Nevertheless, his tragedy stems from dedicating his life to the pursuit of evil. Melmoth accelerates his downfall by allowing himself, the slave of power, to becoming enslaved by passion. This is part of the intoxication of the *elixir vitæ*, which beguiles Melmoth into believing that the falsehood which intoxicates us for a moment is worth more than the truth that would disenchant us for life. Consequently, Melmoth is eventually reduced to becoming an instigator of petty torments. Godwin's *St Leon* also follows out this pattern of moral deterioration, which is a corruption of the Rosicrucian notion of amelioration through self-regeneration. This idealism, which had been transmuted by John Dee into the concept of the Renaissance magus, should have been Melmoth's legacy. In view of this, it is appropriate that he is reputed to have accompanied Dee to Poland.

The possession of the *elixir vitæ* represents an attempt to reverse the effects of the Fall. Ironically, the adept by partaking of forbidden knowledge achieves eternal life. Francis Bacon regarded the claim of the magus to such spiritual enlightenment as constituting a second Fall through pride. This upheaval of the law of divine retribution would have invited the censure of Pope, who writes satirically in his *Essay on Man*, 'Nature lets it fall. / Short and but rare, 'till Man improved it all.'[119] Such disruptions of the order of the Great Chain of Being are aptly described by Pope as forms of madness, pride and impiety. The Rosicrucian sage translates into tangible terms these aspirations which Pope roundly condemns in the following couplet:

> What would this man? Now upward will he soar,
> And little less than Angel, would be more.[120]

Through reason and intellect, the Rosicrucian severs his ties with mortality and thus with humanity. With no place in the cosmic hierarchy, he is forced to wander the world in search of an identity or meaning to his existence. This is also the dilemma of Faust, who has to prove in mankind the stature of a god. Such ambiguity surrounds Melmoth, since Stanton is uncertain whether he is man or beast. Similarly Monçada is undecided whether or not Melmoth is a demon or a god. In all senses, Melmoth is god-like, demonic and human because he operates on both a macrocosmic and microcosmic level. On the larger scale Melmoth has reversed the effects of the Fall for himself, while on a smaller canvas he finds that he has to work out his own redemption for his sin of blasphemy. The universality of Melmoth partakes of the nature of allegory whereby experiences are interpreted by means of images. In this way, Melmoth's spiritual odyssey may be seen as an abbreviation of human evolution. He is a primordial image of the unharnessed energies and boundless aspirations of the human race, which at the same time enables individuals to discover their own being and destiny. As Goethe once pointed out, 'the rational world must be viewed as a great immortal individual which ceaselessly produces the necessary and thereby makes itself master even of the fortuitous.'[121] The story of a wandering immortal has the universality of myth by operating on the level of the generic and of the individual. In *Melmoth*, Maturin's use of the Latin tag *ex uno disce omnes* ('from one learn what all were') is a recognition that the microcosm of the individual unfolds the macrocosm of the species.[122] Examples of such explorations in universal consciousness appear in Goethe's *Faust*:

I'll sound the heights and depths that men can know,
Their very souls shall be with mine entwined,
I'll load my bosom with their weal and woe,
And share with them the shipwreck of mankind.[123]

Gorky assumes that such legends as Faust are not fruits of fancy but 'exaggerations which are necessary and in perfect accord with the laws of real facts.'[124] Likewise in *Melmoth*, the death of an immortal is a poetic exigency which complies with the 'laws of real facts.' Melmoth's death also enables him to emerge as a representative of the human race, and his wanderings to act as a metaphor for humanity's journey between life and death. Here the ontogenetic principle may be seen to recapitulate the phylogenic.

Schiller's assertion that nature 'is unfathomable because one man cannot comprehend it, although all mankind could very well do so'[125] is echoed by Mongada, who reflects in his cell that we have not the strength to comprehend the whole of our calamity. But this strength has not been denied Melmoth, who embodies the tragic conflicts which arise from a liberation from the restraints imposed by time and mortality. Having witnessed the passing of every generation in the 'Wanderer's Dream,' he sees the clock of eternity in a Dantean vision of the Inferno.

The Melmoth theme is a depository of myth ranging beyond European folklore to the story of the disobedient disciple of the Buddha.[126] Maturin's hero is also a classic example of the renegade Rosicrucian wanderer. Melmoth's mastery of the occult arts, his acquisition of the elixir of life, quest for self-regeneration and perpetual wanderings grew out of Rosicrucian legends. But unlike St Leon and St Irvyne, Maturin's hero taps the consciousness of the universal problems of free will and forbidden knowledge which had also been encountered by Adam, Lucifer, Miton's Satan and Goethe's Faust.

Balzac and Melmoth Reconciled

One rather uncharitable critic once noted of Maturin's masterpiece:

> There are two real mysteries about Melmoth, one that it should have fascinated Balzac and Rossetti, the other that in 1892 it should have been deemed worthy of republication, with a memoir, a bibliography, and a "Note on Maturin".[127]

The only valuable comments in this disparagement lie in the critic's recognition that both Rossetti and Balzac admired the work. It was said that Rossetti's 'supreme delight was the blood-curdling romance of Maturin, *Melmoth the Wanderer*,'[128] while Balzac even paid tribute to its author with the sequel, *Melmoth Reconciled.* In Balzac's version of Maturin's novel, at last, Melmoth finds a victim who is willing to accept the elixir. In this way Balzac effectively challenges Maturin's assertion that there would be no fool on earth who would engage in such a transaction. *Melmoth Reconciled* also reflects Balzac's interest in the problems surrounding longevity, which is apparent in the quasi-immortality he grants to some of his characters such as Beringheld, Falthurne and Don Belvidero.[129]

It had been Balzac's intention to devise a formula for protracted existence which would at the same time overcome the disadvantages inherent in the promiscuous use of unlimited power. These abuses are displayed in his short story, *Don Juan or The Elixir of Long Life.*[130] Here the hero steals the secret of immortality from his dying father to find that he becomes 'master of the illusions of life.'[131] Don Juan Belvidero soon discovers his omniscience to be a sobering experience, for after casting matter and soul into the alchemist's crucible, he 'seized on experience like an ape snatches a nut stripping life to the kernel only to be disappointed.' By 'viewing life from the other side of the tomb,'[132] Belvediro finds that he has reached the last degree of cynicism: 'He made a jest of everything, institutions, and ideas.'[133] Like Faust, he meets up with the Pope, but instead of pleading for spiritual absolution he assures him that he has a whole existence in reserve during which he will repent for his sins. Balzac admits that his hero is based on Goethe's *Faust* as well as on Molière's *Don Juan*, Byron's *Manfred*, and 'the *Melmoth* of Maturin, grand figures drawn by the greatest geniuses of Europe.'[134] But as Balzac demonstrates in *Melmoth Reconciled*, there is need of an ethical code which would enable an immortal to resolve the moral conflicts brought about by an extended life span. These are problems germinated by society which Balzac denounces as a race of dupes and conscriptors of genius. In view of this, Balzac concedes that it would be miraculous if some five or six men of genius were to escape from this mediocrity in order to climb the highest heights.

In *Melmoth Reconciled*, Castanier is such a man who eventually allows himself to be persuaded by Melmoth to mortgage his soul for admission into the innermost circles of esoteric knowledge. According to Melmoth, in the passage below, this would imbue Castanier with the powers of an omnipotent being:

> Don't you know that everything here on earth must obey me, that everything is within my power? I read people's hearts, I see the future, I know the past. I am here and can be elsewhere! I do not depend on either time, or space, or distance. The whole world is at my command. I have the power always to feel pleasure, and always to give happiness.[135]

As in Maturin's novel, Melmoth is an Englishman whose presence 'weighed on Castanier like a poisoned atmosphere.'[136] He is in a position to exert power over Castanier, since he threatens to expose the latter for embezzling 5,000,000 francs. Melmoth's offer promises not only to extricate Castanier from his current predicament, but also to provide power and wealth in the future. Unable to resist such an offer, Castanier soon discovers for himself that he can see and know all things, and can do everything. The extent of this mental and physical transformation is a sublunar omnipotence which permits Castanier to comprehend the world as if he has been raised to some high pinnacle above the earth. This image, by evoking the temptation of Christ, emphasises that Castanier's powers are to be wielded in the worldly rather than on a celestial terrain. This is apparent from the way in which he persistently refers to the macrocosm of the infinite from the microcosm of society, even though he has been elevated above the world. Balzac conveys this to the reader by borrowing the language of commerce in order to describe Castanier's experiences as an immortal:

> if it were allowable to compare such great things with social follies, he was like those rich bankers, millionaires several times over, who are refused nothing in society; but who, because they are not admitted in the circles of the nobility, are obsessed with the idea of becoming one of them and think nothing of all the social privileges they have acquired, so long as they lack one of them.[137]

Such chronic discontent is also the hallmark of the mortal immortal. Although Castanier may now satisfy all his desires, perversely he longs for something to which he was entitled during his former state and which is now denied him. After drinking the elixir, he finds that he has acquired a thirst for heaven, particularly since the forces of Hell have brought him a vision of divinity. But this turns out to be a mirage or infernal snare, since the prospect of happiness promised by the transaction proves to be illusory in what turns out to be a fool's bargain, for Castanier has bought 'the terrible power ... at the cost of his eternal happiness.'[138] Couched in the language of commerce, the *elixir vitæ* is a commodity to be bought and sold. As Melmoth's successor now discovers, 'supreme power brought nothingness as a dowry.'[139] The equation of infinity with finite longings proves to be the void in which desire must die. The corollary of this is that the possession of absolute power does not presuppose the ability to use it. Accordingly, omnipotence must remain an abstraction, since eventually it will cease to satisfy every wish of the ordinary individual because all his longings will have been fulfilled. All that remains is the anomaly of desire for desire's sake, which echoes Faust's complaint that in desire he hastens towards enjoyment and then from enjoyment pines to feel desire. As Castanier finds to his chagrin, satiety is the devil's curse. His command over the absolute cannot provide him with an infinity of desires:

> By drawing freely from the treasure of human pleasures whose key he had been given by the devil, he rapidly reached the bottom. This huge power, grasped in one instant, was in one instant evaluated. What had been everything became nothing. It often happens that possession kills the vast poetry of desire, whose dreams the possessed object rarely fulfils.[140]

This imagery recalls Plato's tenet on the moderation of desire. In the *Gorgias*, Callicles argues to Socrates that courage and intelligence ought to be able to cope with unrestrained desire. But he recognises that this would be impossible for the majority. In claiming that only an exceptional individual would be capable of such intemperance, he heralds the superman who may override the moral code:

> If a man is born with a strong enough nature, he will shake off and smash and escape all this. He will trample on all our writings, charms, incantations, all the rules contrary to nature. He rises up and shows himself master.[141]

The Rosicrucian hero must aspire to this dominion through the rule of might, the 'Law' which 'is the sovereign of all,/ Of mortals and immortals alike.'[142] Since Castanier is not a superior being, he follows out the fictional pattern of degradation and disillusionment and consequently follows in the footfalls of Melmoth by attempting to pass on the secret of immortality to another. Like Melmoth, he recognises that the most susceptible victim would be someone in a desperate situation. Subsequently, he visits a prison where he picks out a prisoner condemned to death, who is being tormented by the gibberings of a madman. On this occasion Castanier is unsuccessful, but he does eventually persuade a speculator called Claperon to agree to the pact. Castanier appeals to Claperon's business sense by packaging his proposition as an investment, reminding him that 'we all hold shares in the great speculation of eternity.'[143] Determined to hold a monopoly on the absolute, Claperon takes over from Castanier but soon becomes disillusioned and passes the secret on to a building contractor. He in turn passes on the elixir to an iron merchant, and so it goes on until it arrives in the hands of a clerk. As Balzac informs his reader,

> The huge power discovered and conquered by the Irishman, the offspring of Reverend Maturin's brain, was thus lost.
>
> A few Orientalists, some mystics, some archeologists interested in such matters, found it impossible to ascertain the way of invoking the devil.[144]

Balzac is deliberately ending in absurdity by letting the magic peter out in the petty, money-grabbing society of his own day. The elixir which had started off as the possession of the solitary aristocrat has now become the property of the bourgeois.

Notes

1. Maturin, *The Milesian Chief: A Romance* (London, 1812), preface.
2. For an analysis of the influence of Faust on *Melmoth* see Sydney M. Conger, *Romantic Reassessment: Matthew G. Lewis, Charles Robert Maturin and the Germans: An Interpretative Study of the Influence of German Literature on Two Gothic Novels* (Salzburg, 1977), pp. 163-191.
3. See Dale Kramer, *Charles Robert Maturin* (New York, 1973), p. 14.
4. Lowry Nelson Jr., 'Night Thoughts on the Gothic Novel,' *Yale Review*, 52 (Winter, 1963), p. 236.
5. See Maturin, *Five Sermons on the Errors of the Roman Catholic Church* (Dublin, 1824). In Sermon I, Maturin attacks the Catholic Church for failing to base their doctrines upon the authority of the Bible. In Sermons II and III, he questions the validity of the sacraments of Communion, Confirmation, Penance, Holy Orders and Extreme unction. In Sermon IV, Maturin criticises the Church for not being Apostolic, while in Sermon V, he sums up his arguments.
6. Kramer, *Maturin*, p. 11.
7. As Maturin points out in the preface to his novel, *The Albigenses* (New York, 1974), the fiction was intended to be part of a series being 'the first of three historical romances, illustrative of European feelings and manners in ancient times, in middle, and in modern.' *The Albigenses* represents Maturin's first attempt at the historical novel, a form which was probably suggested to him by his distant friend, Walter Scott. The latter's *Ivanhoe* (1819) had provided Maturin with the incentive to write *The Albigenses. Ivanhoe* deals in part with the Knights Templar who were connected with the Cathars or Albigenses and, according to some sources, inherited their legendary treasure of gold and holy books which was lost during the persecutions. These are believed to form part of the secret tradition which was passed on to the Rosicrucians and Freemasons.
8. Maturin, *The Milesian Chief*, preface.
9. See the essay on '*Explaines Supernatural*' in *Quarterly Review*, III (May, 1810), p. 344:

   > We disapprove of the mode introduced by Mrs Radcliffe and followed by Mr Murphy [Maturin] and her other imitators of winding up their story with a solution by which all the incidents appearing to partake of the mystic and marvellous are resolved by very simple and natural causes ... totally inadequate to its production.

10. Birkhead, *The Tale of Terror*, p. 82.
11. For this novel, Maturin used the pseudonym Dennis Jasper Murphy.
12. Schemoli appears to have been based on Ann Radcliffe's villainous monk, Schedoni, in *The Italian, or The Confessional of the Black Penitents: A Romance*, 3 vols (London, 1797).
13. Maturin distinguishes between the supernatural itself and the fear generated by it, which is akin to superstition. In the preface to *Fatal Revenge*, he writes 'I have allowed myself to base the interest of my novel entirely on the passion of supernatural terror.'
14. Niilo Idman, *Charles Robert Maturin: His Life and Works* (London, 1923), pp. 207-8.

15. Maturin, *Fatal Revenge; or, The Family of Montario: A Romance* (London, 1824), IV, p. 6.
16. Ibid., IV, p. 45.
17. Maturin, *Fatal Revenge*, IV, p. 7.
18. See loc. cit.
19. Ibid., IV, p. 118.
20. Ibid., II, p. 140.
21. Loc. cit.
22. Ibid., II, pp. 140-1.
23. Devendra P. Varma, *The Gothic Flame: Being a History of the Gothic Novel in England: Its Origins, Efflorescence, Disintegration, and Residuary Influences* (New York, 1957), p. 216.
24. Loc. cit.
25. Maturin, *Fatal Revenge*, IV, p. 221.
26. Ibid., II, p. 148.
27. *Fama* in Yates, *The Rosicrucian Enlightenment*, p. 293.
28. Maturin, *Fatal Revenge*, II, pp. 148-9.
29. Loc. cit.
30. Ibid., II, pp. 145-6.
31. Varma, *The Gothic Flame*, p. 216. The appearance of a Satanic stranger is also employed by James Hogg in *The Private Memoirs and Confessions of a Justified Sinner* (1824). The stranger, who is known as Gil-Martin, like Maturin's Orazio, persuades his victim to commit murder.
32. Maturin, *Fatal Revenge*, IV, p. 195.
33. Ibid., II, p. 136.
34. *Fama* in Yates, *The Rosicrucian Enlightenment*, p. 292. For Maturin's interest in necromancy see Maturin, *Leixlip Castle: An Irish Family Legend*, in *The Literary Souvenir, or Cabinet of Poetry and Romance*, ed. Alaric A. Watts (London, 1825), preface.
35. H. W. Piper and A. Norman Jeffares, 'Maturin the Innovator,' *Huntington Library Quarterly*, XXI (May, 1958), pp. 261-84.
36. Leven M. Dawson, '*Melmoth the Wanderer*: Paradox and the Gothic Novel,' *Studies in English Literature*, 8 (Autumn, 1968).
37. Maturin, *Sermons*, p. 20.
38. Ibid., p. 21.
39. The Albigensian persecutions are used as a backcloth to the novel. Dale Kramer points out that some of the Albigenses seem no more heretical than the meekest parishioner in Maturin's own church even though it is clear from the preface that he was attracted to the splendid barbarism of the feudal ages, with their wild superstitions and dubious Christianity. The historical Albigenses, who are also known as the Cathars, originated from the town of Albi, north-east of Toulouse. They were a religious sect whose name means 'pure' and held beliefs which stem from the Gnostics and Manicheans based on the dualistic creed dealing with the polarised forces of good and evil which they believed to be active in the universe. The evil force was epitomised by the presence of the Monster of Chaos who was capable of adopting various physical forms. This was seen as indicative of the power of evil to create that which is material and transitory as opposed to God's creation of the celestial and eternal. Since this doctrine could not be reconciled with the humanity of Christ, the Albigenses not only denied his

material presence but also the cult of the cross. The Albigensian sect was divided into the 'perfect' (*perfecti*) who formed the elite and the 'believers' who made up the bulk of the followers. The neophytes for the order of *perfecti* had to undergo a rigorous initiation ritual before being admitted into the inner circle which prepared them to endure torture rather than betray their faith. This led their enemies to accuse them of being 'favourably disposed towards suicide' but, nevertheless, equipped them for the series of persecutions which punctuate Cathar history. The most famous of these was the Albigensian Crusade which was ordered by Pope Innocent III, at the beginning of the thirteenth century in 1208. In his novel, Maturin recalls the effects of the almost total extirpation of the Cathars. The historical events provide him with the framework for the novel which contains a fictional plot concerning two young noblemen, Sir Paladour de La Croix Sanglante and Amirald. Lord of Courtenaye, for instance, employs a trio of witches to help him summon up the devil while the manifestation of a fiend in Adolpho's dungeon is an incarnation of evil along the lines of the Cathar heresy. But perhaps the most interesting supernatural ingredient of the novel may be found in the presence of a werewolf. This provides one of the earliest examples of lycanthropy in English literature and may link up with the 'beast' in the *Book of Revelation.* This ties up thematically with the 'mark of the beast' which, as Maturin explains, was believed to be part of the Albigensian heresy being:

> the term applied by the Catholics to the professors of the heretical religion, and which was retaliated by the reformers on the Catholics three hundred years afterwards with equal felicity of allusion and acrimony of retort. (op. cit. III, p. 18)

The Albigenses' claim that evil could transmute into the shape of a man or beast may relate to the lycanthrope who admits that even though he has the appearance of a man, he is, in fact, a wolf saying 'trust not my human skin – the hairs grow inward, and I am a wolf within – a man outward only' (ibid. II, p. 263). The werewolf goes on to state that the wolfish heart is within and the wolfish fangs are within. This is similar to Schemoli's description of himself as an intellectual savage once he had been subsumed by the desire for revenge. In *The Albigenses,* the lycanthrope symbolises the malignant change in individuals which not only springs from pure malice, as with Schemoli, but also from dabbling in the occult arts for forbidden knowledge.

40. Maturin, *The Albigenses,* I, pp. 236-7.
41. Maturin, *Sermons,* p. 21.
42. Maturin, *Women, or Pour et Contre: A Tale* (1818), p. 321.
43. Idman, *Maturin,* p. 8.
44. Maturin, *Women or Pour et Contre,* pp. 322-3.
45. Loc. cit.
46. Maturin, *Bertram: or The Castle of Aldobrando: A Tragedy in 5 Acts* (London, 1816), p. 58.
47. Ibid., p. 70.
48. Loc. cit.
49. Loc. cit.
50. Maturin, *Melmoth the Wanderer,* ed. Alethea Hayter (Harmondsworth, 1977), p. 587.

51. Hoffman Nickerson, *The Inquisition: A Political and Military Study of its Establishment* (London, 1832), p. 51.
52. Maturin, *The Universe* (London, 1821), p. 16.
53. Ibid., pp. 32-3.
54. Ibid., pp. 57-8.
55. Maturin, *Melmoth the Wanderer,* p. 41. This is the opening epigram to the novel and is from Shakespeare's *Henry VI Part 2*, iii, 3, lines 12-13.
56. Ibid., preface.
57. Kramer, *Charles Robert Maturin,* p. 126.
58. See Maturin, *Melmoth the Wanderer,* p. 92. Hugh Peters (1598-1660) was an independent preacher who was executed after the Restoration.
59. See Maturin, *Melmoth the Wanderer,* p. 93.
60. See ibid., pp. 13-14.
61. Ibid., p. 337.
62. *Quarterly Review,* 24 (1821), p. 303.
63. Maturin, *Melmoth the Wanderer,* preface.
64. See Jack Null, 'Structure and Theme in Melmoth the Wanderer,' *Papers in Literature and Language,* 13, no. 2 (Spring, 1977), pp. 136-47.
65. Cited in Walter Raleigh, *The English Novel,* pp. 236-8.
66. *Edinburgh Review,* 35 (1821) pp. 353-62. Reprinted in *Famous Reviews* ed. R. Brimley Johnson (New York, 1914).
67. *Quarterly Review,* 24 (1821) pp. 303-11.
68. Quoted by Idman, *Charles Maturin: His Life and Works* (London, 1923), p. 269.
69. Loc. cit.
70. *Quarterly Review,* 24 (1821), p. 303.
71. Maturin, *Melmoth the Wanderer,* p. 55.
72. Ibid., p. 65. See Maturin's fragment, 'The Sybil's Prophecy: A Dramatic Fragment,' in *The Literary Souvenir,* pp. 128-36.
73. The use of the portrait device also mentioned by Godwin in his preface to *St Leon* provided the novelist of a pre-photographic age with a useful means of recording the Rosicrucian's earlier existence. In *Melmoth,* Maturin does not exploit the didactic possibilities provided by the portrait, unlike his descendant Oscar Wilde who in *The Picture of Dorian Gray* (1891), reprinted in *The Works of Oscar Wilde* (London, 1948) reflects that the protagonist's portrait 'was a visible sign of the degradation of sin' (ibid., p. 81). There can be little doubt that Maturin's own novel influenced Wilde who even adopted the name Sebastian Melmoth after his release from prison. Wilde also contributed material to Melmoth's *Memoirs* (1892) and may have been referring to his ancestor in the following passage from *The Picture of Dorian Gray:* 'Yet one had ancestors in literature, as well as in one's own race, nearer perhaps in type and temperament, many of them, and certainly with an influence of which one was more absolutely conscious' (ibid., p. 113). The sin in *Dorian Gray* of which both sitter and painter are guilty lies in their worship of youth and beauty particularly in the Hellenistic concept of physical perfection. But Gray's blasphemy is not merely in the price he is willing to pay for the realisation of this Greek ideal. Although his motivations differ considerably from Melmoth's reasons for prolonging his life, it is likely that Gray's portrait is Wilde's reconstruction of Maturin's hero.
74. Coleridge, *Poetical Works,* ed. Ernest Hartley Coleridge (Oxford, 1969), p. 447.
75. Maturin, *Melmoth the Wanderer,* p. 75.

76. Ibid., p. 75.
77. Loc. cit.
78. Loc. cit.
79. Loc. cit.
80. Ibid., p. 102.
81. Ibid., p. 266.
82. Ibid., p. 306.
83. See Maturin, *Sermons*, p. 21.
84. Maturin, *Melmoth the Wanderer*, p. 361.
85. Loc. cit.
86. See ibid., p. 398.
87. Ibid., p. 400.
88. Ibid., p. 630.
89. Ibid., p. 410.
90. Ibid., p. 516.
91. Robert Kiely, *The Romantic Novel in England* (Cambridge, Mass., 1972), p. 200.
92. See Gabriel Ronay, *The Dracula Myth: The Cult of the Vampire* (London, 1975), pp. 57-8.
93. See Maturin, *Melmoth the Wanderer*, p. 560.
94. Ibid., p. 701.
95. Maturin, *The Milesian Chief*, p. 39.
96. Maturin, *Melmoth the Wanderer*, p. 307.
97. Ibid., p. 697.
98. Ibid., pp. 696-7.
99. Ibid., p. 697.
100. Ibid., preface.
101. Ibid., pp. 568-9.
102. Ibid., p. 569.
103. Loc. cit.
104. Loc. cit.
105. Ibid., p. 696.
106. See *Quarterly Review*, 24, (1821), p. 303.
107. Edgar Allan Poe, *Poems* (1831) (New York, 1936).
108. Maturin, *Melmoth the Wanderer*, p. 696.
109. Judith Wilt, *Ghosts of the Gothic: Austen, Eliot and Lawrence* (New Jersey, 1980) p. 58.
110. Maturin, *Melmoth the Wanderer*, p. 103.
111. Loc. cit.
112. Ibid., p. 697.
113. Ibid., p. 701.
114. Ibid., p. 691.
115. Loc. cit.
116. Ibid., p. 647.
117. See Dawson, '*Melmoth the Wanderer*' pp. 621-32.
118. Maturin, *Melmoth the Wanderer*, pp. 274-5.
119. Pope, *Essay on Man* (1733-4), ed. Maynard Mack (London, 1958), p. 139.
120. Ibid., p. 36.
121. Georg Lukács, *Goethe and his Age*, trans. Robert Anchor (London, 1968) p. 179.
122. Maturin, *Melmoth the Wanderer*, p. 216.

123. Goethe, *Faust* (part 1), trans. Philip Wayne (Harmondsworth, 1976), p. 90.
124. Lukács, *Goethe and his Age*, p. 159.
125. Ibid., p. 179.
126. See Ernest A. Baker, *The History of the English Novel: The Novel of Sentiment and the Gothic Romance* (London, 1934), p. 221.
127. Willem Scholten, *Charles Robert Maturin: The Terror–Novelist* (Amsterdam, 1933), p. 7.
128. Ibid., p. 106.
129. See Gretchen R. Besser, *Balzac's Concept of Genius: The Theme of Superiority in the Comédie Humaine* (Geneva, 1969).
130. Balzac, *Don Juan or The Elixir of Long Life, Shorter Stories from Balzac,* trans. William Wilson and the Count Stenbock (London, 1890), pp. 1-27.
131. Ibid., p. 14.
132. Loc. cit.
133. Loc. cit.
134. Ibid., p. 16
135. Balzac, *Melmoth reconcilié* in *Œuvres Complètes* (Paris, 1960), p. 378:

> Ne sais-tu pas que tout ici-bas doit m'obeir, que je puis tout? Je lis dans les cœurs, je vois l'avenir, je sais le passé. Je suis ici, et je puis être ailleurs! Je ne dépends ni du temps, ni de l'éspace, ni de la distance. Le monde est mon serviteur. J'ai la faculté de toujours jouir, et de donner toujours le bonheur.

136. Ibid., p. 379-80: 'Cet homme était le cauchemar même, et pesait sur Castanier comme une atmosphere empoisonnée.'
137. Ibid., p. 392:

> S'il s'était permis de comparer de si grandes choses aux niaiseries sociales, il ressemblait à ces banquiers riches de plusieurs millions à qui rien ne resiste dans la societé; mais qui n'étant pas admis aux cèrcles de la noblesse, ont pour idée fixé de s'y agreger, et ne comptent pour rien tous les privilèges sociaux acquis par eux, du moment ou il leur en manque un.

138. Ibid., pp. 386-7: 'Castanier s'était promis de faire du terrible pouvoir qu'il venait d'acheter, au prix de son eternité bienheureuse.'
139. Ibid., p. 387: 'la suprème puissance apporta le néant pour dot.'
140. Loc. cit:

> En puisant à pleines mains dans le trésor des voluptés humaines dont la clef lui avait été remise par le Demon, il en atteignit promptement le fond. Cette énorme puissance, en un instant apprehendée, fut en un instant exercée, jugée, usée. Ce qui était tout, ne fut rien. Il arrive souvent que la possession tue les plus immenses po émes du désir, aux rêves duquel l'objet posséde répond rarement.

141. Plato, *Gorgias*, trans. Terence Irwin (Oxford, 1979), p. 57.
142. Ibid. This is a quotation from one of Pindar's Odes which is included amongst the *Fragments of Uncertain Class in The Odes of Pindar including the Principal Fragments,* trans. John Sandys (London, revised, 1957), p. 605: 'Law, the lord of all, mortals and immortals.'

143. Balzac, *Melmoth Réconcilié*, p. 397: 'Nous sommes tous actionnaires dans la grande entreprise de l'éternité.'

144. Ibid., p. 400:

> L'énorme puissance conquise par la découverte de L'Irlandais, fils du Révérend Maturin, se perdit ainsi. Il fut impossible à quelques orientalistes, à des mystiques, à des archeologues occupés de ces choses, de constater historiquement la manière d'évoquer le démon.

The visual representation of the vast power of Melmoth mentioned above may be found in Goya's painting *The Colossus* (see plate 4). As Alethea Hayter points out 'The equivalent in painting for Maturin's novel *Melmoth* would have to be Goya,' *Melmoth the Wanderer*, p. 18.

6

Bulwer-Lytton and the Rose and Cross

Who but a Rosicrucian could explain the Rosicrucian mysteries!

Bulwer-Lytton [1]

Novelist and Rose-Cross Brother

No novelist is more closely associated with Rosicrucianism than Edward Bulwer-Lytton, who, apart from writing Rosicrucian novels and short stories, is reputed to have been a Brother of the Rosy Cross.[2] Any analysis of Bulwer's occult writings would be incomplete without some recognition of the interplay between the novelist, magician and philosopher. The conceptual framework of *Zanoni*, *A Strange Story* and various Rosicrucian tales hinges upon the concepts of the actual and the ideal which are manifestly Hegelian, while the philosophical pursuit of the absolute is expressed through the iconography of the rose and cross.

The neglect of Bulwer studies has been noted by Robert Lee Wolf in *Strange Stories*, where he wryly comments that it is only the occasional wandering scholar who 'ventures into this airless region of literary interstellar space.'[3] At best a lesser luminary dwarfed by brighter constellations, Bulwer has become, according to Michael Sadleir in his biographical and critical study, 'a legend half impressive, half-absurd, to a posterity which can see his faults and read the satire of his enemies, but cannot appreciate wherein lay the power of his age.'[4] Even Sadleir, after completing only the first volume of his biography, wearied of defending Bulwer from time-warped misrepresentations, and admitted 'no one wanted Bulwer nor ever pretended that he did.'[5] Thackeray, who mockingly called Bulwer 'Sawedwardasarlittnbulwig',[6] would have agreed. Out of fashion and with little claim to artistic merit apart from having written one of the best-selling novels of the century, *The Last Days of Pompeii* (1834), Bulwer's reputation may be redeemed by a reappraisal of his Rosicrucian novels, *Zanoni* and *A Strange Story*.

Assuming that Bulwer was a member of a Brotherhood of the Rosy Cross, his achievements in the arcane terrains of occult fiction may be attributable in part to first-hand experience. But his membership has not as yet been verified and claims such as that put forward by his grandson remain unsubstantiated:

> He [Bulwer-Lytton] was himself a member of the Society of Rosicrucians and Grand Patron of the Order. As this was a secret society, it is not surprising that among Bulwer's papers there should be no documents which throw any light on his connection with it, nor any mention of it in his correspondence.[7]

By not revealing his sources of information, Robert Bulwer-Lytton fails to provide evidence that his grandfather was a Rosicrucian. He even implies that the very absence of evidence constitutes proof of Bulwer's loyalty to the secrecy of the brotherhood, thus paving the way for more innuendo and hearsay. The rumour that Bulwer possessed the Rosicrucian powers of invisibility, which would have been an undoubted asset for any politician, is dispelled by his grandson:

> I have even been told wild stories of ridiculous positions into which he was led by his imagined possessions of occult powers; that he would pass through a room full of visitors in the morning, arrayed in a dressing-gown, believing himself to be invisible, and then appear later in the day very carefully and elaborately dressed, and greet his guests as if meeting them for the first time.[8]

The younger Lytton explains that his grandfather spent his mornings in a dressing-gown while engaged on literary work which absorbed him to such an extent that he was oblivious to guests. With pen in hand, Bulwer worked enchantments of a more sublunary than supernatural kind. In many ways, he had been responsible for generating a Rosicrucian mystery about himself along the lines of the original brotherhood's mythopoeia. For example, Bulwer in a letter to the author Hargrave Jennings thanking him for forwarding a copy of his book, *The Rosicrucians: Their Rites and Mysteries* (1870), is deliberately enigmatic:

> There are reasons why I cannot enter into the subject of the "Rosicrucian Brotherhood," a society still existing, but not under any name by which it can be recogn-

> ised by those without its pale. But you have with much learning and much acuteness traced its connection with early and symbolical religions, and no better book upon such a theme has been written, or indeed, could be written, unless a member of the Fraternity were to break the vow which enjoins them to secrecy. Some time ago a sect pretending to style itself "Rosicrucians" and arrogating full knowledge of the mysteries of the craft, communicated with me, and in reply, I sent them the cipher sign of the "Initiate," – not one of them could construe it.[9]

Bulwer's evasiveness is just as cryptic as the cipher sign he refers to above. His claim that the present Rosicrucians are imposters out of touch with the true ancient lore is calculated to suggest that he himself is familiar with the authentic order of Rosicrucians. In the light of this, it is hardly surprising that Bulwer was assumed to have been the mentor of Hargrave Jennings, who allegedly became the Supreme Grand Master of the Rosicrucians in England. Another extravagant claim dealing with Bulwer's alleged membership of the Rosy Cross fraternity states that by 1853 he possessed the following Rosicrucian titles: Highest Arcane Initiate, Order of the Rose, *L'Ordre du Lis*, Member of the Great or World Council, *Fraternitæ Rosæ Crucis*, Supreme Grand Master and Count de L. Hierophant of the World.[10] The office of Hierophant, the highest of the order, had previously been held by the Transylvanian Count Saint-German, a self-styled two-thousand-year-old immortal.[11] E. M. Butler suggests in *The Myth of the Magus* that Saint-German had provided Bulwer with a model for his quasi-Rosicrucian hero, Zanoni.[12] But since Saint-German was reputed to have been a notorious charlatan, it is unlikely that he would have inspired Bulwer's portrait of the most perfect of magi. It is more likely, as John Senior suggests, that Zanoni was modeled on the saintly Saint-Martin,[13] who is mentioned in the novel in hallowed tones: 'no man more beneficent, generous, pure and virtuous, than St Martin, adorned the last century.'[14] Saint-Martin was the most important follower of Pasqualis, who founded a number of secret societies closely associated with the Rosicrucians. Saint-Martin, designated Reau-Croix,[15] as a crusader against charlatans was clearly an occultist of the Zanoni caste. Advancing beyond the teaching of his mentor, Pasqualis, he carved out his own path towards inner truth. Zanoni after witnessing the initiation into Pasqualis's brotherhood of Cazotte, the author of *Le Diable Amoureux* (1772), notes, 'I attended their ceremonies but to see how vainly they sought to revive the ancient marvels of the cabala.'[16]

Another historical character used by Bulwer in his fiction is the Rosicrucian-Cabalist, Eliphas Levi, whose magical practices inspired a number of occult scenes in *A Strange Story*. Here Bulwer refers to Levi as the author of *Dogme et Ritual de La Haute Magic*, which he considers to be 'a book less remarkable for its learning than for the earnest belief of a scholar of our own day in the reality of the art of which he records the history.'[17] Bulwer's reticence in print over Levi does little to verify the claims made by other sources that they both enjoyed a partnership in magic.[18] According to a biographical article called '*Rosicruciæ*,' Bulwer, in his capacity of Supreme Hierophant, allegedly presided over the initiation of Levi and the elevation of Pascal Beverly Randolph, the founder of American Rosicrucianism and exponent of sex magic, to a high degree of the Supreme Grand Dome in Paris some time between 1856 and 1858.[19] Following this, Bulwer is believed to have been present at a ritual described in Levi's *Ritual de la Haute Magic*, an evocation of Apollonius of Tyana, who was a Pythagorean sage from Asia Minor during the first century A. D.[20] It is darkly hinted in *Zanoni* that Apollonius's teachings were the inspiration behind the true Rosicrucian order.[21] Levi claimed that in readiness for this necromantic ceremony, the spirit of Apollonius had sent him instructions between July 20 and 26, 1854, concerning the location of a manuscript of a Greek ritual which he had written himself. According to Levi, a mysteriously veiled woman, the friend of a friend of 'Sir B— L— provided him with a fully-equipped magic room for the complete evocation of Apollonius.'[22] This was to be the setting for the first of three ceremonies intent upon summoning up the magus. The Hellenistic finale took place in Bulwer's presence on the rooftop of the aptly named *Pantheon*, a shop in London's Regent Street. Christopher McIntosh suggests that Bulwer may have initiated Levi into the *Societas Rosicruciana in Anglia*.[23]

As mentioned earlier, some sources claimed that Bulwer was the Grand Patron of this order in 1871. For example, Nelson Steward appears to be referring to this society in his vague and scanty account of Bulwer's Rosicrucian career.[24] Steward's survey begins with a description of the ancient knowledge transmitted by Francis Bacon from the disciples of Christian Rosencreutz. In his foray, Steward makes some unorthodox assumptions about Rosicrucianism, such as referring to their legendary founder as a historical figure. He also suggests that the esoteric teaching of the society was largely theosophical in nature. However true this claim may have been, there is no doubt that the founder of the Theosophical Society, Madame Blavatsky, who admired Bulwer intensely, was convinced that he was a practising Rosicrucian. She proclaimed him a 'prophet who actively participated in the invisible world'[25] and whose

Rosicrucian fiction had dissolved the boundaries between life and art. Convinced that Bulwer's account of the Rosicrucian spirit-world was based on actual observation, she was adamant that 'no author in the world of literature ever gave a more truthful or more poetical description of these beings than Sir E. Bulwer-Lytton, the author of *Zanoni*.'[26] This certainty had been brought about by the power of Bulwer's fiction and his imaginative drive, which for Blavatsky made 'his words sound more like the faithful echo of memory than the exuberant outflow of mere imagination.'[27]

Certainly Bulwer was attracted by the occult themes he wrote about, particularly the quest for the *elixir vitæ,* which he employed as the chief motif of his two Rosicrucian novels, *Zanoni* and *A Strange Story*. For Bulwer, the elixir of immortality was emblematic of the visionary ideal which lay at the heart of his beliefs. In a letter to Lady Blessington, he expresses his hankering for the talismanic philosopher's stone, saying 'if only we can but attain to it!'[28] Bulwer's passionate interest in the elixir was noted by Madame Home, the wife of the spiritualist Daniel Home, in her discussion of Margrave, the villain of *A Strange Story*:

> he is the embodiment of a fancy that takes shape in more than one work of Lytton's – the alchemist's dream of the Elixir of Life. Margrave has renewed his youth with it, and those who read between the lines of *A Strange Story* and *Zanoni* will suspect a fact familiar to some who knew the author of those romances – that Lytton was half-persuaded of the possibility of youth being thus renewed, and had a half-hope that he might one day revive his own.[29]

Bulwer's life-long interest in the occult may have been the legacy of his seventeenth-century ancestor, Dr John Bulwer, who had published a number of treatises on necromancy. The most famous of these, *Anthropo-Metamorphosis or Man-Transformed, or the Artificial Changeling* (1653), maps out the alleged transformations of parts of the body accredited to various astral influences. Undoubtedly this notion of metamorphosis had been derived from Apuleius's *Golden Ass,* subtitled *The Transformations of Apuleius*.[30] For centuries, this Latin novel has been cited as a key to the early mystery cults of Isis which were later associated with Rosicrucian lore and theosophical doctrine. In *The Last Days of Pompeii*, which inspired Blavatsky's *Isis Unveiled*, Bulwer modelled his witch of Vesuvius on the enchantress in *The Golden Ass*.[31] Bulwer's recreation of Pompeii prior to its sulphuric burial had triggered off his interest in the school of Neoplatonists, particularly Iamblichus and Proclus. In turn, this prompted him to delve into the work of other occult writers such as Paracelsus, Cornelius Agrippa, Jean Baptiste Van Helmont and Michael Psellus, who had written a treatise on demons and alchemists.

Such erudition encouraged Bulwer to fill his novels with references to obscure and esoteric philosophies, possibly in defence of his own injunction that 'a novel writer must be a philosopher.'[32] Critics such as W. E. Aytoun capitalised on Bulwer's prosaic Baroque by ridiculing him as a prospective poet laureate who would have admitted:

> Yes, I am he who on the Novel shed
> Obscure philosophy's enchanting light,
> Until the public, 'wildered as they read,
> Believed they saw that which was not in sight.
> Of course, 'twas not for me to put them right.[33]

Edwin Eigner however, by identifying Bulwer as a metaphysical novelist draws attention to the philosophical perspectives to be found in his fiction.[34] By grounding his metaphysics in Hegelian idealism, Bulwer deploys a rationalisation of his mystical beliefs.

The Actual and the Ideal: The Rose and the Cross

In a number of novels such as *Godolphin*, *Ernest Maltravers*, *Alice or the Mysteries*, *Zanoni* and *A Strange Story*, Bulwer traces the dialectical opposition between the actual and the ideal. This conceptual interchange had prevailed throughout the Romantic movement. The dynamic potential of such paradoxes could be unlocked through works of art where, for example, the hero makes a transition from a sceptical state to that of visionary consciousness. As we shall see, Bulwer's metaphysical inclinations gravitate towards a Rosicrucian idealism which seeks to unite the actual and the ideal.

In his early novel, *Godolphin*, Bulwer makes a preliminary excursion into the visionary world which he explores more fully in *Zanoni*. *Godolphin*, which is constructed upon the paradoxical opposition between the actual and ideal, reason and the imagination, tries to reconcile the nineteenth-century dichotomy between utilitarianism and intuition. Attempting to unite immortality with pragmatism, Godolphin's question, 'What then can we say of the desire to be useful, and the hope to be immortal?'[35] could be put to the eternal Rosicrucian striving for social utility. Bulwer, in contrasting the rationality and scepticism of this period with its superstitious and irrational proclivities, shows that he is aware that 'The race of the nineteenth century boast their lights, but run as madly after any folly as their fathers in the eighteenth.'[36] The thrust of his occult novels confronts this Victorian paradox in tracking down mystical Enlightenment and the elixir of life from a vantage point of rationality.

The novel's occult philosopher, Volkman, guides his English protégé, Godolphin, towards the ancient wisdom of Hermes and Zoroaster. He assures him that he will achieve his occult goal by contemplating the ancient arts of alchemy and of an unspecified arcana which is yet 'more gloomy and less rational.'[37] Both Godolphin and Volkman concentrate their energies upon leaping beyond mortal boundaries in the search for the elixir. From the outset they follow the footsteps of 'those pale and unearthly students who, in the darkest ages, applied life and learning to one unhallowed vigil, the Hermes of the Gebir of the alchymists' empty science-dreamers, and the martyrs of their dreams.'[38] The hollow note of this passage re-enacts the forlorn plight of the failed neophyte in the subplot of *Zanoni*. In *Godolphin*, the hero challenges the legitimate limits of knowledge, which he seeks to surpass by discovering the source of knowledge itself. According to Volkman, this is an assignment for the adept who must walk the path of pre-scientific and unearthly knowledge. The imagery here is that of the soul walking with the spirit of the vision. In this allegory of a spiritual journey, Volkman urges that it is from within ourselves that we must discover the alchemical preparations which will elevate us to attaining ancient wisdom.

The hero of Bulwer's later novel, *Ernest Maltravers* (1837), also finds himself drawn towards the obscure and 'half-extinct philosophies'[39] of early civilisations. These cryptic teachings had been transmitted to ancient mystery-religions and cults, and then preserved by secret societies. Bulwer would have been aware of the ancestry of the occult tradition when he decided to subtitle *Maltravers* and its sequel *Alice or The Mysteries, The Eleusiniana.*[40] This subtitle refers to the Eleusian Mysteries of Demeter, into which Apollonius of Tyana was initiated. Apollonius was a magician who, as mentioned earlier, held some importance for Bulwer. It is likely that through the character and name symbolism of Maltravers, Bulwer was able to express his alter-ego.[41] Maltravers is a Gothic character, wild and enthusiastic. Coleridge-like, he steeps himself in German literature and metaphysical speculation. While in the role of a Romantic recluse, Maltravers studies astrology and 'had even been suspected of a serious hunt after the philosopher's stone.'[42] But, as a mystic on the brink of the sublime, Maltravers hankers for that state of enlightenment promised by the Neoplatonists and pursued by the Rosicrucians. It is likely that Bulwer shared these aspirations, for he may have been describing himself in *Ernest Maltravers* when he wrote, 'I am a kind of visionary Rosicrucian.'[43]

Throughout his writings, Bulwer equated the visionary with the ideal, which he regarded as inseparable from the actual. His hero, Ernest Maltravers, whose surname cleverly puns the word 'travel,' journeys through life in the hope of being able to attain both the actual and the ideal. One version of the synthesis between these two concepts may be seen in Maltravers's 'mystic yearning after utility.'[44] The hero's impulses constitute a symbiosis of intuitiveness and utilitarianism, the twin poles of nineteenth-century thought. As the novel reveals, most of Maltravers's yearnings are romantically inclined towards the uneducated peasant girl Alice whom he has befriended. Their love redeems Maltravers from the *taedium vitae* which he believes 'shames and bankrupts the Ideal.'[45] In *Devereux,* Bulwer explains that throughout life, 'it is no real or living thing which we demand; it is the realisation of the idea we have formed within us.'[46] The emphasis on idealism here is not a denial of the experiential world but a reminder of its antipodes. Bulwer's true seekers, particularly those of a Rosicrucian persuasion, strive towards the unity between the actual and the ideal, which in figurative terms completes the circle explained in *Devereux*:

> it has often seemed to me that if there be as certain ancient philosophers fabled, one certain figure pervading all nature, human and universal it is the circle. Round, in one vast monotony, one eternal gyration roll the orbs of space. This moves the spirit of creative life, kindling, progressing, maturing, decaying, perishing, reviving, and rolling again, and so onwards for ever through the same course; and thus even would seem to revolve the mysterious mechanism of human evolution.[47]

According to this overview, the human race is governed by the laws of cyclic change. Likewise the Rosicrucian world-picture is represented by the circular configuration of the rose. As Bulwer points out in *Zanoni*, knowledge is 'but a circle that brings thee back whence thy wanderings began!'[48] This is one of the interlocking circles within the greater circle of life and death which is expressed in *Devereux* through the concept of eternal return:

> we will die in the place where we were born – in the point of space whence began the circle, and there also

> shall it end! This is the grand orbit through which mortality passes only once, but the same figure may pervade all through which it moves on its journey to the grave.[49]

This figure of the ascending circle or spiral expresses the mobility of Romantic thought which has influenced Bulwer's treatment of Rosicrucian fiction. The Romanticist recognises that individuals are concerned with the 'realisation of the idea we have formed within us and which as we are not gods, we can never call into existence.'[50] The Rosicrucian novel advances this concept since it has the potential to bring this inner ideal into actuality through the fusion of the actual and the ideal.

As we shall see later, Bulwer achieves this synthesis in *Zanoni* through his hero, who is redeemed by the love of an opera singer, Viola. In Harriet Martineau's work, *Zanoni Explained*, the two quasi-Rosicrucian characters Zanoni and Mejnour signify the ideal and the actual respectively.[51] Zanoni is also identified with artistic intuition and Mejnour with scientific empiricism, while Viola is equated with the world of instinct whose powers of romantic love eventually tear Zanoni away from his sublunary immortality. As in a Medieval morality play, Bulwer has matched up character to abstraction:

> Idealism [Zanoni] is more subjected than Science [Mejnour] to the Affections, or to Instinct [Viola] because the Affections, sooner or later, force Idealism into the Actual, and in the Actual its immortality departs.[52]

Bulwer derived the ideological framework for the Rosicrucian ideal from Hegel, who, like Andreae, had gained a stipendiary at the famous Tübinger Stift.[53] As Eigner points out in *The Metaphysical Novel in England and America*, Bulwer was responsible for transporting Hegelian Romantic aesthetics into English literature after having rejected British empiricism in a spirit of liberation:

> The great spiritual necessity of his age, as Bulwer understood it, was to free itself from this intellectual bondage, [Lockean materialism] and the tools which he recommended to work this jailbreak were visionary literature and German idealism.[54]

Bulwer also shared Hegel's idealising principle of viewing art as 'the sensuous presentation of the Absolute,'[55] which must retain a unity between the external world and the inner harmony that is contingent upon notional truth. Hegel argued that the fusion between these two states through art would trigger off a cathartic reaction which would give rise to the ideal. More specifically, Hegel expressed his ideas in terms of the Rosicrucian tradition by referring to the rose on the cross which he acknowledged as the symbol of the Brotherhood of the Rosy Cross. Hegel frees the iconography of the Rosy Cross from mystic consciousness, thus enabling it to become the tool of rational enquiry. In the preface to the *Philosophy of Right* (1820), Hegel invites the reader 'to recognise reason as the rose in the cross of the present.'[56] Here the rose represents philosophical truth as a concept of the actual, rather than the ideal. The same metaphor is used in the *Lectures on the Philosophy of Religion.* There Hegel speaks of the ideal as an 'outer rind' through which it is necessary to penetrate in order to recognise the 'substantial kernel of actuality.'[57] Nevertheless, in both texts the rose on the cross represents an ultimate synthesis between the actual and the rational. That Hegel sees these concepts as fluid and interchangeable can be illustrated with reference to his word-play when he describes the beliefs of the Brotherhood of the Rosy Cross as 'Rosicrucianism or Cross-rosism.'[58] Thus the actual may penetrate the ideal or vice versa. But, as Hegel repeatedly insists, it is only those willing to undertake the effort of conceptual thought who will appreciate the ultimate unity between the actual and the ideal. This is expressed symbolically in *The Philosophy of Religion,* where Hegel points out that 'in order to gather the rose in the cross of the Present, we must take that cross itself upon us.'[59] This means that those who undertake the 'severe labour'[60] required to penetrate the kernel of actuality will grasp the truth of philosophical wisdom and take the rose from the cross of the present.

Zanoni is the artistic expression of this philosophical truth. In this novel, Bulwer's hero attains to the true Rosicrucian ideal which refuses to be divorced from the real, depicted here through love and death. Bulwer's other Rosicrucian writings show how the characters fall short of this goal, which in Hegelian terms embodies both the mystical and the rational. M. H. Abrams's comments on the relationship between German philosophy and English Romantic literature have relevance to these convergences in the work of Bulwer and Hegel:

> It is not by chance nor by the influence of a mysteriously noncausal *Zeitgeist*, but through participation in the same historical and intellectual milieu, through recourse to similar precedents in the religious and cultural tradition, and by frequent interaction, that the

> works of philosophy and literature of this age manifest conspicuous parallels in ideas, in design, and even in figurative detail.[61]

Bulwer and Hegel would both agree that at the heart of Romantic Idealism lies the metaphysics of integration or the reconciliation of opposites such as reason and faith. This is an acknowledgment of the moral imperative of reclaiming for self-conscious man the world from which he has become alienated through his own act of self-awareness. The dilemma of fallen humanity found its way into the metaphysical systems of the German Idealists from the Christian Neoplatonists. In turn, the problem of reintegrating a stigmatised and alienated human race with nature was appropriated by the Rosicrucians, who believed that this could be achieved through the possession of esoteric knowledge. This attitude is far removed from Hegel's notion of 'absolute spirit,' symbolised on occasion by the Rose and Cross, which is predicated upon the belief that knowledge of the absolute exists within the boundaries of human understanding. In *Zanoni*, Bulwer's Rosicrucian hero enters into the realm of absolute spirit through the assimilation of the actual and the ideal. This is antithetical to Mejnour, one of the Rosicrucian seekers who devote 'themselves to the knowledge' which they believe to be their 'purification' and 'immortality' but at the same time remain 'deaf and blind to the allurements of the vanity which generally accompanies research.'[62] As the following discussion of Bulwer's Rosicrucian short stories will show, failed adepts or false Rosicrucians, unlike Zanoni, do not fulfil the promise of the manifestos in terms of the reintegration of the individual with nature, nor do they manage to assimilate the actual and the ideal.

Rosicrucian Short Stories

Bulwer's earliest Rosicrucian short story, 'The Tale of Kosem Kesamim: The Magician' was published in 1832. The outline for this Romantic fragment had been written during his school-days. Eventually the tale, which is an invaluable index to Bulwer's early interests in the occult, was recycled into *Zanoni*. The story reflects his epistemological curiosities regarding the limits to knowledge. The magician, Kosem Kesamim, who embarks on an allegoric inner journey, yearns to discover the source of all knowledge and is prepared to hazard everything for the attainment of this goal. Pondering upon this perennial dream stretching back to antiquity which is etched into the earliest folk-memories, Bulwer declares:

'Age after Age Man invents and deserts some worship of idols in his yearning for symbols of a Power beyond the reach of his vision and the guess of his reason.'[63] By striving to make contact with the 'One Great Productive Spirit of all things,' the magus is assuming that knowledge emanates from one single source. In the course of his occult venture, Kosem is confronted by a meteoric fire which he initially believes to be the essence he has been seeking. In *Zanoni*, the self-realisation brought about by immortality is symbolised by a perpetual-burning lamp:

> He who discovers the elixir, discovers what lies in space; for the spirit that vivifies the frame strengthens the senses. There is attraction in the elementary principle of light. In the lamps of Rosicrucius, the fire is the pure elementary principle.[64]

But the spirit of fire turns out to be a demon and, for those who deny their creator, the nightmarish first principle of nature in a godless universe.[65] Kosem's torment, graphically described towards the end of the story, is his punishment for embarking on a false quest. The Platonic idea that the source of knowledge could be found in a world of absolute forms lying beyond the known frontiers of knowledge is no more spurious than Bulwer's belief in metaphysical limits to rational enquiry. The problem for Kosem is that he has been blinded by myth, by succumbing to the ideal and excluding the actual or the real. Consequently, he fails to divine the relationship between knowledge and the knower, believing them to be inseparable. In common with Faust, Kosem's quest for prohibited knowledge is ultimately the search for self-knowledge.[66] The punishment he incurs, thereby banishing his hopes of perpetuity, is manifest in a terrifying vision of death. By wishing to know the 'great arch mystery'[67] of the universe, the source of knowledge, he is also seeking out both its conclusion and completion. Since this may only be realised at the end of time, the magician witnesses an apocalyptic vision of stasis. Once he has entered 'that high and empyreal Knowledge which admits of no dissatisfaction, because [it is] in itself complete'[68] he realises with horror 'I had entered DEATH!'[69] At the end of the story, the hero is redeemed by God, and so looks forward to the prospect of a spiritual immortality in contrast to the death and decay of the flesh. This story provided Bulwer with a model for the failed neophyte in *Zanoni*. Kosem, in common with several Rosicrucian characters in *Zanoni*, has derived his wisdom from ancient Chaldean sources. It is interesting to note that Chaldea is the setting for another Bulwerian account of a seeker who fails in his odyssey for mystical enlightenment.

In 'Arasmanes the Seeker,' the hero is a young Chaldean who searches for the Garden of Eden, referred to throughout as Aden. This fable relates to the mystic goal of the Rosicrucian magus: to redeem fallen mankind from the effects of the Fall. In *Zanoni*, Bulwer evokes the innocence of a time 'when the forbidden fruit is not yet tasted, and we know of no land beyond the Eden which is gladdened by an Eve.'[70] The garden is described to Arasmanes by his dying father in metaphors of a Rosicrucian utopia, classical Arcady, or Golden Age: 'There, is neither age nor deformity; diseases are banished from the air; eternal youth, and the serenity of an unbroken happiness, are the prerogative of all things that breathe therein.'[71] Throughout his travels, Arasmanes comes across many false Adens which embrace spurious ideals such as sensual love or the worship of the alchemist's gold, as in 'the City of Golden Palaces.'[72] Eventually he hits on the idea of forcing his way into Paradise through the barrier of darkness that seals it off from the rest of the world, pleading 'what was the crime of winning the gardens of Paradise by force?'[73] Arasmanes has a brief glimpse of Aden but then loses sight of it forever. Gradually he loses the urge to seek out the garden, and resolves to look for happiness that is within reach. It is not until he rejects all thoughts of entering the abode that he is taken to the garden in an Avalonian ending to the tale. The archetypal image of the paradisal garden containing a fountain of youth reappears in the Rosicrucian legend of the elixir of life. More pertinently, the seeker after the elixir, pining for immortality, perpetual youth and freedom from disease and decay, has the same longings as Arasmanes in Bulwer's short story.

In 1835, Bulwer dreamed of a magus who had manufactured and then drunk the *elixir vitæ*. The instant effect of this potion was to bring about immortality and immunity from all human diseases including old age and natural death. This dream inspired Bulwer to write the fragmentary tale *Zicci* (1838), which turned out to be the blue-print for *Zanoni* (1842).[74] In the preamble to the full-length novel, Bulwer explains that *Zicci* was the shorter version of a hieroglyphic manuscript passed on to the narrator by a suspected Rosicrucian. We are told that the narrator, after spending two years in deciphering the manuscript, published a few chapters in a periodical.[75] These aroused so much interest that when the transliterator realised that he possessed two distinct versions of the tale, he decided to publish the longer one under the title of *Zanoni*. By presenting these publication details to the reader, Bulwer is able to provide a plausible explanation for the overlapping characters in *Zicci* and *Zanoni*. These are Glyndon the initiate, and the magi Mejnour and Zanoni, though the latter is known here as Zicci. Bulwer's fascination with the magus-myth is evident from his treatment of Voltman the astrologer in *Godolphin*, Kosem

Kesamim and Arasmanes from his short stories, and the magician Arbaces in *The Last Days of Pompeii.* Like Albertus Magnus, Bulwer tended to believe that an individual was born a magus, even though he was prepared to accept that this spiritual status could be acquired.[76] It is likely that Madame Blavatsky had derived her theosophical beliefs in the 'masters' from Bulwer's literary treatment of mortals gaining access to immortal states. There can be little doubt that the belief in magi which Bulwer expresses in his novels went beyond his creative writing to his own private convictions. For example, in a letter to his friend John Forster, he writes:

> I do believe in the substance of what used to be called Magic, that is, I believe that there are persons of a peculiar temperament who can effect very extraordinary things not accounted for satisfactorily by any existent philosophy.[77]

In *Zicci*, Glyndon is a character who tries to hijack the power of a magus but fails in the attempt. His frantic yet sublime longings to be initiated are not strong enough to overcome the worldly desires that the neophyte must conquer. Mejnour prescribes the terms of this transcendence in his description of happiness: 'if happiness exist it must be centred in A SELF to which all passion is unknown.'[78] He goes on to alert the aspirant that 'happiness is the last state of being, and as yet thou art on the threshold of the first.'[79] Zicci also tries to dissuade his protégé from adepthood. But Glyndon is determined to join the ranks of the psychic supermen whom he reveres as 'a mighty and numerous race with a force and power sufficient to permit them to acknowledge to mankind their majestic conquests and dominions ... true lords of this planet ... invaders, perchance of others.'[80] This homage, which has overtones of *The Coming Race* (1871), conjures up images of a race of super-beings which had earlier incited the anti-Illuminist alarmists. A less militant picture is presented by Mejnour in his description of an Academy of immortal beings dedicated to the pursuit of magic and science, which bears a striking similarity to the Rosicrucians' Invisible College. Glyndon is greedy not only for occult knowledge in general but also specifically for the immortality of Mejnour and Zicci. The effects of the *elixir vitae* on the latter are described as follows:

> From the shelves Zicci selected one of the phials, and poured the contents into a crystal cup. The liquid was colourless, and sparkled rapidly up in bubbles of light; it

> almost seemed to evaporate ere it reached his lips; but when the strange beverage was quaffed, and sudden change was visible in the countenance of Zicci; his beauty became yet more dazzling, his eyes shone with intense fire, and his form seemed to grow more youthful and etherial.[81]

The description of this crucial moment in the career of a Rosicrucian sage may have inspired Bulwer with the idea of Zanoni, who, as a redeemed Rosicrucian conquering death through spiritual immortality, is portrayed as an embodiment of the ideals of the Brotherhood of the Rosy Cross.

Zanoni: A Novel of Initiation

> He who wishes to catch a Rosicrucian, must take care not to disturb the waters.
>
> Bulwer-Lytton [82]

It is tempting to regard *Zanoni,* an explicitly Rosicrucian text, as emerging from the author's involvement with the Brotherhood of the Rosy Cross. On account of this novel, Bulwer was voted in as Honorary Grand Patron of the English Rosicrucians, *Societas Rosicruciana in Anglia,* extraordinarily without his consent. Dr Wynn Westcott, a prominent member of this society who had read *Zanoni*, alleged that Bulwer had been received into adeptship at a Rosicrucian lodge in Frankfurt, where he had become imbued with the ideas he displayed in *Zanoni* and elsewhere. Walter F. Lord however, in the kind of accusation usually levelled at the alchemist, alleges that Bulwer's interests in the occult had been motivated by the expectation of financial reward, since 'at first for pleasure, and later for curiosity, and at last for business reasons, he saturated his mind with the lore of magic. Its vocabulary was familiar to him; and among crystal globes and steel divining-rods and elixirs of life he moved as a professor in his laboratory.'[83] Yet it is highly unlikely that Bulwer ever imagined that writing a Rosicrucian novel would be lucrative in appealing to popular taste, for as he correctly anticipated, '*Zanoni* will be no favourite with that largest of all asses – the English public.'[84] Predictably, the novel failed to find favour among its readership and was not even given a favorable reception by the critics. Bulwer disregarded adverse criticisms as the outpourings of the 'common herd,' for as he explained in his dedication addressed to the artist John Gibson:

> I love it not the less because it has been little understood, and superficially judged by the common herd. It was not meant for them. I love it not the more, because it has found enthusiastic favours amongst the Few.[85]

Nevertheless, there was a small core of support for the novel in the face of overwhelming criticism. Carlyle reacted positively, by applauding *Zanoni* as 'a liberating voice for much that lay dumb imprisoned in human souls.'[86] But even this high praise falls short of Bulwer's own estimation of the work in a letter to John Forster as 'wonderful' and unique to the English language! In a subsequent letter, Bulwer goes further than this in praising *Zanoni* as 'the loftiest conception in English prose fiction.'[87] But he had to reassure himself that the novel would never be recognised as a masterpiece because it would not be fully understood. His choice of epigraph, borrowed from the *Comte de Gabalis,* signposts this foresight: 'In short, I could make neither head nor tail on't.'[88] This witticism anticipated the reaction of the reviewer of the *Athenæum*, who confessed that he had been confused by the tale.[89] Harriet Martineau, however, defended *Zanoni* against such hostilities, insisting that most reviewers remained perfectly insensible to the true nature of the book. She reassured Bulwer by claiming that though a hundred may read *St Leon* for the one who reads *Zanoni,* he could never be robbed of the true satisfaction derived from writing the novel and of the 'certain moments and hours spent in conceiving and working out such a problem of sacred philosophy.'[90] Martineau realised that one of the reasons why *Zanoni* was not a success with the reading public was because of its erudition.

For this reason she persuaded Bulwer to permit her to provide a key to the allegory, called *Zanoni Explained* on the grounds that the exegesis would not constitute an exposition of the sacred mysteries concealed within the novel but only of the principles upon which they were founded. Bulwer's initial unwillingness to provide a critical commentary was not simply reluctance to divulge Rosicrucian secrets, but a precaution against reducing the novel to a system of allegorical correspondences which would deter the reader from unravelling the enigmas contained in *Zanoni* single-handed. Bulwer also believed that there could be no definitive explanation of the text, since all interpretations would differ. In an annotation, he emphasises this point: "A hundred men," says the old Platonist, "may read the book by the help of the same lamp, yet all may differ on the text; for the lamp only lights the characters – the mind must divine the meaning."'[91] Bulwer regarded the novel as a parable which was not intended to engage the reader in problem-solving but instead to gain moral insights so that 'it takes the thought below the surface of the understanding to the deeper intelligence which the world rarely tasks.'[92]

The hero is a quasi-Rosicrucian whose immortal counterpart is the magus, Mejnour. Between them they represent a series of opposites. Zanoni is an Adonian figure whose perpetual youth and beauty makes him an eternal symbol of art. Mejnour, however, is of a Saturnian disposition, living a contemplative life marked by philosophical reflection. Through these two characters Bulwer expresses the dynamics of art and science, the actual and the ideal. Zanoni becomes the mouthpiece for Bulwer's idealising principle, while Mejnour reflects the actuality of scientific empiricism. Through his love for an opera singer, Viola, Zanoni eventually synthesises the actual and the ideal in his realisation of the absolute. This results in a curious inversion of the Undine legend whereby Zanoni forfeits his immortality for the love of a mortal woman. During the French Revolution, Zanoni sacrifices himself for Viola on the altar of reason, which is the guillotine of the Terror. At one stage he tries unsuccessfully to engineer a romance between Viola and an Englishman called Glyndon. But the latter, who is determined on joining Zanoni's ancient fraternity, devalues human love and subsequently fails as a neophyte. Mejnour has masterminded Glyndon's preparations, which consist of a series of tests and ritualised ordeals. But with Glyndon's failure and Zanoni's death, Mejnour becomes the sole surviving member of the ancient brotherhood and thus continues his perpetual existence alone.

The story, purporting to be the transcription of a mysterious manuscript described in the introduction, is contained within a realistic framework.[93] According to Eigner, this technique is characteristic of the metaphysical novel, for as he points out, 'The metaphysical novel ... uses both its realistic beginning and, sometimes, its allegorical center as means of arriving at the redeeming vision, which transcends and finally reconceives them both.'[94] The authentic opening is immediately apparent in *Zanoni*. In the introduction, the author, who claims to be a Rosicrucian, describes how he has visited a book-shop in Covent Garden in order to find out something about Rosicrucianism. He is particularly keen on reading material which has been written by a member of the brotherhood. While browsing through the books, the author comes across an elderly customer who turns out to be an authority on the subject. The old man indicates that the Rosicrucians never imparted their real doctrines directly to the world but only through an 'obscure hint, and mystical parable.'[95] It is significant that Bulwer describes *Zanoni* as a mystic 'parable' in his explanatory note at the end of the novel. The old man, who describes the Rosicrucians as 'the most jealous of all secret societies,' marvels that the author expects members of the sect to 'lift the veil that hides the Isis of their wisdom from the world.'[96] All this convinces the author that he is addressing a member of the 'August Fraternity.' Yet the old man goes on to point out that knowledge of an older and more illustrious brotherhood than the Rosicrucians may be found in the writing of the elder Pythagoreans and 'the immortal masterpieces of Apollonius.'[97] This is the earlier quasi-Rosicrucian brotherhood to which Mejnour and Zanoni belong. Based on ancient Chaldean wisdom, many of its teachings were transmitted into Rosicrucianism. In *Zanoni*, the old man turns out to be the failed neophyte Glyndon, who joins the Rosicrucians after being rejected from the earlier society. As Mejnour points out to him in connection with the antiquity of this unnamed brotherhood:

> Do you imagine ... that there were no mystic and solemn unions of men seeking the same end through the same means, before the Arabians of Damus, in 1378 [who] taught to a wandering German the secrets which founded the Institution of the Rosicrucians? I allow, however, that the Rosicrucians formed a sect descended from the greater and earlier school. They were wiser than the Alchemists – their masters are wiser than they.[98]

Michael Maier, the Rosicrucian apologist, claimed that the Brothers of the Rosy Cross considered themselves to be the heirs to the ancient wisdom the 'Chaldeans, the Magi, the Gymnosophists, and the Platonists had taught.'[99] This had been the heritage of the 'darker Sons of Magic'[100] which Mejnour believed had been lost to the modern Rosicrucians. It is likely that Bulwer shared this belief, since he described the Rosicrucians to Jennings as imposters. He reveals his knowledge of this mysterious fraternity when he writes to Jennings that the uninitiated would not even recognise the name of this organisation. The old man provides another hint about the older brotherhood when he dismisses 'the mysteries of your Rosicrucians, and your fraternities' as 'mere child's play to the jargon of the Platonists.'[101] Here he seems to be referring to the transmission of ancient lore revived by the Neoplatonists, who had adapted Plato's philosophy to mysticism. In *Zanoni*, no clear distinction is made between Platonism and Neoplatonism.

The manuscript is indebted to Plato's *Phædrus*, which formulates four stages of divine madness. These are the prophetic (*mantike*), initiatory (*telestike*), poetic (*poetike*) and erotic (*erotike*). The *Phædrus* is also renowned for its famous passage on the transcendent idealism of the soul. This links up the relationship of the artist to the ideal and actual, which is of central importance to *Zanoni*. As the old man points out, 'the artist of the higher schools must make the broadest distinction between the Real and the True, – in other words, between the imitation of actual life, and the exaltation of Nature into the Ideal.'[102]

The spoof, *The Dweller of the Threshold* by Sir Ed— D L—tt—n B—lw—r, ridicules Bulwer's veneration of the ideal. It includes a brief lecture on aesthetics delivered to Bulwer by a young Italian boy he has employed to black his boots. Later on, Bulwer suspects that this boy is his son and thus resolves to act towards him 'not like a Father, not like a Guardian, not like a Friend — but like a Philosopher!'[103] Here, Bulwer's unwarranted neglect of an illegitimate child is turned into a comment on the state of his unhappy marriage and mistreatment of his wife. Even his political career is not spared ridicule: 'No one who heard the Baronet that night, in his sarcastic and withering speech on the Drainage and Sewerage Bill, would have recognised the Lover of the Ideal and the Philosopher of the Beautiful.'[104] Finally, the dweller of the threshold is summed up by the vitriolic satirist who describes the initiation of the Italian boy, described as a 'brave child with the Optic'[105] who gazed into the 'Unfathomable Mystery'[106] of the Brotherhood of the Rosy Cross. In a low sweet voice the presiding Rosicrucian declares that 'the real is the sublime and beautiful' and 'the only Ideal is the Ridiculous and Homely.'[107]

Ridicule aside, Bulwer's contribution to the Rosicrucian novel continued Mary Shelley's task of transporting it from the Gothic nether regions to the aerial province of the Romantic writer. He achieved this transition by grafting the Romantic preoccupation with the actual and the ideal onto the Rosicrucian pursuit of the elixir of life.

The Elixir of Life and the Dweller of the Threshold

The concept of an elixir of immortality appealed to the Romantic artist and Rosicrucian sage alike. Even though the idea of perpetual youth and beauty was bound up with the aesthetics of Romanticism, the notion of an immortality dedicated to the pursuit of knowledge had been propagated by Enlightenment figures such as Condorcet, who declares in *Zanoni*: 'Life, I grant, cannot be made eternal; but it may be prolonged almost indefinitely.'[108] Condorcet believed that the brevity of the human life-span, as well as the absence of a common language, hampered the pursuit and accumulation of knowledge.[109] He expands on these theories in the novel during a meeting of intellectuals attended by Zanoni and the prophet Cazotte, who was involved with the Cabalistic order of Saint Martines de Pasqualis.

Significantly, the Rosicrucians as represented by Zanoni have overcome the obstacles to knowledge outlined by Condorcet. Glyndon notices that, in addition to an ability to prolong his life, Zanoni has a perfect, if not uncanny, command over foreign languages. He recalls the writings of a Rosicrucian apologist, John Bringeret, who had asserted that all the languages of the world were known to the genuine Brotherhood of the Rosy Cross.[110] The manifestos look back beyond Babel to the idea of a common language which is communicated in the *Book of Nature*. The Cabalistic idea that language was an integral part of nature and that the cosmos had been created through the spoken word was the forerunner of this aspect of Rosicrucian pansophy. From his observations of Zanoni's proficiency in languages, Glyndon wonders: 'Did Zanoni belong to this mystical Fraternity, who, in an earlier age, boasted of secrets of which the Philosopher's Stone was but the least?'[111]

In *Zanoni*, the dual properties of the philosopher's stone are examined. The first argument concerns the role of the philosopher's stone in the process of transmuting base metal into gold. The contribution made by alchemists towards some of the greatest discoveries in science is also recognised: 'the Philosopher's Stone itself has seemed no visionary chimera to some of the soundest chemists that even the present century has produced.'[112] Glyndon has been drawn towards the Brotherhood of the Rosy Cross in the hope of learning more about the secret of transmutation and life-extension. His attraction may be hereditary, since his ancestor is reputed to have been an alchemist and hermetic philosopher who exceeded the 'allotted boundaries of mortal existence'[113] and halted the ageing process.

Mejnour assures Glyndon that his ancestor attained the secret, though he chose not to prolong his life indefinitely because he did not want to outlive his great-grandchild ('he died rather than survive the only thing he loved').[114] But he is emphatic that the secrets he seeks only involve a shrewd understanding of nature:

> All that we [the adepti, Mejnour and Zanoni] profess to do is but this – to find out the secrets of the human frame, to know why the parts ossify and the blood stagnates, and to apply continual preventatives to the effects of Time. This is not Magic; it is the Art of Medicine rightly understood. In our order we hold most no-

> ble – first, that knowledge which elevates the intellect; secondly, that which preserves the body.[115]

It may be a significant factor in Glyndon's failure as a neophyte that he values the secret of immortality over and above its accompanying wisdom and knowledge. By concentrating on the attainment of the superficial, Glyndon underestimates the more profound benefits of the elixir, for 'To quaff the inner life, is to see the outer life; to live in defiance of time, is to live in the whole. He who discovers the elixir, discovers what lies in space.'[116] Glyndon is so eager to benefit from the elixir that he attempts to short-cut the period of apprenticeship which Mejnour has prepared for him. After teaching Glyndon the works of the 'glorious dupes ... Hermes, and Albert, and Paracelsus,'[117] all of whom have died, Mejnour then leads him towards unrecorded esoteric knowledge including Pythagorean numerology and the chemistry of heat, the agent for renewal. Mejnour delays the final stages of his pupil's training in order to increase Glyndon's self-discipline and control. Full preparation for drinking the elixir was considered vital, since alchemists believed that otherwise it could act as a poison to the unprepared. Then, we are told, 'the philosopher will carry about with him, not the elixir, but the poison.'[118] Ironically, in these circumstances, the elixir of life could even accelerate the ageing process. But the greatest hazard of all lies in the half-prepared neophyte's inability to control the fear generated by his ordeal. For Glyndon, the terror materialises in the form of the Guardians of the Threshold, who are demons intent on preventing the unprepared from attaining the absolute. Glyndon illegally breaks into Mejnour's room and prematurely consumes the elixir, but finds that he is unable to subdue the power of the malevolent forces which he has attracted to himself. Because Glyndon wants the secret of immortality to increase his own sensual enjoyment, he becomes the victim of his own selfish desires, which are symbolised by the fiends. An onlooker has already condemned him for breaking his vow of chastity with a peasant girl, Fillide:

> Oh, pupil of Mejnour! oh, would-be-Rosicrucian-Platonist-Magian – I know not what! I am ashamed of thee! What, in the names of Averroes, and Burri, and Agrippa, and Hermes, have become of thy austere contemplations?[119]

Mejnour criticises Glyndon in much stronger terms in an important passage where he makes a distinction between the false adept and the true:

> Dost thou not comprehend, at last, that it needs a soul tempered, and purified, and raised, not by external spells, but by its own sublimity and valour, to pass the threshold, and disdain the foe? Wretch! all my science avails nothing for the rash, for the sensual – for him who desires our secrets but to pollute them to gross enjoyments and selfish vice? How have the impostors and sorcerers of the earlier times perished by their very attempt to penetrate the mysteries that should purify, and not deprave! They have boasted of the philosopher's stone, and died in rags; of the immortal elixir, and sank to their grave, gray before their time. Legends tell you, that the fiend rent them into fragments. Yes; the fiend of their own unholy desires and criminal designs! What they coveted thou covetest; and if thou hadst the wings of a seraph, thou couldst soar not from the slough of thy mortality. Thy desire for knowledge, but petulant presumption; thy thirst for happiness but the diseased longing for the unclean and muddied waters of corporeal pleasure; thy very love, which usually elevates even the mean, a passion that calculates treason, amidst the first glow of lust; – *thou,* one of us! Thou, a brother of the August Order![120]

False seekers such as Melmoth in Maturin's novel and Margrave in *A Strange Story* are destroyed eventually by their own corrupt desires. Although Glyndon does not completely destroy himself he does in fact attract the wrath of a fiend which symbolises the negative force of his frustrated desire. Nevertheless he would have experienced a sense of frustration even if his wish for immortality had been gratified, because the realisation of perpetual life cannot cure him of relentless desire. In Glyndon's case, the philosopher's stone is symbolic of yearning being tantamount to desire for its own sake. Thus the possession of the *elixir vitæ* will never satisfy the kind of individual who will always be consumed by longings. Zanoni draws attention to this state of perpetual dissatisfaction in his reply to Glyndon's enquiry about his failure as a neophyte:

> why to thee have been only the penance and the terror – the Threshold and the Phantom? Vain man! look to the commonest elements of the common learning. Can every tyro at his mere wish and will become a mas-

> ter? – can the student, when he has bought his Euclid, become a Newton? ... yea, can yon pale tyrant, with all the parchment-laws of a hundred system-shapers, and the pikes of his dauntless multitude, carve, at his will, a constitution not more vicious than the one which the madness of a mob could overthrow?[121]

As the final image suggests, this is the failed idealism which can set into motion the forces of collective tyranny, which Bulwer illustrated through the degeneration of the French Revolutionary ideal. Theodor Adorno and Max Horkheimer, who looked at the pattern of revolution from a different standpoint in *Dialectic of Enlightenment,* concluded that 'The spirit of enlightenment replaced the fire and rack by the stigma it attached to all irrationality, because it led to corruption.'[122] Similarly, Bulwer highlights the tragic consequences which spring from the artificial separation of reason and faith by drawing parallels between the fictional incidents in *Zanoni* and the train of historical events leading up to the Reign of Terror.

The French Revolution and the Failed Ideal

It is significant that Bulwer, the last Rosicrucian novelist of any note, set his novel in the Enlightenment, the period during which the first Rosicrucian novel, *St Leon,* was written. The intellectual trends governing this era, like those influencing Renaissance Neoplatonism, seemed to invite the separation of reason from sentiment. In abstract terms, human frailties and weaknesses were cast aside for the pursuit of higher knowledge in the fallacious belief that rationality must remain unhampered by instinctive or irrational impulses. This had also been the error of mystics and seekers after spiritual enlightenment who, along the lines of the ideological constructs contained within *Zanoni,* had sought the ideal through the exclusion of the actual. The message of Bulwer's Rosicrucian novel is that the two states are inseparable and integral, since true enlightenment may only be achieved by acknowledging this fusion. Thus a parallel may be drawn between the role of the aspiring Rosicrucian adept and that of the political revolutionary.

Bulwer's treatment of the French Revolution in *Zanoni* takes place on a spiritual level. This was not unusual since in the minds of a number of prominent thinkers such as Blake, the mystical significance of the French Revolution was inseparable from its historic dimension. But for Blake, and many other onlookers, the glorious promise of the Revolution as a harbinger to a golden age eventually turned into a dark hiatus in the spiritual history of mankind. In Blake's poem *The French Revolution* (1791), one of the villains laments the departure of religion, which has been outlawed by the rationality of the Revolution:

> ... and God, so long worshipped, departs like a lamp
> Without oil; for a curse is heard hoarse through the
> land, from a godless race
> Descending to beasts.[123]

For Bulwer, the Revolution of France was 'that hideous mockery of human aspirations.' Its atheism had taken on the trappings of a fanatical religion spawned from 'the most stubborn of all bigotries – the fanaticism of unbelief.'[124] Robespierre's attack in *Zanoni* on the suppression of religion is a response to this anomaly:

> Who then invested you with the mission to announce to the people that there is no God? – What advantage find you in persuading man that nothing but blind force presides over his destinies, and strikes hap-hazard both crime and virtue?[125]

Bulwer was sufficiently interested in the implications of the Revolution to produce a treatise entitled *The Reign of Terror: Its Causes and Results,*[126] where he argues that the great experiment in liberty had turned into the antithesis of itself and, like the titan Saturn, had started to devour its own children. This image of the serpent eating its own tail is a circular image of the self-destruction which gained momentum during the Reign of Terror. The internal conflict of the French Revolution effected a barrier between reason and faith, the actual and the ideal. In Cabalistic terms, such ideologies accelerated the Fall of mankind into greater division. The Rosicrucians aimed to arrest this process and reintegrate fallen mankind. Some mystics welcomed the French Revolution as a prelude to the moment of this integration. But Zanoni, the true visionary, is quick to recognise that, since the Revolution took shape from the artificial division of the actual and the ideal, then it is unlikely to act as an agent for unification. According to Hegel, the tragedy of the French Revolution lay in its paradoxical nature which embodied a faith without content. The residue of this was a sense of sheer yearning, since its inner truth consisted of an empty kernel. In his treatise, Bulwer shows how the facade of religious tolerance disintegrates, thus revealing the scourges of partisan persecution:

> It was then the period, when a feverish spirit of change was working its way to that hideous mockery of human aspiration, the Revolution of France .... Need I remind the reader, that while that was the day for polished scepticism and affected wisdom, it was the day also for the most egregious credulity and the most mystical superstitions, – the day in which magnetism and magic found converts amongst the disciples of Diderot, – when prophecies were current in every mouth, – when the salon of a philosophical deist was converted into an Heraclea, in which necromancy professed to conjure up the shadows of the dead – when the Crosier and the Book were ridiculed, and Mesmer and Cagliostro were believed.[127]

For Bulwer, the French Revolution encapsulates the 'False Ideal that knows no God,'[128] a concept endorsed by the materialistic philosophers. Antagonistic towards those Enlightened thinkers whom he regards 'not as philosophers rejoicing in the advent of light, but as ruffians exulting in the annihilation of law,'[129] Bulwer blames the Terror on the 'philosophizing excuses and argumentative dogmas'[130] of the philosophers who have opened up the floodgates of absolute freedom, which Hegel points out removes the antithesis between the universal and individual will.[131] The removal of all moral restraint paves the way for domination by the will of those who are intent upon destruction. According to Bulwer, these liberties had been sanctioned by the Encyclopaedists, whose practical philosophy reduced egotism to a system, a recipe for the metamorphosis of freedom into tyranny. In this way, the absolute freedom preached by the revolutionaries may be seen to contain the seeds of totalitarianism.[132]

The transition of the revolutionary to a new form of tyrant may be represented allegorically in the downfall of the false magus who succumbs to the power of his own selfish desires. In the following passage from *Zanoni*, Bulwer compares the paths of the Rosicrucian aspirant and the agent for revolutionary change:

> And what in truth are these would-be builders of a new world? Like the students who have vainly struggled after our supreme science, they have attempted what is beyond their power; they have passed from this solid earth of usages and forms, into the land of shadow; and its loathsome keeper has seized them as its prey.[133]

The loathsome keeper Bulwer refers to above is the monster of the Reign of Terror, who is the 'dim shapelessness going before the men of blood, and marshalling their way.'[134] This corresponds to the 'Dweller of the Threshold' who challenges the neophyte working towards Enlightenment along a Rosicrucian path. Glyndon is overcome by terror when confronted by the fiend, described in *Zanoni* as the 'Ghostly One that dwells on the Threshold, and whose victims are the souls that would *aspire*, and can only *fear*.'[135] Similarly, the revolutionaries in France fight for ideals which later degenerate into fear, epitomised by the Reign of Terror. According to Mejnour, on a spiritual level the individual cannot soar but will remain earth-bound 'for FEAR is the attraction of man to earthiest earth.'[136] It was this fear and superstition which defeated the noble revolutionary principles of equality and freedom, reducing them to that close-knit option: 'Fraternity or Death.' Glyndon's downfall is also symptomatic of the erosion of idealism. Bulwer's intention to parallel the fates of the spiritual seeker and the political revolutionary is evident from the way in which he describes Robespierre's downfall in the language of the failed neophyte: '*He,* and not the starry Magician, [is] the *real* Sorcerer! And round *his* last hours gather the Fiends he raised!'[137] Bulwer completes the equation by addressing Glyndon in terms appropriate to Robespierre, thus recognising that Glyndon's desire for power is similar to that of the megalomaniac desires of a tyrant who is consumed by his own hunger for power. [138]

The revolutionary who only succeeds in throwing up a dictator is little better than the failed neophyte who has released against himself the negative forces of his own frustrated desires. Glyndon, who is blinded by his own desire for adeptship, is also 'dazzled by the dawn of the Revolution,' and fails to see that:

> In that Heliacal Rising heralding the new sun before which all vapours were to vanish, stalked from their graves in the feudal ages all the phantoms that had flitted before the eyes of Paracelsus and Agrippa.[139]

The Terror eventually destroys Zanoni, who sacrifices himself for Viola, knowing that on the next day she will be freed. Liberated into immortality through death, Zanoni ascends to the regions of eternal sunshine in a Dantean vision of the Apocalypse. In doing so, he fulfils his own credo, imparted to Glyndon, that the prolongation of life becomes unimportant to those who have attained sublime knowledge.

Glyndon's tragic flaw as a neophyte may be traced back to his pursuit of the analytic rather than of the synthetic. Through the act of separation, the secular and spiritual seekers seek the ideal to the exclusion of the actual. As Zanoni himself has discovered, there is an inbuilt hazard for the immortal, since 'even the error of our lofty knowledge was but the forgetfulness of the weakness, the passions, and the bonds, which the death we so vainly conquered only can purge away.'[140] Nevertheless, while Zanoni is portrayed as the true sage who achieves the absolute, Mejnour is conceived as a more restricted being who is incapable of making the supreme sacrifice of self for another. Having purged away his human frailties, passions and desires, he has made himself indifferent to whether his knowledge produces weal or woe, and is content to remain the mechanical instrument of a more benevolent will, saying 'I live but in knowledge – I have no life in mankind.'[141] This one-sidedness, which was also the error of the revolutionaries in France, is the antithesis of the Rosicrucian ideal, evident in Zanoni's synthesis of the actual and the ideal, and enacted through his sacrificial love for Viola. By forfeiting his life for another, Zanoni believes that he will attain the true ideal and the genuine victory.

Just before his execution, Zanoni urges Mejnour to abandon the elixir of life. Even though Mejnour turns out to be the sole surviving Rosicrucian, it is Zanoni who becomes the embodiment of poetic truth after having passed through the Platonic stages of divine madness or inspiration to a level of transcendence where he renounces earthly immortality for spiritual eternity. In this way the Rosicrucian is redeemed through the realisation of the ideal, which is the ultimate synthesis of the actual and the ideal. *Zanoni* is the manifesto for a metaphysical idealism which enables the reader to glimpse the invisible ideal through the visible real. By this token alone, Bulwer has transformed himself from being merely a Romantic novelist into a magus who has mastered the art of revealing both the sacred and the profane.

Artist and Magician

Bulwer proclaimed it to be the duty of the artist to disclose the ideal or transcendent goal by invoking the sublime in human nature. Through his novels he acts as a mystagogue equating his art with the supernatural in a kind of metaphysics of Romanticism. The artist, in this context, becomes the visionary who is able to unlock the absolute. According to Bulwer:

> Art is the effort of man to express the ideas which nature suggests to him of a power above Nature, whether

> that power be within the recesses of his own being or in the Great First Cause of which Nature like himself, is but the effect. Art employs itself in the study of Nature, for the purpose of implying though but by a hint or a symbol, the supernatural.[142]

He recognised the supernatural to be a legitimate preoccupation of the Romantic artist, as a pivot between the inner nature of the individual and the outer nature of the cosmos. Accordingly the art of fiction enables the practitioner to conjure up that mystic union of the real and the ideal emulated by the Rosicrucian. The novel mediates between the dialectical opposition of the real and the ideal, since the narrative framework contains the real, at the same time giving voice to the greater abstraction of the ideal. Bulwer, in accordance with theorists such as Schelling,[143] defines art as the expression of the infinite spirit made manifest in the finite. This may be described as a form of Magic Idealism, a concept derived from Novalis, which Roger Cardinal interprets as an alchemical process fusing spirit and matter through the creative power of language:

> From the magician's point of view, to speak is not simply to voice abstract concepts, but to create literal forms out of figures of speech. Poetic utterance is after all a medium of heightened expression which seeks to give maximum reality to metaphors: the Magic Idealist is saying that metaphors become literal truth when uttered by the true poet.[144]

It is in this way that *Zanoni* becomes 'a truth for those who can comprehend it.'[145]

Friedrich Leopold Von Hardenberg (1772-1801), better known as 'Novalis,' author of *The Disciples at Sais (Die Lehrlinge zu Sais)* (1798-9) was the first Romantic theorist to evolve the theory of Magic Idealism, outlining the concept of the poet as magician. Wolf suggests that Novalis may have exerted a considerable though hitherto unrecognised influence on *Zanoni*.[146] Wolf confines his attention to the blue flower image in *Zanoni*, the symbol of the German Romantic poets which Novalis used in his novel *Heinrich von Ofterdingen* (1802). Though Wolf refers to a Jungian connection between the blue flower and the medieval alchemist's rose, he senses that the real significance of the symbol is to identify the hero, Zanoni, with the Romantic tradition. But Wolf does not emphasise the close connection between Novalis's Magic Idealism and Bulwer's concept of the Rosicrucian ideal.

Like Bulwer, Novalis believed that self-knowledge restored individuals to a sense of unity with nature. Furthermore, art could remove the veil of the finite to reveal the infinity sought by the aspirant. Romantic art, by functioning to heighten the everyday significance of things, dissolved 'the absorbing tyranny of every-day life.'[147] Because of this, the claims of the finite must remain subordinate to the demands of the infinite. Only then may a magical transformation take place which betokens the liberation of the imagination and the unity between mankind and nature. The goals which may be achieved through art, as revealed by Novalis, may also be realised through initiation. In his novel *The Disciples at Sais,* Novalis tells the story of a number of novitiates who are studying to become initiates into the mysteries of Isis at the ancient Egyptian city of Sais. Bulwer uses an extract from Schiller's version of this story in a poem entitled *The Veiled Image at Sais,* for the epigraph of his fourth book called 'The Dweller of the Threshold,' which concerns the preparation for the initiation of Glyndon:

> *Sey hinter ihm was will! Ich heb ihn auf*
> (Be behind what there may – I raise the veil)[148]

Like *Zanoni*, Novalis's *Disciples at Sais* is a fable of the mystic goal of the novitiates towards self-awareness and integration. The key to this self-knowledge concerns that which lies beyond the veil. They strive to regain the unity with nature in the face of increasing alienation, and complain of their inner being splitting into ever-increasing division.

According to Novalis, 'a true seeker never becomes old, every Eternal Quest is outside the bonds of life, and the more the outer husk withers, the clearer, the brighter, the more potently glows the kernel.'[149] By way of illustrating this point he inserts into the text a *Märchen* which tells of how Hyazinth leaves his sweetheart and homeland behind to search for a veiled maiden. He dreams that he enters the temple of Isis and, on lifting the veil that conceals the goddess, sees before him the sweetheart he has abandoned. This corresponds to the final stage of divine madness dealing with love, which is outlined in the *Phædrus*. An alternative ending to the novel lays greater stress on the theme of self-knowledge by describing how the seeker discovers only himself behind the veil of the goddess of Sais. Eventually, the seeker who lifts up the veil of forbidden knowledge is found dead by the priests behind it. The mystery and the seeker are now one.

The idea of mystic unity is central to *Zanoni*. Here we have the Hegelian reconciliation of polarities such as the actual and the ideal brought about by the hero. This synthesis illustrates the recovery of mankind from the effects of the Fall. The Romantic artist is in tune with the Rosicrucian idealist, who recognises that once the veil of the finite has been removed, then the unity between inner and outer nature will be revealed, and the correspondence between the above and below will show that nature and the human mind are one. The distinctions between macrocosm and microcosm collapse into one another in the face of the anthropocentric subjectivity of the Romantic sensibility. This is the point at which the artist-magician declares himself a god in the solipsistic exercise of his own creative powers.

The image of the artist in *Zanoni* reinforces Bulwer's romantic conception of the Rosicrucian hero. The most important example may be seen in the typology of Zanoni who represents art, in contrast to Mejnour who embodies science. It is significant that the novel is dedicated to the artist John Gibson. The author describes himself as a literary artist, while the introduction concerns the fate of the creative writer who subsequently transcribes the manuscript. The figure of the artist emerges in the opening chapter, which contains an account of the musician Gaetano Pisani and his daughter the singer Viola, who falls in love with Zanoni. There is a correlation between the artist and the Rosicrucian, since the former may be seen as a species of the real while the latter may be seen to be indicative of the ideal. These polarities are reunited in Zanoni himself, symbolically through his union with Viola. Because of the close ties between the artist and the Rosicrucian, Zanoni suggests to Glyndon that he should try to discover the answers to his quest through art rather than by joining the Rosicrucian fraternity. He asks him:

> is not there a magic also in the art you would advance? Must you not, after long study of the Beautiful that has been, seize upon new and airy combinations of a beauty that is to be? See you not that The Grander Art, whether of poet or of painter, ever seeking for the TRUE, abhors the REAL .... You would conjure the invisible beings to your charm; and what is painting but the fixing into substance the Invisible? Are you discontented with this world? This world was never genius! To exist, it must create another. What magician can do more; nay, what science can do as much? There are two avenues from the little passions and the drear calamities of earth; both lead to heaven and away from hell – Art and Science. But art is more godlike than science; science discovers, art creates .... The astronomer who catalogues the stars cannot add one atom to the

> universe, the poet can call a universe from the atom; the chemist may heal with his drugs the infirmities of the human form; the painter, or the sculptor, fixes into everlasting youth forms divine, which no disease can ravage, and no years impair.[150]

As this passage reveals, Zanoni makes a clear equation between art and magic, and reminds the artist that 'your pencil is your wand.' The notion of art as a substitute for initiation into a Rosicrucian fraternity as proposed by Zanoni to Glyndon, opens up some fascinating insights into literature and the occult. Both give expression to the whole through the particular. Also, as representations of the ideal, art and magic become gateways to the actual. This synthesis of the actual and the ideal may also be seen through the Rosicrucian novel, where the distinctions between form and content merge into a total expression of the absolute. As Bulwer explains:

> The work of art still has something in common with enchantment: it posits its own, self-enclosed area, which is withdrawn from the context of profane existence, and in which special laws apply. Just as in the ceremony the magician first of all marked out the limits of the area where the sacred powers were to come into play, so every work of art describes its own circumference which closes it off from actuality .... As an expression of totality art lays claim to the dignity of the absolute.[151]

The point of correspondence between the accomplished artist and magus is that while each may acquire the power of earthly immortality, eternal youth and beauty may become the province of both.

Perpetual youth and beauty are the themes of Bulwer's later novel, *A Strange Story*. But in contrast to *Zanoni*, where the secret of perpetual life is employed as a tool of morality, here the Rosicrucian hero abuses his occult knowledge and shows how the elixir of life may be subverted to become an instrument of moral and spiritual depravity.

A Strange Story

> Have the Rosicrucians bequeathed to you a prescription for the elixir of life?
>
> Bulwer[152]

A Strange Story contains a number of occult motifs including ritual magic, alchemical and hermetic lore and the pursuit of the elixir of life. Its main interest, however, concerns the Faustian figure, Margrave, who is determined to discover the Rosicrucian secret of immortality. Unlike *Zanoni*, with its setting during the Enlightenment in an atmosphere of illuminism and revolution, *A Strange Story* takes place during the Victorian age, dominated by the tensions existing between science and religion.

This setting provided Bulwer with an opportunity to explore the topical reason-faith dichotomy, which reworks the actual-ideal dialectic in *Zanoni*. As both novels demonstrate, the Rosicrucian mind-set provided a synthesis for such oppositions as magic and science, mysticism and rationality. *A Strange Story,* in its attempt to demystify the inexplicable, can be seen as a continuation of *Zanoni*. Furthermore, *A Strange Story* represents a traditional approach to Rosicrucian fiction by returning to the moral orthodoxies which Bulwer had abandoned in *Zanoni*. For example, in the earlier novel he had shown through Zanoni and Mejnour that earthly immortality did not necessarily lead to a state of spiritual degeneracy. But in *A Strange Story* he reverts to the formulaic view of the Rosicrucian sage as the fallen magus who has re-enacted Original Sin. In addition to this, Bulwer sets out to show 'how the supernatural resolves itself into the natural when faced and shifted.'[153] As the following synopsis will reveal, the rationalisation of the occult is central to the novel's narrative purpose.

The main character is the narrator, Allen Fenwick, a young doctor who has taken up the practice of Julius Faber, now retired and gone abroad. From the outset, Fenwick establishes his ideological position as a materialist and arch-empiricist. In medicine, Fenwick professes to be the pupil of François Broussais, while in metaphysics he claims to be the disciple of Etienne Bonnot de Condillac.[154] As a consequence, Fenwick strongly opposes the views of his immediate rival in the medical profession, Dr Lloyd, who ardently believes in the reality of somnambular clairvoyance and mesmerism. Lloyd has the support of the most lucrative section of the local community. These are the inhabitants of Abbey Hill, whose Cranford-gentility is orchestrated by the formidable Mrs Poyntz. Through her influence, the patronage of the Hill is transferred to Fenwick, whose victory over the now demoralised Lloyd precipitates the premature death of his rival. Prior to this, Lloyd has denounced Fenwick as a false scientist who was willing to bow down before the gods of bigotry. He accuses him:

> You are of the stuff of which inquisitors are made. You cry that truth is profaned when your dogmas are questioned. In your shallow presumption you have meted the dominions of nature, and where your eye halts its vision, you say, 'There nature must close;' in the bigotry which adds crime to presumption, you would stone the discoverer who, in annexing new realms to her chart, unsettles your arbitrary landmarks. Verily, retribution shall await you! In those spaces which your sight has disdained to explore you shall yourself be a lost and bewildered straggler.[155]

Even more ominously, Lloyd warns Fenwick that 'The gibbering phantoms are gathering round you.'[156] This imagery is suggestive of the sinister Dweller of the Threshold in *Zanoni*. After dismissing these warnings, Fenwick falls in love with one of Lloyd's distant relatives, the heiress Lilian Ashleigh. Her spiritual and frail sensibility is the antithesis of Fenwick's robust materialism. He perceives her as a delicate being from another world who is in touch with forces and energies existing beyond the limitations of his empirical and scientific outlook. Lilian, who frequently falls prey to a nervous illness ostensibly activated by her innate nervous disposition, is particularly susceptible to the presence of a young man called Margrave, who exudes an animal energy and magnetic influence over everyone he meets. His radiance and beauty are accompanied by a wide and erudite knowledge. These qualities combine to make him a fascinating and enigmatic character. It is revealed later that he is an adept of Eastern magic whose youth has been renewed by the elixir of life. But unfortunately, Margrave does not possess the formula for the potion. Therefore he needs to acquire Fenwick's scientific knowledge in order to procure the elixir. Fenwick's scepticism, however, makes him unwilling to embark on such a project, which he compares to the search for a unicorn or some other mythological being.

Instead, Fenwick believes that the inexplicable should be subjected to the rigour of rational scientific explanation. This attitude is backed up by his predecessor, Dr Faber, who has recently returned from abroad. During the course of lengthy philosophical dialogues,[157] Faber encourages Fenwick to respond to the strange happenings which have overtaken him by persisting in his rigidly empirical approach. These arguments are supported by quotations from Beattie's *Essay on Truth,* David Brewster's *Letters on Natural Magic,* William Hamilton's *Lectures on Metaphysics and Logic* and Muller's *Physiology of the Senses.* Conversely, Margrave tries to break down Fenwick's resistance to the visionary through the mediumistic Lilian, who is receptive to his powers. Gradually Fenwick's screen of common sense disintegrates, thus exposing him to a barrage of psychic phenomena. Margrave is not responsible for all of Fenwick's visionary experiences, for some are invoked by Sir Philip Derval, a Rosicrucian and local aristocrat who, until recently, has been travelling in the East.

Derval maintains that Margrave's true identity is that of Louis Grayle, an elderly and unscrupulous occultist who has murdered the Rosicrucian sage Haroun of Aleppo for the elixir of life. Though Grayle has been restored to youth, he has failed to secure the formula for the compound. Furthermore, he has lost his soul in the attempt. It is possible that his name 'Grayle' is intended as a pun on the Holy Grail for the purpose of making an ironic comment on the degeneration of the search for the ideal. His spiritual downfall is revealed by Derval to Fenwick, who, while in a trance-state, sees Margrave-Grayle as a man without a soul. Following this revelation, Fenwick agrees to help Derval bring Margrave to the authorities, but before this takes place Derval himself is murdered. Convinced that his death has been brought about by Margrave, Fenwick resolves to escape from the evil influence which frequently haunts him in the guise of the *Scin-Læca* or shining corpse of Scandinavian folklore. Fenwick leaves the country for Australia, taking Lilian as his wife. In the hope that Fenwick will help him find the formula for the elixir, Margrave eventually tracks him down. Now that the effects of the potion are wearing off, revealing Margrave to be old and infirm, he grows desperate for the secret of immortal youth. Reluctantly Fenwick agrees to help him perform the occult ceremony to achieve his rejuvenation. But as the elixir is boiled and the moment approaches, the demonic powers turn against Margrave and succeed in overturning the cauldron. Fenwick, however, survives this ordeal to be reunited with Lilian, who has been restored to normality. Having abandoned his earlier scepticism, Fenwick is now willing to believe in the existence of an immortal soul.

The Metaphysics of Immortality

A Strange Story presents a powerful philosophical argument for the immortality of the soul. The novel ends on the same note as *Zanoni* in its advocacy of spiritual immortality as a state preferable to infinite life-extension. Much against the advice of Dickens, Bulwer set out to explain the theoretical basis of his novel in his preface.[158] He pointed out that the pattern of the book correlated to the intellectual development of the French thinker Maine de Biran, whose brand of anti-empirical metaphysics had attracted him. Biran had not always been receptive to such visionary dimensions of existence, having had to proceed towards an understanding of mystical traditions from an originally empirical standpoint. Bulwer regarded Biran as representative of the evolution of European thought during the nineteenth century.

The beginning of Biran's career reflected the influence of the Enlightenment, as characterised by a blind faith in Condillac and materialism. In *A Strange Story*, Biran's starting point corresponds to Fenwick's initial adherence to Condillac's mechanistic and materialistic doctrines. At this stage, intellect is represented as having separated all its enquiries from any spiritual or physical consideration. But gradually, like Biran, Fenwick moves away from materialism towards a more vitalist view of the world which had become disseminated through Condillac's theory of the senses. Finally Fenwick and Biran acquire the wisdom which enables them to embrace 'the simple faith which unites the philosopher and infant.'[159] Thus, through his protagonist, Fenwick, Bulwer embarks on an exposition of the three stages of human evolution, the animal or instinctive nature, the rationality which is mediated through self-consciousness, and finally the life which exists in the soul. Forging a link between Biran's metaphysics and the career of his protagonist, he shows how romance conducts its 'bewildered hero,' Fenwick, towards the same goal to which philosophy leads its luminous student. Using Biran's words, Bulwer explains this evolutionary process:

> The relations (*rapports*) which exist between the elements and the products of the three lives of Man are the subjects of meditation, the fairest and finest, but also the most difficult. The Stoic Philosophy shows us all which can be most elevated in active life; but it makes abstraction of the animal nature, and absolutely fails to recognise all which belongs to the life of the spirit. Its practical morality is beyond the forces of humanity. Christianity alone embraces the whole Man. It dissimulates none of the sides of his nature, and avails itself of his miseries and his weakness in order to conduct him to his end in showing him all the want that he has of a succour more exalted.[160]

This Christian hermeneutic also provides an exegesis of the ending of *Zanoni*, where the supreme Rosicrucian quest is measured in terms of Christian eschatology. Though this has obvious implications for the followers of Christian Rosencreutz, it also identifies Zanoni rather than Mejnour as the true Rosicrucian type. Fenwick, however, engages with both, since initially he embraces Mejnour's empirical outlook before acquiring Zanoni's spirituality. Thus Fenwick eventually succeeds in becoming the fully integrated individual, unlike the 'sensuous, soulless Nature'[161] of Margrave or the purely ethereal spirituality of Lilian, who is described as 'the erring but pure-thoughted visionary, seeking overmuch on this earth to separate soul from mind, till innocence itself is led astray by a phantom, and reason is lost in the space between earth and the stars.'[162] Contrary to Jacobi's idea (quoted by Bulwer in his preface)[163] that only through reason may the supernatural be revealed, Lilian's mystical experiences arise from the separation of faith and reason. Thus the dislocation of the individual's spiritual self from the real is indicative of the necessity for that union between the actual and the ideal which provides the conclusion for both *Zanoni* and *A Strange Story*. This fusion between the actual and the ideal was noted enthusiastically by Chauncey Hare Townsend who, after having sent Bulwer 'a brain-message by mesmeric post,'[164] wrote to him:

> To strike at once the diapason of life which includes the two extremes of the Ideal and the Real was, in itself, a grand idea. To idealise the Real and to make the Ideal seem Real, is a triumph of art in the execution of your Idea.[165]

In *Zanoni*, interaction between the actual and the ideal takes place on two levels: first in the union between Viola and Zanoni, and then in terms of the hero's inner self. These two levels complement one another since now Zanoni finds that he achieves through love the mystic unity he has been seeking which will enable him to enter the absolute. In both *A Strange Story* and *Zanoni*, marriage symbolises the unity between the actual and the ideal. In *A Strange Story,* the synthesis between reason and faith is symbolised by the marriage of Fenwick and Lilian. At the same time, Fenwick undergoes a sea-change which involves the acceptance of a metaphysical dimension to his existence, coinciding with his acknowledgement of an immortal soul. Until this point, however, Fenwick is shown to oppose as unreal all that refers to the spirit. In this way he becomes a caricature of the Enlightened thinker who looks to the disenchantment of the cosmos. Such bare schematisation is prepared to purge the world of all spiritual forces, for as Fenwick has boasted, 'I felt as if it were a royal delight to scorn Earth and its opinions, brave Hades and its spectres.'[166] He formulates his views into a system designed to attack German metaphysicians, whom he regards as the chief exponents of the dangerous mysticism of pseudo-philosophy. Fenwick describes his methodology in the following passage:

> I clamped and soldered dogma to dogma in the links of my tinkered logic, till out from my page, to my own complacent eye, grew Intellectual Man, as the pure formation of his material sense; mind, or what is called soul, born from and nurtured by them alone; through them to act, and to perish with the machine they moved.[167]

Fenwick's reliance on sense-experience alone engenders the ascendancy of reason, which in turn excludes belief in the existence of the soul. This is a denial of the *spiritus mundi* of the Renaissance Neoplatonists mentioned earlier. But more immediately, Fenwick's conceptual position and his ensuing doubts encapsulate the Victorian crisis of faith and rising scepticism, which had been exacerbated by the Darwinian Revolution. Darwinism had made a major impact upon Bulwer's fiction, particularly *A Strange Story*, which had appeared two years after the publication of Darwin's *Origin of Species*. In this context, frequent references are made to sceptics like the evolutionist Lamarck, and Laplace, the theorist of celestial mechanics.[168] Throughout the novel, Bulwer makes overtures towards Darwin's belief in a definitive evolutionary theory which does not accommodate a belief in the immortality of the soul.

Science and Sorcery

For Bulwer the controversies and debates surrounding the Darwinian question invited comparison with the problems relating to the spiritual evolution of the magus culminating in the Rosicrucian ideal. This may be seen through a number of similarities between Fenwick and the occultist Margrave, who both realise that the elixir of life is the inheritance of the Rosicrucians. Each character is polarised between reason and faith, the actual and the ideal. Fenwick has rejected his spiritual self through the mechanisation of his own soul, while Margrave, by losing his, has become a purely mechanical and heartless being. Each spiritually condemning himself, Margrave has abandoned his soul while Fenwick has denied his immortal existence. In a curious twist at the end of the story, Fenwick eventually achieves the immortality which Margrave has sought. These two characters have existed in a strange symbiotic relationship ever since Margrave has recognised that he needs science to bring about his Rosicrucian immortality. But Fenwick rejects Rosicrucianism and the supernatural in the mistaken belief that the frontiers of 'legitimate science' may not be extended to the 'fables of wizards'[169] thus refusing to descend from the 'Academe of decorous science' to the level of a 'slumbering sibyl.'[170] In Bulwer's eyes, magic could be validated in the new scientific age, since it contained agencies of communication analogous to the boasted powers of the Renaissance philosophical magicians.

The partnership between magic and science which had been dissolved during the Enlightenment had been upheld by the Rosicrucian fraternity who regarded them as inseparable. As mentioned earlier, Yates identifies the Renaissance scientist as the true Rosicrucian type, and certainly the figure of the scientist-magus dominated the Invisible College. This centre of learning was later eclipsed by the emergence of the Royal Society, whose fellows adhered to an analytical approach to knowledge, excluding magic in favour of the new Baconian scientific method.[171] Such a strict demarcation between magic and science was contrary to the occult world-view, an outlook incorporating a belief in an animated universe where the cosmic forces could be tapped by ritual magic, similar to the 'vril' energy or 'atmospheric magnetism' described by Bulwer in *A Coming Race*.[172] Once again, the polarisation between traditional magic and modern science may be viewed in terms of the opposition between the ideal and the actual, which could be reconciled through Rosicrucianism. Bulwer endorsed a synthetic approach to knowledge and felt optimistic that some scientists were willing to acknowledge their debt to magical traditions. In *A Strange Story* Bulwer tries to converge the views of a contemporary chemist, Liebig, with the conclusions reached by the alchemist and Rosicrucian precursor Van Helmont in his treatise *Long Life*.[173] Both Liebig and Van Helmont believed that the animating spirit of life may be found in a gaseous substance.[174] According to Bulwer, Van Helmont claimed to have rationalised spiritual existence through his discovery of invisible bodies or gases. Margrave, however, by assuming that the secret of the *elixir vitæ* must be contained in some gaseous substance, in fact overlooks the spiritual preparation to be made by the individual before partaking of such sacred knowledge. The correlation between the attainment of the elixir of life and some chemical reaction relates to the tripartite structure of the novel, since Derval's description of the three stages of mind, the instinctive, intellectual and spiritual, corresponds to the three states of matter – solid, liquid and gas. Margrave's mechanistic approach, however, sets out to reduce the mystery of the *elixir vitae* to a formula which he claims chemistry should not despair of producing. Such a reductionist notion resembles Balzac's suggestion that the absolute may be found in a test-tube.[175]

Bulwer's message is that reason should not banish spirituality, and that a balance should be retained between the two. As a way of demonstrating how individuals automatically reach for this equilibrium in their lives, he gives the example of the sceptic, Lord Herbert of Cherbury, who while writing a book against the reality of divine revelation, asked for a sign from heaven to assure him of his creator's approval.[176] Such incidents do not merely illustrate human inconsistency but actively demonstrate the complementary workings of the rational and irrational sides of human nature, as pointed out earlier by Godwin. Similarly, the true scientist would be misguided to cut him or herself off from the springs of magic and mysticism. Ideologically, Biran's brand of empirical metaphysics reconciles these polarities. Another thinker who embraced both science and magic was Newton. Margrave makes this point by asking 'did Newton ... hold the creed of the alchemists in scorn?'[177] He then goes on to cite Descartes's interest in rationality and the occult in support of his argument for the material reality of the elixir of immortality:

> that other great sage, inferior only to Newton – the calculating doubt-weigher, Descartes – had he not believed in the yet nobler hope of the alchemists, – believed in some occult nostrum or process by which human life could attain to the age of the Patriarchs?[178]

In a footnote, Bulwer describes how Descartes over a period of twenty-four years sought to obtain membership of the Brotherhood of the Rosy Cross but was unable to discover a single member who could introduce him. The relevance of Descartes to *A Strange Story* lies in the Cartesian distinction between spirit and matter, which is upheld by Fenwick at the beginning of the novel and then later abandoned. In terms of the plot, the interaction between magic and science is essential to Margrave's campaign to enlist Fenwick's help in manufacturing the elixir of life. Since Margrave believes that the secret is purely a chemical compound, he sets out to try and convince Fenwick that the legend of immortality has some scientific basis. Fenwick, however, persists in dismissing this as the 'old illusion of the medieval empires'[179] while Margrave insists 'the elixir of life is no fable,' for:

> That elixir was bright in my veins when we last met. From that golden draught of the life – spring of joy I took all that can gladden creation. What sage would not have exchanged his wearisome knowledge for my

> lusty revels with Nature? What monarch would not have bartered his crown, with its brain-ache of care, for the radiance that circled my brows, flashing out from the light that was in me?[180]

The discourse of the above echoes the speech traditionally made by the Rosicrucian aspirant before partaking of the *elixir vitæ*. In common with St Leon and Melmoth, Margrave has many attributes of the Rosicrucian sage, such as an erudite knowledge extending to a firsthand experience of events which predate his own natural life-span. Nevertheless, Bulwer emphasises that Margrave is not a member of the Rose Cross fraternity, even though his longevity and power over nature lead Fenwick to believe that he must be a member of the brotherhood. But later, Fenwick doubts his adversary's Rosicrucian powers while observing the innocent appearance of the sleeping Margrave. Relying on sense-impressions, Fenwick asks himself, 'was this indeed, the potent magician whom I had so feared! – this the guide to the Rosicrucian's secret of life's renewal, in whom, but an hour or two ago, my fancies gulled my credulous trust?'[181] It is clear, nonetheless, that Margrave does not possess the formula for the elixir of life, otherwise he would not be soliciting the assistance of Fenwick. Apart from this, there are clear indications that Margrave is in fact a travesty of the true Rosicrucian type. For example, Fenwick detects major moral defects in his nature, since Margrave has no sense of compassion or remorse. His instinctive cruelty is indicative of a nature red in tooth and claw. On one occasion, by ruthlessly killing a squirrel that bites him, he reveals himself to be as 'callous to the sufferings of another as a deer who deserts and butts from him a wounded comrade.'[182] When Derval condemns Margrave as a monster without metaphor, he is assigning him literally to the first stage of human development. This is the instinctive or animal level which cannot house a human soul. Margrave, after murdering Aleppo, has forfeited his soul, hence his intense hunger for life and inordinate fear of death. He expresses the horror of having bartered away the promise of life beyond the grave, telling Fenwick: 'could you live but an hour of my life you would know how horrible a thing it is to die!'[183] Because of the quality of his human existence, Margrave dreads the prospect of death. In view of his soulless and perpetual existence, it is predictable that he fails to recognise that the *elixir vitæ* has a spiritual dimension. Instead he attempts to subvert the Rosicrucian ideal of mortal immortality for his own selfish gain:

> When the mortal deliberately allies himself to the spirits of evil, he surrenders the citadel of his being to the

> guard of its enemies; and those who look from within can only dimly guess what passes within the precincts abandoned to Powers whose very nature we shrink to contemplate, lest our mere gaze should invite them.[184]

Margrave's desire to arrest this downward moral spiral is indicated by his resolution to reform his character and re-enter the world as its benefactor, provided that he can retake the elixir. Yet even before Margrave commits the blasphemy of stealing it from the Rosicrucian, Haroun, his victim has realised already that he is depraved. Significantly, Haroun refers to Margrave as 'fallen' prior to his act of taking forbidden fruit. This judgement is mirrored in Haroun's response to Margrave's request for eternal life.

> Fallen and unhappy wretch, and you ask me for prolonged life! – a prolonged curse to the world and to yourself. Shall I employ spells to lengthen the term of the Pestilence, or profane the secrets of Nature to restore vigour and youth to the failing energies of crime?[185]

From the beginning, Haroun rightly suspects that Margrave will abuse the secret of immortality. In this respect, the latter falls into the category of pseudo-Rosicrucians who possess many attributes of the brotherhood but who lack the idealism and compassion which distinguishes the virtuous sage from the charlatan. Through nature, Margrave embraces the life of the actual and rejects the idealising principle. Robert Lee Wolf suggests that Bulwer had derived the concept of Margrave from the first draft of his short story 'The Haunted and the Haunters,' where there is a description of a man who has a 'Zanoni-like (or Cagliostro-like) gift of immortality.'[186] This Gothic immortal starts out as a sixteenth-century profligate who then becomes an eighteenth-century charlatan only to end up as a nineteenth-century adventurer. He is blamed as the source of the evil haunting a house, which takes the form of a mysterious darkness not unlike the Dweller of the Threshold in *Zanoni*.

Likewise, in *A Strange Story* Margrave and his hopes of an immortal existence are dashed by the demonic forces which he unleashes as a result of his illicit quest for the secret of eternal life. As Margrave comes near to possessing the Rosicrucian secret, ironically he accelerates his own destruction. Beside the cauldron within which the elixir of life bubbles, Margrave urges Fenwick to observe the process of the *opus magnum* in its final stages, saying: 'Behold how the Rose of the alchemist's dream enlarges its blooms from the folds of its petals! I shall live, I shall live!'[187] Fenwick notes that the coruscations which have formed on the surface of the liquid are 'literally' in the shape of a rose. As mentioned previously, one of the theories regarding the etymology of the term 'Rosicrucian' is that it was a derivative from the Latinate word *rosa*, a reference to the alchemist's dew. Bulwer appears to be describing the dew or the effects of condensation which also demarcate a stage in the process of transmutation. Once the elixir is ready, it gives off a flame symptomatic not merely of its purgative quality but also of its life-giving properties, since heat was believed by the Rosicrucians to be the first principle of life. On another occasion, Fenwick has witnessed Margrave chanting a wild Persian fire-worshipping hymn to the sun. The elixir shares with fire the ability to act as an agent of annihilation or purification. But for Margrave the quest proves to be destructive. Just before the completion of the *opus magnum*, the cauldron is overturned by the phantoms of the threshold at the crucial moment when Margrave is on the verge of renewing his youth. Though not torn limb from limb by the demons in Faustian fashion, he is nevertheless destroyed, in spite of the intervention of Ayesha, who personifies nature, because he has failed to face the phantoms he has invoked. This incident parallels Glyndon's failure to pass through the initiation ordeals of the brotherhood in *Zanoni*. Glyndon is defeated by the Dweller of the Threshold, whose malevolent influence is eventually exorcised by Zanoni. In *A Strange Story*, Fenwick, like Zanoni, has been redeemed by the power of love for Lilian which has made him strong enough to withstand the stride of the demon and the hoofs of the beast. As Bulwer notes in his preface to *Night and Morning*, 'he who would arrive at the Fairy Land, must face the Phantoms.'[188] The fairy land may be seen in terms of the Rosicrucian ideal, a part of the 'Poetry of the Modern Civilisation and Daily Existence' which is 'shut out from us ... by the shadowy giants of Prejudice and Fear.'[189]

Bulwer's preoccupation with the actual and the ideal, which Hegel explored through the metaphor of the Rose and Cross, emerges through his Rosicrucian novels. Rosicrucianism as a living and historical tradition may be interpreted as the actual which is idealised in terms of fiction. Bulwer correctly anticipated that *A Strange Story* would not meet with a favourable reception because of the reading public's dislike of mysticism and allegory. Even his hopes for critical acclaim were disappointed by a number of unsympathetic reviews. The response of the *Athenæum* reviewer typified the hostilities directed at the novel by describing it as a concoction of 'magic and science, poetry and prose' which 'meet here in a sort of witch-dance. The tale will be a torment for any bystander who has not eaten of the insane root.'[190] For those who have sampled the 'insane root' of the Rosicrucian novel, the metaphor may be applied most appropriately to the *elixir vitæ* as the forbidden fruit of the Tree of Knowledge of Good and Evil.

Among the symbolic truths presented in *A Strange Story* is mankind's desire to reintegrate with nature and to become the conqueror of death. In this novel, Bulwer includes a keynote to Romantic thought: 'there in the ... new world ... man seeks to renew his own youth, and there the magician long estranged from Nature finds her [Ayesha].'[191] Through his fiction Bulwer confronted the problems of immortality, prohibited knowledge and the alienation from nature. He proved that these fundamental human problems, which are central to Rosicrucianism, could be adequately explored by the novelist through the medium of the Rosicrucian novel.

Notes

1. Bulwer, *Zanoni*, (London, 1842), preface, vii, [x]. Most of the references to *Zanoni* have been taken from the first edition of 1842. The other references come from the 1853 edition, as this contains Bulwer's dedicatory epistle to John Gibson (which was prefaced originally to the 1845 edition), the author's preface to the 1853 edition, post-script and Harriet Martineau's key *Zanoni Explained.* To avoid inconsistency, references to the 1853 edition appear alongside those referring to the 1842 edition. Unless stated otherwise, references to the 1853 edition will be contained within square brackets. Allusions to Bulwer refer to Bulwer-Lytton.
2. Kenneth Mackenzie was so convinced of Bulwer's membership that he remarked on Bulwer's ignorance of the higher Rosicrucian degrees: 'Even Lytton who knew so much was only a neophyte and could not reply when I tested him years ago.' See Ellic Howe, *The Magicians of the Golden Dawn: A Documentary History of a Magical Order* 1887-1923 (London, 1972), pp. 30 ff.
3. Robert Lee Wolf, *Strange Stories and other Explorations in Victorian Fiction* (Boston, 1971), p. 145.
4. Michael Sadleir, *Bulwer: A Panorama* (London, 1931) p. 1.
5. Ibid., p. 19.
6. Quoted by Joseph I. Fradin, 'The Absorbing Tyranny of Every-day Life: Bulwer-Lytton's *A Strange Story,' Nineteenth-Century Fiction*, 16 (June, 1961), pp. 1-16.
7. Robert Bulwer-Lytton, *The Life of Edward Bulwer, First Lord Lytton by his grandson*, 2 vols (London, 1913), p. 41. Hereafter cited as *Life* (1913).
8. Ibid., p. 40.
9. Christopher McIntosh would disagree with this, since he doubts that Jennings was ever initiated into Rosicrucianism, even though the latter had published *The Rosicrucians: Their Rites and Mysteries* (London, 1870) and *Adventure Among the Rosicrucians* (London, 1910).
10. See Wolf, *Strange Stories*, p. 234.
11. Reports of Count German's age vary. For instance, Christopher McIntosh describes how he was reputed to have possessed an elixir which had kept him alive for 400 years. Saint-German's coachman was unable to confirm this, though he admitted that the Count had changed little in the 130 years he had served him! See *The Rosy Cross Unveiled*, p. 76.
12. See E. M. Butler, *The Myth of the Magus* (Cambridge, 1948), pp. 244ff.
13. See John Senior, *The Way Down and Out: The Occult in Symbolist Literature* (New York, 1959), p. 51.
14. Bulwer, *Zanoni*, I, p. 62 [pp. 22-3n].
15. One of Pasqualis's advisers, Jean-Baptiste Willermoz, claimed to be both Reau-Croix and Rose-Cross. Reau-Croix denoted the highest degree of the order, the eleventh. The adept was identified with 'Great Adam,' who symbolised the process of reintegration with nature, which represented the ultimate aim of the rituals. For Pasqualis's ideology, see his treatise *On the Reintegration of Beings* (1899). The most famous of Saint-Martin's writings is his *Book of Errors and of Truth*, which was heavily attacked for reflecting more of the spirit of error than of truth!
16. Bulwer, *Zanoni*, I, p. 63 [p. 23].
17. Bulwer, *A Strange Story*, p. 387.
18. For a description of the meeting between Bulwer and Levi see Paul Chacornac, *Eliphas Levi: Renovateur de L'Occultisme en France* (1810-1875) (Paris, 1926), pp. 149-56.

19. Randolph describes his own version of Rosicrucianism in the following version from his book, *Eulis! The History of Love: Its Wonderous Magic, Chemistry, Rules, Laws, Modes, Moods and Rationale; Being the Third Revelation of Soul and Sex* (Ohio, 1874), which is concerned with sex magic:

> I studied Rosicrucianism, found it suggestive and loved its mysticisms. So I called myself The Rosicrucian, and gave my thought to the world as Rosicrucian thought; and lo! the world greeted with loud applause what it supposed had its origin and birth elsewhere than in the soul of P. B. Randolph .... I became practically, what I was naturally, a mystic, and in time chief of the lofty brethren; taking the clues left by the masters, and pursuing them farther than they had ever been before; actually discovering the ELIXIR OF LIFE; the universal solvent, or celestial Alkahest; the water of beauty and perpetual youth, and the philosopher's stone, – all of which this book contains; but only findable by him who searches well. Randolph, op. cit. pp. 15–16.

20. Apollonius was the hero in Christoph Martin Wieland's *Agathodamon* (1799), a book which Bulwer had read. He mentions Apollonius in the following passage from *Last Days in Pompeii*:

> Apollonius knew the language of birds, read man's thoughts in their bosoms, and walked about with a familiar spirit. He was a devil of a fellow with a devil, and induced a mob to stone a poor demon of venerable and mendicant appearance, who ... changed into a huge dog. He raised the dead, passed a night with Achilles, and when Domitian was murdered he called out aloud (though in Ephesus at the time) 'Strike the tyrant!' The end of so honest and great a man was worth his life. It would seem that he ascended into heaven. What less could be expected of one who had stoned the devil? Bulwer-Lytton, op. cit. I, p. 314.

21. The importance attached to Apollonius is evident from the following description of the secret teaching by a mysterious Rosicrucian at the beginning of the novel:

> their knottiest problems have never yet been published. Their sublimest works are in manuscript, and constitute the initiatory learning, not only of the Rosicrucians, but of the nobler brotherhoods I have referred to. More solemn and sublime still is the knowledge to be gleaned from the elder Pythagorean, and the immortal masterpieces of Apollonius. *Zanoni*, preface, xiii.

22. See Wolf, *Strange Stories*, pp. 260ff.
23. See McIntosh, *Eliphas Levi and the French Occult Tradition* (London, 1972), p. 164.
24. See C. Nelson Steward, *Bulwer-Lytton as Occultist* (London, 1927).
25. See S. B. Liljegren, *Bulwer-Lytton's Novels and Isis Unveiled,' Essays and Studies on English Language and Literature*, XVIII, Harvard University Press, Cambridge, 1957. Madame Blavatsky claimed that Bulwer's *Last Days in Pompeii* inspired her book, *Isis Unveiled.* But perhaps it would be unwise to attach too much significance to this, since according to Beechofer:

> when the book was published ... as *Isis Unveiled*, a statistically minded critic discovered in it no fewer than two thousand plagiarisms from modern books on occultism, together with seven hundred blunders in names, words and numbers, and six hundred misstatements of fact. Liljegren, op.cit., p. 66.

26. Blavatsky, H. P., *Isis Unveiled: A Master-key to the Mysteries of Ancient and Modern Science and Theology*, 2 vols (London, 1877), I, p. 285.
27. Loc. cit.
28. Letter to Lady Blessington, October 23, 1834. Reprinted by Bulwer's grandson in *Life* (1913), pp. 459-60.
29. Wolf, *Strange Stories*, p. 173. Before making this statement, Madame Home pointed out that Bulwer had intended to portray her husband in *A Strange Story* instead of the character Margrave.
30. Lucius Apuleius also wrote a *Discourse on Magic*.
31. See Apuleius, *The Golden Ass*, trans. Robert Graves (Harmondsworth, 1980), p. 43.
32. Bulwer, *Pelham or Adventures of a Gentleman* (London, 1840), p. 174. Bulwer's son stated 'my father's creations responded to the guidance of no single philosopher, and contain no artistic illustration of the maxims of any particular school or system of philosophy,' in *The Life, Letters and Literary Remains of Edward Bulwer, Lord Lytton by his Son* (London, 1883), p. 97.
33. Aytoun published this under the pseudonym of Bon Gaultier in 'Lays of the would-be Laureates,' *Tait's Edinburgh Magazine*, 19 (May, 1843), p. 276.
34. See Edwin M. Eigner, *The Metaphysical Novel in England and America: Dickens, Bulwer, Melville, and Hawthorne* (London, 1978), p. 12.
35. Bulwer, *Godolphin* (Manchester, 1840), p. 186. See Jerome B. Schneewind, 'Moral Problems and Moral Philosophy in the Victorian period,' *English Literature and British Philosophy: A Collection of Essays*, ed. S. P. Rosenbaum (London, 1971), pp. 185-207.
36. Bulwer, *Godolphin*, p. 291.
37. Ibid., p. 136.
38. Ibid., p. 142. This imagery is reminiscent of Mary Shelley's *Frankenstein*. Direct reference is made in *Ernest Maltravers* (London, 1837) preface, vii 'As we grow older we observe less, we reflect more, and, like Frankenstein, we dissect in order to create.'
39. Bulwer, *Ernest Maltravers*, p. 393.
40. See Bulwer, *Alice or the Mysteries* (London, 1838).
41. This superficially conflicts with Bulwer's Rosicrucian idealism. P. F. Strawson looks at this problem of conflicting ideals in relation to such literary forms as the novel in 'Social Morality and Individual Ideal,' *Philosophy*, XXXVI, no. 136 (January, 1961), p. 2. The hero of *Ernest Maltravers* reveals that he cannot be 'satisfied merely by ideal images' (p. 271).
42. Bulwer, *Ernest Maltravers*, p. 20.
43. Ibid., p. 271.
44. Ibid., p. 204. This paradox may also be viewed in terms of 'word-weighing and picture writing,' ibid., p. 271.
45. Bulwer, *Alice or the Mysteries*, p. 471.
46. Bulwer, *Devereux* (London, 1852), p. 120.
47. Ibid., p. 438.
48. Bulwer, *Zanoni*, III, p. 38 [p. 214].
49. Bulwer, *Devereux*, p. 438.
50. Ibid., p. 120.
51. See Bulwer, *Zanoni* (1853), p. 302. Here Martineau points out that 'Mejnour [represents the] Contemplation of the Actual ... Zanoni – [the] Contemplation of the Ideal'.
52. Ibid. (1853), p. 302n.
53. It is likely that here Hegel had been exposed to Rosicrucian idealism.
54. Eigner, *The Metaphysical Novel*, pp. 8 and 70.

55. Loc. cit.
56. Hegel, *Grundlinien der Philosophie des Rechts* (Hamburg, 1955), pp. 16-17, trans. by Robert B. Pippin in 'The Rose and the Owl: Some Remarks on the Theory-Practice Problem in Hegel,' *The Independent Journal of Philosophy*, III (1979), p. 10.
57. Hegel, *Lectures on the Philosophy of Religion together with a Work on the Proofs of the Existence of God*, ed. Rev. E. B. Speirs trans. E. B. Speirs and J. Burdon Sanderson (London, 1895), p. 284.
58. This appears in his essay 'Who thinks abstractedly?' reproduced by Walter Kaufmann, *Hegel: A Reinterpretation* (London, 1966), p. 463.
59. Hegel, *Philosophy of Religion*, p. 285.
60. Ibid., p. 284.
61. M. H. Abrams, *Natural Supernaturalism: Tradition and Revolution* (London, 1971), p. 193.
62. Bulwer, *Eugene Aram: A Tale* (London, 1847), p. 66.
63. Bulwer, 'The Tale of Kosem Kesamim the Magician' was first published in *The Student* (1832) but is cited here from *Miscellaneous Prose Works* (London, 1868), 11, pp. 211-28. Quotation is from pp. 214-15.
64. Bulwer, *Zanoni*, II, p. 194 [p. 168].
65. But if we take this problem beyond Christian morality, then we may see the fundamental error of trying to reduce nature to a single entity by attempting to extract and then isolate its 'essence.' According to Novalis, who may have influenced Bulwer, 'it is very hazardous ... to reconstruct Nature from external forces and phenomena, and to declare her now a monstrous fire ... or some other portentous force,' *The Disciples at Sais and Other Fragments*, trans. F. V. M. T. and U. C. B (London, 1903), p. 125.
66. In *Genesis*, Adam, by eating the fruit of the Tree of Knowledge of Good and Evil, gained knowledge of himself in the form of self-consciousness. His punishment lies in the burden of this responsibility.
67. Bulwer, 'Kosem Kesamim: The Magician,' p. 221.
68. Ibid., p. 224.
69. Ibid., p. 226.
70. Bulwer, *Zanoni*, I, pp. 195-6 [p. 69].
71. Bulwer, 'Arasmanes the Seeker,' *Miscellaneous Prose Works*, 11, pp. 112-45. Quotation taken from p. 113. Later on in the story reference is made to 'a mystic virtue which can cure all the diseases of kings.' The method suggested which would enable the 'King to live for ever' is to glide down the stream in a gilded bark scattering myrrh and frankincense. Ibid., p. 144.
72. Ibid., p. 130.
73. Ibid., p. 136.
74. Bulwer, *Falkland* and *Zicci* (London, 1878).
75. *Zicci* was first published in *The Monthly Chronicle*, which Bulwer edited.
76. See Bulwer, *A Strange Story*, p. 433.
77. Letter to John Forster reprinted in *Life* (1913), p. 48.
78. Bulwer, *Zicci*, p. 222.
79. Loc. cit.
80. Bulwer, *Zanoni*, II, p. 230 [p. 97].
81. Bulwer, *Zicci*, p. 146.
82. Bulwer, *Zanoni*, preface, I, xi [xii].
83. Walter Frewen Lord, *The Mirror of the Century* (London, 1906), pp. 172-3.
84. *Life* (1913), II, p. 35.
85. Bulwer, *Zanoni*, preface (1853), vi.
86. *Life* (1913), II, p. 39.

87. Ibid., II, p. 35.
88. This is the end of the epigraph for book 2, chapter 6.
89. See *Athenaeum*, 748 (Saturday, February 26, 1842), pp. 181-3.
90. Bulwer, *Life* (1913), p. 36.
91. Bulwer, *Zanoni*, (1853), p. 302.
92. Loc. cit.
93. *Life* (1913), II, p. 39. Here Bulwer reveals that the book-seller in the tale is based on a real character.
94. Eigner, *The Metaphysical Novel*, p. 226.
95. Bulwer, *Zanoni*, preface, vii [x].
96. Loc. cit.
97. Ibid., preface, xiii [xiii].
98. Ibid., II, p. 150 [p. 154].
99. Ibid., I, p. 174 [p. 62].
100. Loc. cit.
101. Ibid., xvii [xiv]. Technically Zanoni and Mejnour are quasi-Rosicrucians, but they fall into the wider definition of Rosicrucianism.
102. Ibid., x [xi]. See 'Readings and Re-readings: *Zanoni*,' *Theosophical Review*, 31 (December, 1902), pp. 338-46 for a discussion of the antagonism between the emotions and the intellect which may be synthesised through art.
103. Bret Harte, *Condensed Novels* (London, 1903), p. 74.
104. Loc. cit.
105. Ibid., p. 75.
106. Loc. cit.
107. Ibid., p. 76.
108. Bulwer, *Zanoni*, I, p. 61 [p. 22].
109. The misguidedness of this kind of thinking is explained by Hans-Georg Gadamer in the following passage from *Truth and Method* (London, 1979), p. 243:

    > In fact the presupposition of a mysterious darkness in which there was a mythical collective consciousness that preceded all thought is just as dogmatic and abstract as that of a state of perfection achieved by a total enlightenment or that of absolute knowledge.

    This argument would also provide an effective attack against the Rosicrucians' pansophic ideal.
110. See Bulwer, *Zanoni*, I, p. 173 [p. 62].
111. Loc. cit.
112. Ibid., I, p. 170 [p. 61].
113. Ibid., I, p. 125 [p. 47]. Here Bulwer may have been recalling his own ancestor.
114. Ibid., II, p. 150 [p. 154].
115. Ibid., II, p. 151 [loc.cit.].
116. Ibid., II, p. 194 [p. 168].
117. Ibid., II, p. 167 [p. 159].
118. Ibid., I, p. 65 [p. 23].
119. Ibid., II, p. 188 [p. 165].
120. Ibid., II, p. 264 [p. 190].
121. Ibid., II, p. 218 [pp. 269-70]. See also Bulwer, *Rienzi: The Last of the Tribunes* (London, 1908), p. 268, where Bulwer uses the metaphors of magic, for as he discovers, 'I am in the middle of a magician's spell .... If I desist, the fiends will tear me to pieces.'
122. Theodor W. Adorno and Max Horkheimer, *Dialectic of Enlightenment* (London, 1973), p. 31.
123. *Blake: The Complete Poems*, ed. W. H. Stevenson, text by David V. Erdman (London, 1971), p. 133.

124. Bulwer, *Zanoni*, I. p. 123 [p. 46].
125. Ibid., (1853) p. 25. See also ibid., I, p. 62 [p. 23], where Bulwer describes St Martin as a man who combated 'materialism, and vindicated the necessity of faith amidst a chaos of unbelief.'
126. See Bulwer, 'The Reign of Terror: Its Causes and Results,' *Miscellaneous Prose Works*, I, pp. 1-48.
127. Bulwer, *Zanoni*, I, p. 124 [p. 46].
128. Ibid., III, p. 136 [p. 244].
129. Ibid., p. 12 [p. 204].
130. Bulwer, *Miscellaneous Prose Works*, I, p. 4.
131. See Hegel's treatise on the *French Revolution* in *The Phenomenology of Spirit*, trans. A. V. Miller (Oxford, 1977). See also Marcuse's sympathetic interpretation of Hegel's political philosophy published in 1941: *Reason and Revolution: Hegel and the Rise of Social Theory* (London, 1986).
132. This is explained by Adorno and Horkheimer, *Dialectic of Enlightenment*, p. 28:

> In the enlightened world, mythology has entered into the profane. In its blank purity, the reality which has been cleansed of demons and their conceptual descendants assumes the numinous character which the ancient world attributed to demons.

This seeks to demonstrate how 'Enlightenment behaves towards things as a dictator towards men,' p. 9.
133. Bulwer, *Zanoni*, III, p. 147 [p. 247].
134. Ibid., III, p. 146 [Loc. cit.].
135. Loc. cit.
136. Ibid., III, p. 51 [p. 218].
137. Ibid., III, p. 318 [p. 298].
138. See Ibid., III, p. 219 [p. 270].
139. Ibid., I, p. 124 [p. 46].
140. Ibid., II, p. 218 [p. 269].
141. Ibid., II, p. 149 [p. 154].
142. Bulwer, 'Caxtons,' *Blackwood's Edinburgh Magazine*, 92 (1862), p. 163.
143. See Roger Cardinal, *German Romantics in Context* (London, 1975), p. 84.
144. Ibid., p. 38.,
145. Bulwer, *Zanoni*, xviii [xv].
146. See Wolf, *Strange Stories*, p. 223.
147. Bulwer, *A Strange Story*, p. 303.
148. Bulwer, *Zanoni*, II, p. 107 [p. 141].
149. Novalis, *The Disciples at Sais*, p. 141.
150. Bulwer, *Zanoni*, I, p. 197 [pp. 67-8].
151. Ibid., III, p. 139 [p. 246].
152. Bulwer, *A Strange Story*, p. 147.
153. This letter from Bulwer to Dickens was dated late 1861 or early 1862 by Bulwer's grandson. It is quoted by Wolf in *Strange Stories*, p. 292. Here Bulwer contends that the supernatural furnishes a legitimate province of fiction. In a letter to John Forster, December 1861, Bulwer discusses the supernatural in general and 'recorded marvels' in particular, suggesting: 'There must be a natural cause for them – if they are not purely imposture. Even if that natural cause be the admission of a spirit world around us...?' It is likely that Bulwer's interest in natural supernaturalism had been aroused by Thomas Carlyle's essay on that subject in his *Sartor Resartus* (1833-4). The popularity of this subject is also attested by Reverend James M'Cosh's 'The Supernatural in Relation to the Natural' (1862), which was reviewed alongside *A Strange Story* in 'The Literature of

the Supernatural,' *The Eclectic Review*, 115 – New Series 2 – (April, 1862), pp. 302–26.

154. Broussais (1772-1838) was a physician whose theory of medicine was explained in *Examen de la doctrine médicale généralement adoptée* (1816). Here he asserts that life was sustained only through irritation or excitement. Condillac (1714-80) was a French philosopher who wrote *Traité des systèmes* (1749), where he outlined his theory that the source of knowledge and the thinking faculties were derived from sensation alone.
155. Bulwer, *A Strange Story*, pp. 14–15.
156. Ibid., p. 15.
157. See Bulwer, *A Strange Story*, chapters 44-6 and 71-3. There was controversy over whether or not to include these dialogues. Bulwer expressed his own uncertainties to his son by pointing out 'in poetry they would be inexcusable. I am not sure that in prose they are justified. But still they are essential...' Quoted by Wolf, *Strange Stories*, p. 299.
158. Dickens had a vested editorial concern in *A Strange Story*, since it was to be published in a serialised form in his journal *All the Year Round*. He advised Bulwer against a lengthy preface for the same reason as he had criticised the Faber-Fenwick dialogues as follows:

    > I counsel you most strongly NOT to append the proposed dialogue between Fenwick and Faber, and NOT to enter upon any explanation beyond the title-page and the motto unless it be in some very brief preface.... Let the book explain itself. It speaks for itself with a noble eloquence.

    Quoted by Wolf, *Strange Stories*, p. 295.

    Bulwer, however, insisted on his explanatory preface, which came under fire from a number of critics. The *Saturday Review* declared that the preface obtrudes itself clamorously upon the reader as well as being too difficult for the average intelligence even after three readings!
159. Bulwer, *A Strange Story*, preface, vi, Biran ((1766-1824) was a French philosopher who devoted himself to psychology. In his *Influence de l'habitude* (1802) he subscribed to Locke and Condillac's sensualist philosophy, which he eventually rejected in favour of mystical Theosophy.
160. Loc. cit. Here Bulwer is quoting from Œvres *Inédites de Maine de Biran*, ed. Ernest Naville and Marc Debrit (Paris, 1859), III, p. 524.
161. Ibid., preface, ix.
162. Loc. cit.
163. Ibid. preface, viii. Here Bulwer quotes from Friedrich Heinrich Jacobi's *Von der Göttlichen Dingen* (1811):

    > Is it unreasonable to confess that we believe in God, not by reason of the Nature which conceals Him, but by reason of the Supernatural in Man which alone reveals and proves him to exist? ... Man reveals God: for Man, by his intelligence, rises above Nature, and in virtue of this intelligence, is conscious of himself as a power not only independent of, but opposed to, Nature, and capable of resisting, conquering, and controlling her.
164. Wolf, *Strange Stories*, p. 307.
165. Loc. cit.
166. Bulwer, *A Strange Story*, p. 341.
167. Ibid., p. 90.
168. Jean-Baptiste Lamarck (1744-1829) was a French naturalist who became a tutor to Buffon's son. He made important contributions to Botany and wrote the *Dic-*

tionnaire de botanique and *Illustrations de genres* (published in the *Encyclopédie méthodique*, 1785). In 1793 he was appointed as a professor of Zoology and between 1815 and 1822 wrote *Histoire des animaux sans vertebres.* He is most renowned for his philosophical concept of evolution as being a direct result of heredity and adaptation which is expounded in his *Philosophie Zoologique* (1809). Pierre Simon Laplace (1749-1827) was a French mathematician who in 1796 published his *Exposition du système du Monde* on astronomy, where he explains his famous nebular hypothesis on the origin of the solar system. His monumental work dealing with the problems of the solar system was *Traité de Mécanique céleste* (1799-1825).

169. Wolf, *Strange Stories*, p. 199.
170. Bulwer, *A Strange Story*, p. 151.
171. See Balzac, 'A Treatise on the Occult Sciences' in *Cousin Pons* (Harmondsworth, 1968), pp. 128-38, where Balzac complains about the division between science and magic, stating that:

    > the occult sciences, like so many phenomena of nature, are spurned by sceptics or materialist philosophers, that is to say by those who cleave solely to solid, visible facts, to the results shown by the retorts and balances of modern physics and chemistry.

    Bulwer suggests that the reason for this is because magic has been dismissed as the art of the absurd, and alleges:

    > But this criterion of absurdity once ruled out the harnessing of steam; it still rules out aerial navigation, it ruled out many inventions: gunpowder, printing, the telescope, engraving, and also the most recent great discovery of our time, the daguerreotype.... Nowadays so many attested and authenticated facts have emerged from the occult sciences that the time will come when these sciences will be professed as chemistry and astronomy are professed. Just now, when so many professorial chairs are set up in Paris – chairs in Slavonic, in Manchurian studies, and in literature so *unprofessable* as those of the North; chairs which, instead of offering instruction, stand in need of it themselves; chairs whose titular holders eternally grind out articles on Shakespeare or the sixteenth century – is it not a matter of surprise that, under the name of anthropology, the teaching of occult philosophy, one of the glories of the old-time university, has not been restored? Balzac, op. cit., p. 133

    In a note to *Les Misérables*, August 12, 1860, Victor Hugo writes

    > Science, under the pretext that such things are 'marvels,' abandoned its scientific duty. To the great profit of the charlatans she left the mass of the people a prey to visions mingled with reality. She stumbled and lost her footing, and where she should have advanced she retreated.
    >
    > Quoted by Wolf, *Strange Stories*, p. 322.

172. Bulwer, *The Coming Race* (New York, 1874). 'Vril' is described as a 'quasi-nuclear force' in Geoffrey Wagner, 'A Forgotten Satire: Bulwer-Lytton's *The Coming Race*' in *Nineteenth-Century Fiction*, 19 (March, 1964-5), p. 382.
173. See Bulwer, *A Strange Story*, pp. 113-4.
174. Justus, Freiherr von Liebig (1803-73) was the first scientist to prove that the activity of chemical forces is similar to that of the organic substance of the mineral world. Helmont (1577-1644) studied mysticism, which led him through the

influence of Paracelsus to chemistry. He investigated 'gases' and the chemical fluids contained within the human body.

175. See Balzac, *The Quest for the Absolute* (London, 1908), p. 211.
176. See Bulwer, *A Strange Story*, p. 394.
177. Ibid., p. 436.
178. Ibid., p. 437.
179. Ibid., p. 113
180. Ibid., p. 429.
181. Ibid., p. 425
182. Ibid., p. 122.
183. Ibid., p. 119.
184. Ibid., p. 217.
185. Ibid., p. 55.
186. Wolf, *Strange Stories*, p. 257. See Bulwer, 'The Haunted and the Haunters' (London, 1925). Bulwer's rationalisation of the occult in this story is discussed by Richard Kelly in 'The Haunted House of Bulwer-Lytton,' *Studies in Short Fiction*, 8 (1971), pp. 581-7.
187. Bulwer, *A Strange Story*, p. 490.
188. Bulwer, *Night and Morning* (London, 1892), preface, viii.
189. Loc. cit.
190. Quoted by Wolf, *Strange Stories*, p. 303.
191. *Life* (1913), 11, pp. 347-50 (to Robert Lytton, April 15, 1862).

7

The Problem of Immortality

> I do not want to die – no, I neither want to die nor do I want to want to die; I want to live for ever and ever and ever. I want this "I" to live – this poor "I" that I am and that I feel myself to be here and now, and therefore the problem of the duration of my soul, tortures me.
>
> Unamuno[1]

The underlying problem of the Rosicrucian novel is that the immortal hero may be spiritually redeemed only through death. Even the supremely virtuous Zanoni, submits to death for greater spiritual fulfilment by sacrificing his eternal existence for love. Yet for Bulwer-Lytton, the real riddle in the novel is why Zanoni and Mejnour should have chosen to prolong their lives beyond the allotted span.[2]

Arguments in favour of limits to life are quick to point out that life-extension magnifies and multiplies the miseries of human existence. Certainly the majority of the Rosicrucian characters are portrayed as having to endure the suffering and tedium of perpetual 'mortality.' But why should this be so? Perhaps the five novelists discussed, by conceptualising immortality in this way, are consciously expressing a moral responsibility towards their readers in order to reconcile them to an acceptance of death's inevitability. As a defender of mortality, the Rosicrucian novel reinforces the belief that protracted life would eventually produce an eternity of boredom and frustration. The assumption here is that the cessation of life is preferable to its perpetuation. Bernard Williams argues against the case for immortality by drawing attention to Karel Capek's drama, *The Makropulos Case*, which documents the interminable boredom of Elena Makropulos, who has lived for 342 years, having remained the biological age of 42.[3] Williams concludes that her eternal ennui is inevitable, since the individual can only fulfil a series of finite possibilities within a lifetime. But, given the resilience of human nature, would it not be more likely that if immortality were possible then individuals would manufacture appropriate goals? The tragedy for both the Rosicrucian hero and Makropulos is that they have lost the ability to recreate perpetual goals and, therefore, find meaning to life. The implication of this is that life can be meaningful only in the face of death. Broadly speaking, the Rosicrucian novelists analysed here subscribe to this view.

It was not until the early twentieth century that the acceptance of mortality was questioned seriously within a literary context. Bernard Shaw challenges the traditional view of death as necessary and ethically desirable. He appeals to an evolutionary model of life-extension in the preface to his play *Back to Methuselah*, a Bergsonian exploration of creative evolution in which he claims to 'exploit the external interest of the philosopher's stone which enables men to live for ever.'[4] Shaw argues:

> Conceivably, however, the same power that has taken us thus far can take us further. If Man now fixes the term of his life at three score and ten years he can fix it at three hundred or three thousand, or even until a sooner-or-later-inevitable accident makes an end. Surely our ruinous world-wars should convince him of the necessity for at least outliving his taste for golf and cigars if the race is to be saved.
>
> This is not fantastic speculation: it is deductive biology, if there is such a science as biology.[5]

The notion of death and mortality as both natural and morally desirable is preserved and sanctioned by religion. Even Rosicrucian novelists like the radicals Godwin and Shelley deny in their fiction the idea that unlimited life could be more appealing than mortality. The problem of immortality lies not merely in overcoming the practical difficulties of life-extension but also in preserving the quality of life itself. Apart from materialist considerations, it is bound up with factors ranging from inner peace to human dignity which are, according to Pascal, indicative of self-consciousness since 'even if the universe were to crush him, man would still be nobler than his slayer, because he knows that he is dying and the advantage the universe has over him. The universe knows nothing of this.'[6] Yet the Rosicrucian hero whose very existence flies in the face of these platitudes behaves as though he knows nothing of his advantage over the universe. Ironically, it is his inability to cope with a life circumscribed by death that attracts him most to the *elixir vitae*. This pattern of failure and moral weakness emerges most clearly in Godwin's *St Leon* and Bulwer-Lytton's *A Strange Story*, where the pursuit of immortality reveals the inability of the Rosicrucian hero, to find meaning within mortality. Consequently, he is unable to make meaningful an infinite life-extension. In many cases, the Rosicrucian is a caricature of our need to endow meaning upon human existence, which involves living by that which is unattainable. Fundamental to this condition is the striving after unattainable goals, a reaching out for the 'imaginable, eternally unreachable Gardens of Eden' where 'idle dreams bloom' for 'individuals behind every rock face whose sheerness they can never conquer.'[7] To create or recreate uncertainties is essential to human existence. The tragedy of the Rosicrucian, who misguidedly believes that he has attained everything, lies in his unwillingness to devise goals for living and to be satisfied with a static and unchanging state by deluding himself into believing that there are no more Gardens of Eden to discover. In contrast to this, Shaw's defence of immortality is based on its inherent dynamism and mutability. He claimed that human beings have an infinity of desires to satisfy, since 'nothing remains beautiful and interesting except thought, because the thought is the life.'[8]

As we have seen, the Rosicrucian novelists have bestowed immortality on characters whose chronic dissatisfaction with existence, prolonged or otherwise, ensures that they will always remain discontented. Immortality is wasted on those who are prepared to squander life. As Mephistopheles emphasises to Faust, life is really given to be lived.[9] But its intrinsic value is often overlooked by Rosicrucians heroes like Ginotti, Melmoth and Margrave, who are already bored with the set of experiences contained within mortality, and thus crave for the new sensations which they believe may be attained through the elixir. Often this leads to purely sensory gratification, which ends in moral debauchery and spiritual degeneration. These destructive tendencies do not necessarily suggest that immortality is intrinsically bad, rather that it can be misused. It depends upon the individual whether or not the infinity of positive possibilities present throughout an immortal existence will be denied. In the Rosicrucian drama *Back to Methuselah*, an ancient informs a young immortal that 'If you should turn out to be a person of infinite capacity, you will no doubt find life infinitely interesting.'[10] The Rosicrucian's failure in the novel to cope with immortality also testifies to his inability to face up to the reality of an eternal existence which he himself has earlier desired. The hero's self-destruction and subsequent willingness to die then become an escape into the only enduring fiction: death, which lies beyond human experience.

Rosicrucian heroes who get caught up in this spiral include Maturin's Melmoth and Bulwer's Margrave, who traverse eternity as incarnations of evil. In contrast, Mejnour and Zanoni, who have obtained mystic enlightenment, devote their lives to peaceful pursuits. While Zanoni eventually realises that spiritual salvation may be attained through death, Mejnour finds that the only way in which he can sustain his immortal state is by having no life in humanity, but in living purely through the intellect. A variation on this insular state may be seen in Mary Shelley's 'Mortal Immortal' and Frankenstein's creation, where characters experience the suffering of an alienated immortal existence. In keeping with the prevailing precepts illustrated by the Rosicrucian novels discussed, Godwin and Shelley never allow their anarchistic Rosicrucian heroes to triumph over the moral code which is ratified by death. Both St Leon and Ginotti confirm, through their longing to die, the social and theological values which they previously denied.

According to the manifestos, adepts must work out their own spiritual redemption, elevate themselves to a god-like state of being, and master nature through the power of the will. The main emphasis, however, is placed upon the evolutionary nature of this spiritual development which, like Bergson's concept of creative evolution, rests on the notion that psychic forces could effect a gradual physiological change which would enable human beings to evolve an extended life-cycle and elevated spirituality. In contrast, the fictional Rosicrucian hero attempts to accelerate this gradual process by grasping the secrets of the philosopher's stone prematurely. But in the final analysis the Rosicrucian immortal can never be defeated, even though he has incurred eternal damnation, because he represents the supreme triumph of the individual will. This is best expressed by Goethe's assessment of Faust: 'if the moment provided by Mephistopheles would be so sweet that he could wish it to last for ever, he will willingly allow himself to be cast into chains and perish in Hell.'[11] Likewise Goethe recognises nobility in the sacrifice of the soul for perpetual existence. The Rosicrucian's decision to mortgage or even forfeit his soul for prolonged existence must be among the greatest tributes ever paid to the value of life.

The importance of immortality is emphasised by Shaw in his futuristic *Back to Methuselah*, where Lilith, the mythical parent of Adam and Eve, ponders upon how at last mankind has evolved into a race of immortals. She reflects upon the time when individuals were mortal and notes that then 'they did terrible things: they embraced death, and said that eternal life was a fable.'[12] But hope had loomed for Lilith when one man, like the Rosicrucian hero, defied mankind's mortality by living for three hundred years and so enabled a race of immortals to emerge who 'accepted the burden of eternal life.'[13] Lilith describes immortalised humanity, the dream of the Rosicrucians, as follows:

> They have taken the agony from birth; and their life does not fail them even in the hour of their destruc-

> tion .... I am Lilith; I brought life into the whirlpool of force, and compelled my enemy, matter, to obey a living soul. But in enslaving Life's enemy I made him Life's master: for that is the end of all slavery .... Of life only is there no end.[14]

The hopes and beliefs for immortality which were channelled through the tradition of the Rosy Cross and expressed through the Rosicrucian novel continue up to the twentieth century. For example, Temple Thurston's narrative *The Rosicrucian,* which was first published in 1930, recounts the now familiar circumstances surrounding the mysterious stranger whose knowledge of past events is at odds with his youthful appearance. Thurston's hero, who is based on the legendary Saint-Germain, is discovered by the narrator to be a Rosicrucian – 'a brother of the secret order of the Rosy Cross! Walking in the Haymarket in broad daylight in the twentieth century.' The narrator is particularly amazed since 'prior to this, he had only read of Rosicrucians in the later Middle Ages.'[15]

Christopher McIntosh in *The Rosy Cross Unveiled* acknowledges that the Rose-Cross legends provided an important source of inspiration for a variety of poetry and prose fiction which he regards as a 'strange literary progeny.'[16] The Rosicrucian novel draws upon the myths of the Rosy Cross to allegorise the universal spiritual odyssey. Encompassed within this is the longing to reverse the effects of the Fall through the philosopher's stone and *elixir vitæ,* in the belief that these would bring about a pansophic utopia. The persistent Rosicrucian dream of universal knowledge is described by the novelist John Hargrave:

> The idea of a synthesis of science to be applied to the regeneration of mankind may not have intrigued the popular mind as did the notion of a secret brotherhood of anonymous adepts holding the key to the mysteries; yet this Universal and General Reformation of the Whole Wide World is the only significant residuum after evaporating the "Celestial Slime" of Rosicrucian philomagical lore.[17]

He goes on to quote Robert Burton's perhaps ironic comment in *The Anatomy of Melancholy* (1621) that we are in need of 'some general vistor' a 'just army of Rosie-cross men' a body of undeceiving Jesuits 'that shall reform which is amiss.'[18] The Rosicrucian novel of the nineteenth century was a faint echo of the reform movement heralded by the Brotherhood of the Rosy Cross.

The Rosicrucian tradition functions as a synthesis for opposing principles. Bulwer expresses the polarisation of the actual and the ideal in *Zanoni* through the opposition between art and magic. In *Frankenstein*, Mary Shelley explores the antinomies of magic and science through the Rosicrucian Renaissance amalgam of the magician-scientist. In *A Strange Story*, Bulwer-Lytton takes a Rosicrucian position by arguing that the scientist is wrong to cut himself off from the springs of magic and mysticism. The background to the novel concerns the debate between scientific scepticism and religious faith which had taken place in the wake of Darwin. The antagonism between reason and faith is represented by Fenwick and Lilian respectively. The third Rosicrucian manifesto, *The Chemical Wedding*, which allegorises a political alliance, is an alchemical romance which unites the binary oppositions between the sun and the moon and the male and the female principles.

The Brotherhood of the Rosy Cross advocated such a holistic approach. The move towards synthesis and unity was the message of Rosicrucianism. This is the common factor to be found in novels as disparate as *St Leon* and *Zanoni*, in which both heroes aspire towards the ideals of the Rose and Cross. But where Zanoni succeeds, St Leon fails. More notable failures include Ginotti, Melmoth, and Margrave, who spiral downwards into a hell of their own making. In most of the other novels looked at, the Rosicrucian wanderer has been portrayed as a charlatan whose greed for the secret of perpetual life has alienated him from nature, mankind and even himself. For the monster in *Frankenstein*, perpetual life brings only the isolation and anguish of the wandering immortal. Bulwer shows how this inability to integrate may be remedied through his Romantic concept of the Rosicrucian hero in *Zanoni*, who achieves complete reconciliation. Through this characterisation, he demonstrates how the true conquest of death may be achieved through the assimilation of the actual and the ideal, which may be represented by the Rosy Cross, the symbol of the Rosicrucian tradition.

The novel is able to express effectively the idealism of the Rosy Cross, for as Bulwer-Lytton notes in his *Strange Story*, 'I do not elaborate a treatise submitted to the logic of sages,' since it is only when in 'fairy fictions drest that Romance gives admission to truths severe.'[19] The Rosicrucian novelists, by concentrating upon the seeker of immortality focus, upon the universal problems of life and death. Their fictional exploration of the dilemmas encountered by the mortal immortal is really an allegory of the spiritual crises which confront every mortal individual.

Notes

1. Miguel de Unamuno y Jugo, *The Tragic Sense of Life* (1913) trans. J. E. Crawford Flitch (London, 1962), p. 60.
2. See Bulwer-Lytton, *Zanoni*, p. 270.
3. See Bernard Williams, '*The Makropulos Case:* Reflections on the Tedium of Immortality' in *Problems of the Self* (Cambridge, 1973), pp. 82-100.
4. Bernard Shaw, *Back to Methuselah: A Metabiological Pentateuch* (Harmondsworth, 1939), p. 62.
5. Ibid., p. 15.
6. Blaise Pascal, *Pensées* (Harmondsworth, 1981), p. 95.
7. Quoted from Georg Lukács's essay, 'The Metaphysics of Tragedy' in *Soul and Form*, trans. Anna Bostock (Cambridge, Mass., 1974), p. 153.
8. Shaw, *Back to Methuselah*, p. 298.
9. See Richard Friedenthal, *Goethe: His Life and Times* (London, 1963), p. 500.
10. Shaw, *Back to Methuselah*, p. 263.
11. Quoted by Friedenthal, *Goethe*, p. 503.
12. Shaw, *Back to Methuselah*, p. 304.
13. Ibid., p. 304.
14. Ibid., pp. 304-5.
15. Quoted by McIntosh in *The Rosy Cross Unveiled*, p. 128.
16. Loc. cit.
17. Hargrave, *The Confessions of the Kibbo Kift: A Declaration and General Exposition of the Work of the Kindred* (London, 1927), p. 48.
18. Burton, *The Anatomy of Melancholy* (Oxford,1621). This quotation does not appear in the first edition. Instead it is cited in the modern edition published by J. M. Dent in 1972 in vol. 1 on p. 96. According to this version, one would have expected to find the quotation on p. 55 of the original.
19. Bulwer-Lytton, *A Strange Story*, preface, vii.

Appendix

Sadak The Wanderer

He through storm and cloud has gone,
To the mountain's topmost stone;
He has climb'd to tear the food
From the eagle's screaming brood;
By the turbid jungle tide,
For his meal, the wolf has died;
He has brav'd the tiger's lair,
In his bleeding prey to share.
Hark! the wounded panther's yell,
Flying from the torn gazelle!
By the food, wild, weary, wan.
Stands a thing that once was man!

Look upon that wither'd brow,
See the glance that burns below!
See the lank and scatter'd hair!
See the limb, swart, wither'd bare!
See the feet, that leave their mark
On the soil in bloodstains dark!
Who thus o'er the world doth roam,
Hath the desert for his home?
Hath his soul been steep'd in crime
That hath smote him in his prime?
Stainless as the newborn child,
Strays this wanderer through the wild;
Day by day, and year by year,
Must the pilgrim wander there:
Through the mountain's rocky pile,
Through the ocean, through the isle,
Through the sunshine, through the snow,
Still in weariness and woe;
Pacing still the world's huge round,
Till the mystic fount is found,
Till the waters of the Spring
Round the roofs their splendours fling,
Round the tyrant, Amurath,

SADAK THE WANDERER

Leaves the harem for the throne:
– Then shall all his woe be done.
Onward, Sadak, to thy prize!
But what night has hid the skies?
Like a dying star the sun
Struggles on through cloud-wreaths dun;
From yon mountain's shelter'd brow
Burst the lava's burning flow:
Warrior! wilt thou dare the tomb
In the red volcano's womb!
In he plunges: spire on spire
Round him shoots the living fire;
Rivers round his footsteps pour,
Where the wave is molten ore;
Like the metal in the mould
Springs the cataract of gold;
O'er the warrior's dazzled glance
Eddying flames of silver dance;
By a thousand fountains fed
Roar'd the iron torrents red;
Still, beneath a mighty hand,
Treads he o'er the fiery land.
O'er his head thy purple wing,
Angel spirit of the Spring!
Through the flood, and through the field,
Long has been the warrior's shield.

Never fell the shepherd's tread
Softer on the blossom's mead,
Than, thou man of anguish! thine,
Guided through this burning mine.

Hanging now upon the ledge,
That the precipice doth edge;
Warrior! take the fearful leap,
Though 't were as the ocean deep:
Through the realm of death and night
Shall that pinion scatter light
Till the Fount before thee lies,
Onward, warrior, to the prize!
Till thy woes are all repaid:
Thine, all thine, young Kalasrade.

Bibliography

Primary Sources

Ainsworth, William Harrison *Auriol: The Elixir of Life* (George Routledge and Sons, London, 1881)

Andreæ, Johann Valentin *Christianopolis: An Ideal of the Seventeenth Century* trans. Felix Emil Held (Oxford University Press, New York, 1916)

Anon. 'Cabala: Sive Scrina Sacra: Mysteries of State and Government' in *Letters of Illustrious Persons and great agents; in the Reigns of Henry the Eighth, Queen Elizabeth, K. James and the late King Charles* (M. M. G. Bedell and T. Collins, London, 1654)

Apuleius, Lucius *The Transformations of Lucius otherwise known as The Golden Ass* trans. Robert Graves (Penguin, Harmondsworth, 1980)

Balzac, H. *Don Juan or The Elixir of Long Life, Shorter Stories from Balzac* trans. William Wilson and Count Stenbock (Walter Scott, Camelot Classics, London, 1890)

——— *Œuvres Complètes* (Guy lePrat, reprint, Paris, 1960)

——— *The Quest for the Absolute* (J. M. Dent, London, 1908)

——— *Cousin Pons* trans. Herbert J. Hunt (Penguin, Harmondsworth, 1968)

Barruel, Abbé *Memoirs Illustrating the History of Jacobinism* trans. Robert Clifford, 2nd edition, 4 vols (T. Burton, London, 1797)

de Biran, Maine *Œuvres Inédites* ed. Ernest Naville and Marc Debrit (Bezobrv E. Magdelaine et Cie., Paris, 1859)

Blake, William *The Complete Poems* ed. W. H. Stevenson, text by David V. Erdman (London, 1971)

Bond, Donald F. ed. *The Spectator* (Clarendon Press, Oxford, 1965)

Boswell, James *Life of Johnson* (1791) 2 vols (J. M. Dent, London, 1958)

Bulwer-Lytton, Edward *Alice or The Mysteries* (George Routledge and Sons, London, 1838)

——— *A Strange Story: An Alchemical Novel* (Shambola, London, 1973)

——— 'Caxtons,' *Blackwood's Edinburgh Magazine,* 92 (1862)

——— *Devereux* (Collins, London, 1852)

——— *Ernest Maltravers* (G. J. Howell, London, 1837)

——— *Eugene Aram: A Tale* (George Routledge and Sons, London, 1847)

——— *Falkland* and *Zicci* (George Routledge and Sons, London, 1878)

——— *Godolphin* (George Routledge and Sons, Manchester, 1840)

——— *The Coming Race* (George Routledge and Sons, New York, 1874)

——— *The Haunted and the Haunters* (Simpson, Marshall, and Hamilton, London, 1925)

——— *Miscellaneous Prose Works* 3 vols (Richard Bentley, London, 1868)

——— *Night and Morning* (George Routledge and Sons, London, 1892)

——— *Pelham or Adventures of a Gentleman* (Walter Scott, London, 1840)

——— *Rienzi: The Last of the Tribunes* (Collins, London, 1908)

——— *Zanoni* 3 vols (Saunders and Otley, London, 1842)

——— *Zanoni* (Chapman and Hall, London, 1853)

Burton, R. *The Anatomy of Melancholy* (Henry Cripps, Oxford, 1621)

——— *The Anatomy of Melancholy* (1621) (J. M. Dent, London, 1972)

Byron, George Gordon *Poetical Works* ed. Frederick Page and John Jump (Oxford University Press, London, 1970)

Campanella, Tommaso *La Citta del Sole: Dialogo Poetico — The City of the Sun: A Poetical Dialogue* (1623) trans. with introduction by Daniel J. Donno (University of California Press, London, 1981)

Cohausen, Johann Heinrich *Hermippus Redivivus: or the Sage's triumph over old age and the grave. Wherein, a method is lain down for prolonging the life and vigour of man. Including a commentary upon an ancient inscription in which this great secret is revealed* trans. John Campbell (J. Nourse, London, 1744)

Coleridge, Samuel Taylor *Coleridge: Poetical Works* ed. Ernest Hartley Coleridge (Oxford, University Press, Oxford, 1974)

Croly, George *Tarry thou till I come or Salathiel, the Wandering Jew* (Funk and Wagnalls Company, London, 1901)

Darwin, Erasmus *The Botanic Garden* (J. Johnson, London, 1789-91)

——— *The Temple of Nature* (J. Johnson, London, 1803) (A Scholar Press Facsimile, London, 1973)

De Quincey, Thomas *Works* ed. David Masson reprint, 16 vols (A. and C. Black, Edinburgh, 1880)

Dubois, Robert [Count Reginald de St Leon] *St Godwin: A Tale of the 16th, 17th, and 18th Century* (J. Wright, London, 1800)

Fairclough, Peter ed. *Three Gothic Novels* (Penguin, Harmondsworth, 1974)

Flammenberg, Lawrence *The Necromancer* trans. Peter Teuthold (Folio Press, London, 1968)

Godwin, William *Antonio: A Tragedy in 5 Acts* (G. G. and J. Robinson, London, 1800)

——— *Adventures of Caleb Williams or Things as They Are* (1794) (New English Library, London, 1966)

——— *Catalogue of the Curious Library of that very eminent and distinguished author, William Godwin* (Sotheby, London, 1836)

——— *Enquiry Concerning Political Justice and Its Influence on Modern Morals and Happiness* (1798) ed. Isaac Kramnick (Harmondsworth, 1976)

——— *Essay on Sepulchres or, A Proposal for Erecting some memorial of the illustrious dead in all ages on the spot where their remains have been interred* (W. Miller, London, 1809)

——— *Faulkener: A Tragedy* (Richards Phillips, London, 1807)

——— *Fleetwood or The Man of Feeling* 3 vols (Richard Phillips, London, 1805)

——— *Imogen: A Pastoral Romance from the Ancient British* (1784) (New York Publishing Library, New York, 1963)

——— *Italian Letters of The History of the Count de St Julian* ed. Burton R. Pollin (University Nebraska Press, Lincoln, 1965)

——— *Lives of the Necromancers or, An account of the most eminent persons in successive ages, who have claimed for themselves or to whom has been imputed by others, the exercise of magical power* (Frederick J. Mason, London, 1834)

——— *Mandeville, A Tale of the Seventeenth Century in England* 3 vols (Archibald Constable, and Longman, Hurst, Rees, Orme and Brown, London, 1817)

——— *Of Population — An Enquiry concerning the Power of Increase in the Numbers of Mankind, Being an answer to Mr Malthus's essay on that subject* (Longman, Hurst, Rees, Orme and Brown, London 1820)

——— *St Leon, A Drama* (Edward Churton, London, 1835)

——— *St Leon, A Tale of the Sixteenth Century* (Mcgarth, New York, 1972)

——— *Thoughts on Man, His Nature, Productions and Discoveries. Interspersed with some particulars respecting the author* (Effingham Wilson, London, 1831)

——— *Tragical Consequences or A Disaster at Deal being an unpublished letter of William Godwin dated Wednesday, November 18th, 1789 and Remarks thereon by Edmund Blunden* (Fytton Armstrong, London, 1921)

Goethe, Johann Wolfgang *Faust* Part one, trans. Philip Wayne (Penguin, Harmondsworth 1976)

Grosse, Carl Friedrich August *Horrid Mysteries: A Tale from the German of the Marquis of Grosse* (1796) 2 vols, trans. P. Will (Robert Holden, London, 1927)

Hargrave, John *The Confessions of the Kibbo Kift: A Declaration and General Exposition of the Work of the Kindred* (Duckworth, London, 1927)

Harte, Bret *Condensed Novels* (Chatto and Windus, London, 1903)

Hazlitt, William, 'Conversations with Northcote' in *Complete Works of William Hazlitt* ed. P. P. Howe, 21 vols (J. M. Dent and Sons, London, 1930-31)

Hegel, Georg Friedrich Wilhelm *Grundlinien der Philosophie des Rechts* (Felix Meiner, Hamburg, 1955)

——— *Lectures on the Philosophy of Religion together with a Work on the Proofs of the Existence of God* ed. Rev. E. B. Speirs, trans. Rev. E. B. Speirs and J. Burdon Sanderson (Kegan Paul, Trench, Trubner and Co. London, 1895)

——— *Phenomenology of Spirit* trans. A.V. Miller (Oxford University Press, Oxford, 1977)

Hoffmann, Ernest Theodor Amadeus *The Devil's Elixir* (1815-16) trans. Ronald Taylor, 2 vols (T. Cadell, London, 1829)

Hogg, James *The Private Memoirs and Confessions of a Justified Sinner* (Oxford University Press, Oxford, 1981)

Jennings, Hargrave *The Rosicrucians: their Rites and Mysteries* (John Camden-Hotten, London, 1910)

——— *With the Adepts; An Adventure among the Rosicrucians* (W. Rider, London, 1910)

Jones, Frederick L. ed. *Mary Shelley's Journal* (University of Oklahoma Press, Norman, 1947)

——— *The Letters of Percy Bysshe Shelley* 2 vols (Clarendon Press, Oxford, 1964)

Jonson, Ben *The Alchemist* ed. Douglas Brown (Ernest Benn, London, 1966)

Lamb, Charles and Mary *The Letters of Charles and Mary Lamb* ed. E.V. Lucas, 3 vols (J. M. Dent, London, 1935)

Malthus, Thomas Robert *An Essay on the Principle of Population, as it Affects the Future Improvement of Society, with Remarks on the speculations of Mr Godwin, M. Condorcet and Other Writers* (1798) (facsmile reprint, Macmillan, London, 1966)

Marx, Karl *Early Texts* ed. David McLellan (Basil Blackwell, Oxford, 1972)

——— *Economic and Philosophical Manuscripts* (1844) ed. David McLellan (Basil Blackwell, Oxford, 1972)

Maturin, Charles Robert *The Albigenses: A Romance* 4 vols (Arno Press, New York, 1974)

——— *Bertram: or The Castle of St Aldobrando: A Tragedy in 5 Acts* 9th edition (John Murray, London, 1817)

——— 'Conversations of Maturin' no. 1, *New Monthly Review* XIX (May, 1827), pp. 401-11

——— 'Conversations of Maturin' no. 11, *New Monthly Magazine* XIX (June, 1827), pp. 570-7

——— *The Correspondence of Sir Walter Scott and Charles Robert Maturin* ed. Fannie E. Rotchford and William H. McCarthy (University at Austin, Texas, 1937)

——— *Fatal Revenge: or The Family of Montario: A Romance* 4 vols, 2nd edition (A. K. Newman, London, 1824)

——— *Five Sermons on the Errors of the Roman Catholic Church* (William Folds, Dublin, 1824)

——— 'Lexlip Castle: An Irish Family Legend' in *The Literary Souvenir or Cabinet of Poetry and Romance* ed. Alaric A. Watt (Hurst, Robinson and Co. London, 1825), pp. 211-32

——— *Manuel: A Tragedy* in 5 Acts (John Murray, London, 1817)

——— *Melmoth the Wanderer: A Tale* ed. Douglas Grant (Oxford University Press, London, 1968)

——— *Melmoth the Wanderer: A Tale* ed. Alethea Hayter (Penguin, Harmondsworth, 1977)

——— *The Milesian Chief: A Romance* 4 vols (Henry Colburn, London, 1812)

——— 'The Sybil's Prophecy: A Dramatic Fragment' in *The Literary Souvenir or Cabinet of Poetry and Romance* ed. Alaric A. Watts (Hurst, Robinson and Co. London, 1826), pp. 128-36

——— *The Universe: A Poem* (Henry Colburn, London, 1821)

——— *Women: or Pour et Contre: A Tale* 3 vols (Longman, Hurst, Rees, Orme and Brown, London, 1818)

Novalis [Friedrich Leopold Von Hardenberg] *The Disciples at Sais and Other Fragments* trans F.V.M.T. and U.C.B. (Methuen, London, 1903)

Pindar *The Odes of Pindar including the Principal Fragments* trans. John Sandys (William Heinemann, London, 1915, revised 1987)

Poe, Edgar Allan *Poems* (1831) (facsimile reprint, Columbia University Press, New York, 1936)

Radcliffe, Ann *The Italian, or the Confessional of the Black Penitents: A Romance* 3 vols (T. Cadell Jr and W. Davies, London, 1797)

Shakespeare, William *Complete Works* ed. Peter Alexander reprint (Collins, London, 1970)

Shaw, George Bernard *Back to Methuselah: A Metabiological Pentateuch* (Penguin, Harmondsworth, 1939)

Shelley, Mary *Collected Tales and Stories* ed. Charles E. Robinson (Johns Hopkins University Press, London, 1976)

——— *Falkner: A Novel* 3 vols (Saunders and Otley, London, 1837)

——— *Frankenstein: or The Modern Prometheus* (1818), ed. James Rieger (Bobbs-Merrill, New York, 1974)

——— 'Lives of the Most Eminent Literary and Scientific Men of Italy, Spain and Portugal' (1835-37) in *Dionysius Lardner, The Cabinet Cyclopædia* (London, 1830-49)

——— *The Last Man* (1826) ed. Hugh J. Luke, Jr (University of Nebraska Press, Lincoln, 1965)

——— Review of *Cloudesley* in *Blackwood's Edinburgh Magazine* 27 (May, 1830), pp. 711-16

——— *Tales and Stories by Mary Wollstonecraft Shelley* ed. Richard Garnett (William Oaterson and Co. London, 1891)

——— *Valperga or The Life and Adventures of Castruccio, Prince of Lucca* 3 vols (G. and W. B. Whittaker, London, 1823)

Shelley, Percy Bysshe *The Complete Works of Percy Bysshe Shelley* ed. Roger Ingpen and Walter Edwin Peck, 10 vols (Ernest Benn, London, 1965)

——— *Zastrozzi: A Romance* and *St Irvyne or The Rosicrucian* (Arno Press, New York, 1977)

Wilde, Oscar *Works* ed. G. F. Maine (Collins, London, 1948)

Yeats, W. B. *W. B. Yeats: the Poems; A New Edition* ed. Richard J. Finneran (Macmillan, London, 1983)

Secondary Sources

Abrams, M. H. *Natural Supernaturalism: Tradition and Revolution* (Oxford University Press, London, 1971)

Adorno, Theodor W. and Horkheimer, Max *Dialectic of Enlightenment* trans. J. Cumming (Allen Lane, London, 1973)

Albrecht, W. P. and Pulas C. E. 'Godwin and Malthus' *Publications of the Modern Language Association* 70 (June, 1955), pp. 552-5

Allen, Paul M. *A Christian Rosenkreutz Anthology* (Rudolph Steiner, New York, 1968)

Anderson, George, K. 'The Legend of the Wandering Jew' *Books at Brown* 19 (May, 1963), pp. 143-59.

——— *The Chymical Wedding of Christian Rosenkreutz* trans. Edward Foxcroft (Minerva Books, London)

Anon. '*Frankenstein, or the Modern Prometheus*' *Quarterly Review* XVIII (March, 1818), pp. 379-85

——— 'On the Prolongation of Life' *The Retrospective Review* 7 (1832), pp. 64-87

——— 'The Literature of the Supernatural' *The Eclectic Review* 115 New Series 2 (April, 1862), pp. 302-26

——— 'Readings and Rereadings: *Zanoni*' *Theosophical Review* 31 (December, 1902), pp. 338-46

Antippas, Andy P. 'The Structure of Shelley's *St Irvyne*: Parallelism and the Gothic Mode of Evil' *Tulane Studies in English* 18 (1970), pp. 59-71

Baker, Ernest A. *The History of the English Novel: The Novel of Sentiment and the Gothic Romance* (H. F. and G. Witherby, London, 1934)

Baldick, Chris *In Frankenstein's Shadow: Myth, Monstrosity and Nineteenth-Century Writing* (Clarendon Press, Oxford, 1987)

Barnard, Ellsworth *Shelley's Religion* (University of Minnesota, Minneapolis, Minnesota, 1937)

Besser, Gretchen R. *Balzac's Concept of Genius: The Theme of Superiority in the 'Comedie humaine'* (Libraire Droz, Geneve, 1969)

Birkhead, Edith *The Tale of Terror: A Study of the Gothic Romance* (Constable, London, 1921)

Blavatsky, H. P. *Isis Unveiled: A Master-key to the Mysteries of Ancient and Modern Science and Theology* 2 vols (Bernard Quaritch, London, 1877)

Blunden, Edmund 'Godwin's Library Catalogue' *Keats-Shelley Memorial Bulletin* 9 (1958), pp. 27-9

——— *Shelley: A Life Story* (Collins, London, 1948)

Booth, Bradford A. 'The Pole: A Story by Clare Clairmont' *English Literary History* V (1938), pp. 67-70

Briggs, Katherine M. 'Legends of Lilith and the Wandering Jew' *Folklore* 92, 11 (1981), pp. 132-40

Brockman, John and Rosenfeld, Edward *Real Time* (Picador, London, 1973)

Brown, Ford K. *The Life of William Godwin* (J. M. Dent, London, 1926)

Bulwer Lytton, Edward Robert *The Life, Letters and Literary Remains of Edward Bulwer, Lord Lytton* 2 vols (Kegan Paul and Co. London, 1913)

——— *The Life of Edward Bulwer* 2 vols (Macmillan, London, 1913)

Butler, E. M. *The Myth of the Magus* (Cambridge University Press, Cambridge, 1948)

Cameron, Kenneth Neill *The Young Shelley: Genesis of a Radical* (Victor Gollancz, London, 1951)

BIBLIOGRAPHY

Cardinal, Roger *German Romantics in Context* (Macmillan Publishers, London, 1975)

Carlye, Thomas *Sartor Resartus: The Life and Opinions of Hertr Teufelsdrockh* (Harrap, London, 1927)

Chacornac, Paul *Eliphas Levi, Renovateur de l'Occultisme en France (1810-1875)* (Paris, Chacornac Frères, 1926)

Chailley, Jacques *The Magic Flute, Masonic Opera: An Interpretation of the Libretto and the Music* (Victor Gollancz, London, 1972)

Colby, E. *A Bibliography of Thomas Holcroft* (New York Public Library, New York, 1922)

Conger, Syndy M. *Matthew G. Lewis, Charles Robert Maturin and the Germans: An Interpretative Study of the influence of German Literature on two Gothic Novels* ed. James Hogg (Salzburg University, Salzburg, 1977)

Cook, Davidson 'Sadak the Wanderer: An Unknown Shelley Poem' *Times Literary Supplement* 16 May 1936, p. 424

Croker, John Wilson Review of *Melmoth the Wanderer* in *Quarterly Review* 24 (1821), pp. 303-11

Dawson, Leven M. 'Melmoth the Wanderer: Paradox and the Gothic Novel' *Studies in English Literature* 8 (1968), pp. 621-32

Dawson, Paul *The Unacknowledged Legislator: Shelley and Politics* (Oxford University Press, London, 1980)

Disraeli, Benjamin *Lord George Bentinck: A Political Biography* revised edition (Colburn and Co. London, 1852)

Disraeli, Isaac *Curiosities of Literature* ed. B. Disraeli, 3 vols (Routledge, Warne, Routledge, London, 1863)

Dodds, M. H. 'Shelley's Use of Abbé Barruel's Work on Secret Societies' *Notes and Queries* CXIII (March 10 1917), p. 196

Donne, John *Poems* ed. J. C. Herbert Grierson (Oxford University Press, London, 1912)

Dowden, Edward *The Life of Percy Bysshe Shelley* (Routledge and Kegan Paul, London, 1969)

Drummond, William *Academical Questions* (W. Bulmer and Co., London, 1805)

Eigner, Edwin M. *The Metaphysical Novel in England and America: Dickens, Bulwer, Melville and Hawthorne* (University of California press, London, 1978)

Eliot, Simon and Stern, Beverley ed. *The Age of Enlightenment: An Anthology of Eighteenth-Century Texts* 2 vols (Ward Lock Educational in association with Open University Press, London, 1979)

Fest, Alexander, 'Bethlem Gabor in English Literature' *The Hungarian Spectator* 89 (November, 1913)

Fradin, Joseph I. 'The Absorbing Tyranny of Every-day Life: Bulwer-Lytton's *A Strange Story*' *Nineteenth-Century Fiction* 16 (June, 1961), pp. 1-16

French, Peter *John Dee: the World of the Elizabethan Magus* (Routledge and Kegan Paul, London, 1972)

Friedenthal, Richard *Goethe: His Life and Times* (Weidenfeld and Nicolson, London, 1963)

Florescu, Radu *In Search of Frankenstein* (New English Library, London, 1975)

Gadamer, Hans-Georg *Truth and Method* (Sheed and Ward, London, 1979)

Gaer, Joseph *The Wandering Jew* (Mentor, New York, 1961)

Gardener, F. Leigh *Bibliotheca Rosicruciana: A Catalogue Raisonné of Works on the Occult Sciences* (Privately printed, 1923)

Glut, Donald F. *The Frankenstein Legend: A Tribute to Mary Shelley and Boris Karloff* (Scarecrow Press, New Jersey, 1973)

Grabo, Carl *A Newton among Poets — Shelley's Use of Science in Prometheus Unbound* (University of North Carolina, Chapel Hill, 1930)

——— 'Electricity, the Spirit of the Earth in Shelley's Prometheus Unbound' *Philological Quarterly* Vll, no. 2 (April, 1927), pp. 133-50

——— *The Magic Plant: The Growth of Shelley's Thought* (University of North Carolina, Chapel Hill, 1936)

Gruman, Gerald J. 'A History of Ideas about the Prolongation of Life: The Evolution of Prolongevity hypotheses to 1800' *Transactions of the American Philosophical Society* vol. 56, part 9 (1966), pp. 1-97

Gualtier, Bon, 'Lays of the would-be Laureates' *Tait's Edinburgh Magazine* 19 (May, 1843), p. 276

Hartley, Harold *Humphrey Davy* (Scholar Press, Yorkshire, 1972)

Harvey. Paul ed. *The Oxford Companion to English Literature* (1967) revised by Dorothy Eagle (Clarendon Press, Oxford, 1975)

Hogg, James *The Private Memoirs and Confessions of a Justified Sinner* (1824) ed. John Carey (Oxford University Press, Oxford, 1981)

Hogg, Thomas Jefferson and Tralawny, John Edward *The Life of Percy Bysshe Shelley* 2 vols (J. M. Dent, London, 1933)

Holmes, Richard *Shelley the Pursuit* (Weidenfeld and Nicolson, London, 1974)

Howe, Ellic *The Magicians of the Golden Dawn: A Documentary History of a Magical Order: 1887-1923* (Routledge and Kegan Paul, London, 1972)

Idman, Niilo *Charles Robert Maturin: His Life and Works* (Constable, London, 1923)

Jack, Ian *Augustan Satire: Intention and Idiom in English Poetry, 1660--1750* (Oxford University Press, London, 1952)

Jacobi, Friedrich Heinrich *Van der gottlichen Dingenund ihrer Offenbarung* (Fleischer, Leipzig, 1811)

Jeaffreson, John Cordy *The Real Shelley: New Views of the Poet's Life* 2 vols (Hurst and Blackett, London, 1885)

Johnson, R. Brimley ed. *Famous Reviews* (Pitman, New York, 1914)

Johnstone, Charles *Chrysal or the Adventures of a Guinea* 4 vols (T. Becket, London, 1761)

Kaufmann, Walter *Hegel: A Reinterpretation* (Weidenfeld and Nicolson, London, 1966)

Kelley, Richard 'The Haunted House of Bulwer-Lytton' *Studies in Short Fiction* 8 (1971), pp. 581-7

Ketterer, David *Frankenstein's Creation: The Book, The Monster, and Human Reality* (English Literary Studies, University of Victoria, Canada, 1979)

Kiely, Robert *The Romantic Novel in England* (Harvard University Press, Cambridge, Mass., 1972)

King-Hele, Desmond *Erasmus Darwin* (Macmillan, London, 1963)

——— *Shelley: His Thought and Work* (Papermac, London, 1960)

Kinsley, James ed. *The Poems and Fables of John Dryden* (Oxford University Press, London, 1970)

Kirk, G. S. and Raven, J. E. *The Presocratic Philosophers* (Cambridge University Press, London, 1957)

Knoop, D. Jones, G. P. and Hamer, D. *Early Masonic Pamphlets* (Manchester University Press, Manchester, 1945)

Kramer, Dale *Charles Robert Maturin* (Twayne, New York, 1973)

Landsberg, Paul-Louis *The Experience of Death: The Moral Problem of Suicide* (Salisbury Square, London, 1953)

Levine, George *One Culture: Essays in Science and Literature* (University of Wisconsin Press, London, 1988)

Levine, George and Knöpflmacher, U. C. *The Endurance of Frankenstein: Essays on Mary Shelley's Novel* (University of California Press, London, 1979)

Lewis, Matthew *The Monk* (Sphere Books, London, 1974)

Liljegren, S. B. 'Bulwer-Lytton's Novels and *Isis Unveiled*' *Essays and Studies on English Language and Literature* XVlll (Uppsala, Harvard University Press, Cambridge, Mass., 1957)

Locke, Don *A Fantasy of Reason: The Life and Thought of William Godwin* (Routledge and Kegan Paul, London, 1980)

Lord, Walter Frewen *The Mirror of the Century* (John Lane, London, 1906)

Lukács, George *Goethe and his Age* trans. Robert Anchor (Merlin Press, London, 1968)

——— *Soul and Form* trans. Anna Bostock (MIT Press, Cambridge, Mass., 1974)

Mackenzie, Norman ed. *Secret Societies* (Aldus Books, London, 1967)

Madaule, J. *The Albigensian Crusade* (Burns and Oates, London, 1967)

Marcuse, Herbert *Reason and Revolution: Hegel and the Rise of Social Theory* (Routledge and Kegan Paul, second edition, London, 1986)

McManners, John *Death and the Enlightenment: Changing Attitudes to Death among Christians and Unbelievers in Eighteenth-Century France* (Clarendon Press, Oxford, 1981)

McIntosh, Christopher *Eliphas Levi and the French Occult Tradition* (Rider, London, 1972)

——— *The Rosy Cross Unveiled: The History, Mythology and Rituals of an Occult Order* (Acquarian Press, Wellingborough, 1980)

Montgomery, J. W. *Cross and Crucible: J.V. Andreæ (1586-1654), Phoenix of the Theologians* 2 vols (Martinus Nijhoff, The Hague, 1973)

Moody, Christopher 'Godwin's *St Leon*: *A Tale*' *The Monthly Review* 33, September, 1800, pp. 23-29

Moore, Thomas *The Epicurean: A Tale* (A. and W. Galignani, Paris, 1827)

Moretti, Franco 'The Dialectic of Fear' *New Left Review* 136 (1982), pp. 67-87

Morley, Edith J. ed. *Crabb Robinson in Germany: 1800--1895: Extracts from his Corrrespondence* (Oxford University Press, London, 1929)

Morton, A. L. *The English Utopia* (Lawrence and Wishart, London, 1978)

Nelson, Lowry, Jr 'Night Thoughts on the Gothic Novel' *Yale Review* 52 (Winter, 1963), pp. 236-57

Nickerson, Hoffman *The Inquisition: A Political and Military Study of its Establishment* (John Bale, Sons and Danielssohn, London 1832)

Nitchie, Elizabeth *Mary Shelley: Author of Frankenstein* (Rutgers University Press, New Brunswick, 1953)

Norman, Sylva *Flight of the Skylark: The Development of Shelley's Reputation* (Max Reinhardt, London, 1954)

Null, Jack 'Structure and Theme in Melmoth the Wanderer' *Papers in Literature and Language* 13, no. 2 (Spring, 1977), pp. 136-47

Pascal, Blaise *Pensées* trans, A. J. Krailsheimer (Penguin, Harmondsworth, 1981)

Paul, C. Regan *William Godwin: His Friends and Contemporaries* (Henry S. King, London, 1876)

Peacock, Thomas Love *Nightmare Abbey* (1818) ed. Raymond Wright (Penguin, Harmondsworth, 1979)

Peck, Walter Edwin 'Shelley and the Abbé Barruel' *Publications of the Modern Language Association of America* XXXVI, no. 3 (September, 1921), pp. 347-53

Piper, H. W. and Jeffares Norman, A. 'Maturin the Innovator' *Huntington Library Quarterly* XXI (May, 1958), pp. 261-84

Pippin, Robert B. 'The Rose and the Owl: Some Remarks on the Theory-Practice Problem in Hegel' *The Independent Journal of Philosophy* III (1979)

Plato *Gorgias* trans. Terence Irwin (Clarendon Press, Oxford, 1979)

Pollin, B. R. 'Philosophical and Literary Sources of Frankenstein' *Comparative Literature* 17 (Spring, 1965) pp. 97-108

Pope, Alexander *Essay on Man* ed. Maynard Mack (Methuen, London, 1958)

Powell, Neil *Alchemy, the Ancient Science* (Danbury Press, London, 1976)

Powers, Katherine Richardson *The Influence of William Godwin on the Novels of Mary Shelley* unpublished Ph.D. thesis (University of Tennessee, August, 1972)

Punter, David *The Literature of Terror: A History of Gothic Fictions from 1765 to the Present Day* (Longman, London, 1930)

Raleigh, W. *The English Novel* (University Extension Manual, New York, 1894)

Ranald, Margaret Loftus and Ralph, Arthur Ranald 'Shelley's Magus Zoroaster and the Image of the *Doppelgänger*' *Modern Language Notes* LXXVI (January, 1961), pp. 7-12

Randolph, Pascal Beverly *Eulis! The History of Love: Its Wonderous Magic, Chemistry, Rules, Laws, Modes, Moods and Rationale; Being the Third Revelation of Soul and Sex* (Randolph Publishing Company, Toledo, Ohio, 1874)

Rieger, James *The Mutiny Within: The Heresies of Percy Bysshe Shelley* (George Braziller, New York, 1967)

Roberts, Marie *British Poets and Secret Societies* (Croom Helm, London, 1986)

——— 'Rosicrucianism or Cross-Rosism in Hegel's Phenomenology' *History of European Ideas* 6, no. 1 (1985), pp. 99-100

——— 'The English Rosicrucian Novel' *Cauda Pavonis* 8 no. 1 (Spring, 1989), pp. 7-11

——— 'The Flying Island and the Invisible College in Book Three of *Gulliver's Travels*' *Notes and Queries* (September, 1984), pp. 391-3

Robinson, Charles E. 'Mary Shelley and the Roger Dodsworth Hoax' *Keats-Shelley Journal* 24 (1975), pp. 20-8

Ronay, Gabriel *The Dracula Myth: The Cult of the Vampire* (Pan books, London, 1975)

Rosenbaum, S. P. *English Literature and British Philosophy: A Collection of Essays* (University of Chicago Press, London, 1971)

Rossetti, William Michael *A Memoir of Shelley* (Shelley Society, London, 1886)

Sadleir, Michael *Bulwer, A Panorama* (Constable, London, 1931)

Scarborough, Dorothy *The Supernatural in Modern English Fiction* (G. P. Putnam, The Knickerbocker Press, London, 1917)

Scholten, William *Charles Robert Maturin: The Terror-Novelist* (H. G. Paros, Amsterdam, 1933)

Scott, Shirley Clay *Myths of Consciousness in the Novels of Charles Maturin* unpublished Ph.D. thesis (Kent State University, August, 1973)

Scott, Walter, Review of *Frankenstein* in *Blackwood's Edinburgh Magazine* no. xii, II (March, 1818), pp. 613-20

——— *Waverley or 'Tis Sixty Years Since* (J. M. Dent, London, 1910)

Senior, John *The Way Down and Out: The Occult in Symbolist Literature* (Cornell University Press, New York, 1959)

Singleton, Charles S. ed. *Art, Science and History in the Renaissance* (Johns Hopkins Press, Baltimore, 1968)

Sophocles *Œdipus at Colonus* trans. F. Storr (Loeb Classical Library, London, 1924)

Stettin, M. Theo *The Rosicrucian Emblems of Daniel Cramer: The True Society of Jesus and the Rosy Cross* (1614) ed. Adam Mclean, trans. Fiona Tait (Magnum Opus Hermetic Sourceworks, Edinburgh, 1980)

Steward, C. Nelson *Bulwer-Lytton as Occultist* (Theosophical Publishing House, London, 1927)

Strawson, P. F. 'Social Morality and Individual Ideal' *Philosophy* XXXVI, no. 136 (January 1961)

Tennyson, A. *The Poems of Tennyson* ed. Christopher Ricks (Longmans, London, 1969)

Terrasson, Jean Abbé, *The Life of Sethos: Taken from Private Memoirs of the Ancient Egyptians* trans. Mr Lediard (J. Walthoe, London, 1732)

Thompson, E. P. *The Making of the English Working Class* (Penguin, Harmondsworth, 1968)

——— 'Time, Work-Discipline, and Industrial Capitalism' *Past and Present: A Journal of Historical Studies* 38 (1967), pp. 56-97

Tillotson, Geoffrey ed. *The Poems of Alexander Pope* 10 vols (Methuen, London, 1939-67)

Tomory, Peter *The Life and Art of Henry Fuseli* (Thames and Hudson, London, 1972)

Unamunco, Y. de Jugo, Miguel *The Tragic Sense of Life* (1921), trans. J. E. Crawford Flitch (Fontana Library edition, London, 1921)

Varma, Devendra P. *The Gothic Flame: Being a History of the Gothic Novel in England: Its Origin, Efflorescence, Distintegration and Residuary Influences* (Russell and Russell, New York, 1957)

Wagner, Geoffrey 'A forgotten Satire: Bulwer-Lytton's *The Coming Race*' *Nineteenth-Century Fiction* 19 (March, 1964-5), pp. 379-88

Waite, Arthur Edward *The Brotherhood of the Rosy Cross: Being Records of the House of the Holy Spirit in its Inward and Outward History* (Riderk, London, 1924)

Walling, William A. *Mary Shelley* (Twayne, New York, 1972)

Webster, Charles *From Paracelsus to Newton: Magic and the Making of Modern Science* (Cambridge University Press, London, 1982)

Webster, Nesta H. *Secret Societies and Subversive Movements* (Britons Publishing Co. London, 1964)

White, Newman Ivey *The Unextinguished Hearth: Shelley and His Contemporary Critics* (Duke University Press, Durham, 1938)

Williams, Bernard *Problems of the Self* (Cambridge University Press, Cambridge, 1973)

Wilt, Judith *Ghosts of the Gothic: Austen, Eliot and Lawrence* (Princeton University Press, New Jersey, 1980)

Wolf, Robert Lee *Strange Stories and Other Explorations in Victorian Fiction* (Gambit, Boston, 1971)

Yates, Frances A. *The Art of Memory* (Penguin, Harmondsworth, 1978)

——— *The Rosicrucian Enlightenment* (Paladin, St Albans, 1975)

Young, A. B. 'Shelley and M. G. Lewis' *Modern Language Review* 1 (1906), pp. 322-4.

Index

C

G

H

T